ZAMBIA

CRIMINAL LAWS, REGULATIONS AND PROCEDURES HANDBOOK

VOLUME 1

STRATEGIC INFORMATION AND BASIC LAWS

International Business Publications, USA
Washington DC, USA - Zambia

ZAMBIA

CRIMINAL LAWS, REGULATIONS AND PROCEDURES HANDBOOK

VOLUME 1 STRATEGIC INFORMATION AND BASIC LAWS

UPDATED ANNUALLY

We express our sincere appreciation to all government agencies and international organizations which provided information and other materials for this handbook

Cover Design: International Business Publications, USA

2019 Edition Updated Reprint International Business Publications, USA
ISBN 1-5145-0830-3

For additional analytical, business and investment opportunities information, please contact Global Investment & Business Center, USA at (703) 370-8082. Fax: (703) 370-8083. E-mail: ibpusa3@gmail.com Global Business and Investment Info Databank - www.ibpus.com

Printed in the USA

ZAMBIA

CRIMINAL LAWS, REGULATIONS AND PROCEDURES HANDBOOK

VOLUME 1
STRATEGIC INFORMATION AND BASIC LAWS

TABLE OF CONTENTS

STRATEGIC AND BUSINESS PROFILES

Capital and largest city	Lusaka 15°25′S 28°17′E15.417°S 28.283°E
Official languages	English > 0.5%
Recognised regional languages	
	> 0.5%
Ethnic groups	
Demonym	Zambian
Government	Presidential republic
• President	Edgar Chagwa Lungu
• Vice President	Inonge Mutukwa Wina
Legislature	National Assembly
Independence	
• from the United Kingdom	24 October 1964
• Current constitution	24 August 1991
Area	
• Total	752,618 km² (39th) 290,587 sq mi
• Water (%)	1
Population	
• 2015 estimate	16,212,000 (69th)
• 2010 census	13,092,666
• Density	17.2/km² (191st) 44.5/sq mi
GDP (PPP)	2014 estimate
• Total	$61.786 billion[5]
• Per capita	$4,113
GDP (nominal)	2014 estimate
• Total	$26.611 billion
• Per capita	$1,810
Gini (2010)	57.5 high
HDI (2014)	▲ 0.586[7] medium · 139th
Currency	Zambian kwacha (ZMW)
Time zone	CAT (UTC+2)
Drives on the	left
Calling code	+260
ISO 3166 code	ZM
Internet TLD	.zm

The **Republic of Zambia** is a landlocked country in Southern Africa, neighboring the Democratic Republic of the Congo to the north, Tanzania to the north-east, Malawi to the east, Mozambique, Zimbabwe, Botswana and Namibia to the south, and Angola to the west. The capital city is Lusaka, in the south-central part of the country. The population is concentrated mainly around Lusaka in the south and the Copperbelt Province to the northwest.

Originally inhabited by Khoisan peoples, the region was colonised during the Bantu expansion of the thirteenth century. After visits by European explorers in the eighteenth century, Zambia became the British protectorate of Northern Rhodesia towards the end of the nineteenth century. For most of the colonial period, the country was governed by an administration appointed from London with the advice of the British South Africa Company.

On 24 October 1964, the country became independent of the United Kingdom and then-prime minister Kenneth Kaunda became the inaugural president. Kaunda's socialist United National Independence Party (UNIP) maintained power from 1964 until 1991. From 1972 to 1991 Zambia was a single-party state with the UNIP as the sole legal political party under the motto 'One Zambia, One Nation'. Kaunda was succeeded by Frederick Chiluba of the social-democratic Movement for Multi-Party Democracy in 1991, beginning a period of social-economic growth and government decentralisation. Levy Mwanawasa, Chiluba's chosen successor, presided over the country from January 2002 until his death in August 2008, and is credited with campaigns to reduce corruption and increase the standard of living. After Mwanawasa's death, Rupiah Banda presided as Acting President before being elected President in 2008. Holding office for only three years, Banda stepped down after his defeat in the 2011 elections by Patriotic Front party leader Michael Chilufya Sata.

In 2010, the World Bank named Zambia one of the world's fastest economically reformed countries. The Common Market for Eastern and Southern Africa (COMESA) is headquartered in Lusaka.

STRATEGIC PROFILE

Background:	The territory of Northern Rhodesia was administered by the South Africa Company from 1891 until takeover by the UK in 1923. During the 1920s and 1930s, advances in mining spurred development and immigration. The name was changed to Zambia upon independence in 1964. In the 1980s and 1990s, declining copper prices and a prolonged drought hurt the economy. Elections in 1991 brought an end to one-party rule, but the subsequent vote in 1996 saw blatant harassment of opposition parties.

GEOGRAPHY

Location:	Southern Africa, east of Angola
Geographic coordinates:	15 00 S, 30 00 E
Map references:	Africa

Area:	total: 752,614 sq km land: 740,724 sq km water: 11,890 sq km
Area - comparative:	slightly larger than Texas
Land boundaries:	total: 5,664 km border countries: Angola 1,110 km, Democratic Republic of the Congo 1,930 km, Malawi 837 km, Mozambique 419 km, Namibia 233 km, Tanzania 338 km, Zimbabwe 797 km
Coastline:	0 km (landlocked)
Maritime claims:	none (landlocked)
Climate:	tropical; modified by altitude; rainy season (October to April)
Terrain:	mostly high plateau with some hills and mountains
Elevation extremes:	lowest point: Zambezi river 329 m highest point: unnamed location in Mafinga Hills 2,301 m
Natural resources:	copper, cobalt, zinc, lead, coal, emeralds, gold, silver, uranium, hydropower
Land use:	arable land: 7% permanent crops: 0% permanent pastures: 40% forests and woodland: 39% other: 14%

Irrigated land:	460 sq km
Natural hazards:	tropical storms (November to April)

Environment - current issues:	air pollution and resulting acid rain in the mineral extraction and refining region; chemical runoff into watersheds; poaching seriously threatens rhinoceros, elephant, antelope, and large cat populations; deforestation; soil erosion; desertification; lack of adequate water treatment presents human health risks
Environment - international agreements:	party to: Biodiversity, Climate Change, Desertification, Endangered Species, Hazardous Wastes, Law of the Sea, Nuclear Test Ban, Ozone Layer Protection, Wetlands signed, but not ratified: Climate Change-Kyoto Protocol
Geography - note:	landlocked; the Zambezi forms a natural riverine boundary with Zimbabwe

Base 802736 (B00492) 2-01

PEOPLE

Population:	9,770,199 note: estimates for this country explicitly take into account the effects of excess mortality due to AIDS; this can result in lower life expectancy, higher infant mortality and death rates, lower population and growth rates, and changes in the distribution of population by age and sex than would otherwise be expected (est.)
Age structure:	0-14 years: 47.36% (male 2,324,128; female 2,303,349) 15-64 years: 50.14% (male 2,433,250; female 2,465,747) 65 years and over: 2.5% (male 105,694; female 138,031)
Population growth rate:	1.93%
Birth rate:	41.46 births/1,000 population
Death rate:	21.97 deaths/1,000 population
Net migration rate:	-0.16 migrant(s)/1,000 population
Sex ratio:	at birth: 1.03 male(s)/female under 15 years: 1.01 male(s)/female 15-64 years: 0.99 male(s)/female 65 years and over: 0.77 male(s)/female total population: 0.99 male(s)/female
Infant mortality rate:	90.89 deaths/1,000 live births
Life expectancy at birth:	total population: 37.29 years male: 37.06 years female: 37.53 years
Total fertility rate:	5.53 children born/woman
HIV/AIDS - adult prevalence rate:	19.95%
HIV/AIDS - people living with HIV/AIDS:	870,000
HIV/AIDS - deaths:	99,000
Nationality:	noun: Zambian(s) adjective: Zambian
Ethnic groups:	African 98.7%, European 1.1%, other 0.2%
Religions:	Christian 50%-75%, Muslim and Hindu 24%-49%, indigenous beliefs 1%
Languages:	English (official), major vernaculars - Bemba, Kaonda, Lozi, Lunda, Luvale, Nyanja, Tonga, and about 70 other

	indigenous languages
Literacy:	definition: age 15 and over can read and write English total population: 78.2% male: 85.6% female: 71.3% (1995 est.)

GOVERNMENT

Country name:
conventional long form: Republic of Zambia
conventional short form: Zambia
former: Northern Rhodesia
etymology: name derived from the Zambezi River, which flows through the western part of the country and forms its southern border with neighboring Zimbabwe

Government type:
presidential republic

Capital:
name: Lusaka; note - a proposal to build a new capital city in Ngabwe was announced in May 2017
geographic coordinates: 15 25 S, 28 17 E
time difference: UTC+2 (7 hours ahead of Washington, DC, during Standard Time)

Administrative divisions:
10 provinces; Central, Copperbelt, Eastern, Luapula, Lusaka, Muchinga, Northern, North-Western, Southern, Western

Independence:
24 October 1964 (from the UK)

National holiday:
Independence Day, 24 October (1964)

Constitution:
history: several previous; latest adopted 24 August 1991, promulgated 30 August 1991 (2017)
amendments: proposed by the National Assembly; passage requires two-thirds majority vote by the Assembly in two separate readings at least 30 days apart; passage of amendments affecting fundamental rights and freedoms requires approval by at least one-half of votes cast in a referendum prior to consideration and voting by the Assembly; amended 1996, 2015, last in 2016

Legal system:
mixed legal system of English common law and customary law

International law organization participation:
has not submitted an ICJ jurisdiction declaration; accepts ICCt jurisdiction

Citizenship:
citizenship by birth: only if at least one parent is a citizen of Zambia
citizenship by descent only: yes, if at least one parent was a citizen of Zambia
dual citizenship recognized: yes
residency requirement for naturalization: 5 years for those with an ancestor who was a citizen of Zambia, otherwise 10 years residency is required

Suffrage:
18 years of age; universal

Executive branch:
chief of state: President Edgar LUNGU (since 25 January 2015); Vice President Inonge WINA (since 26 January 2015); note - the president is both chief of state and head of government
head of government: President Edgar LUNGU (since 25 January 2015); Vice President Inonge WINA (since 26 January 2015)
cabinet: Cabinet appointed by president from among members of the National Assembly
elections/appointments: president directly elected by absolute majority popular vote in 2 rounds if needed for a 5-year term (eligible for a second term); last held on 11 August 2016 (next to be held in 2021)
election results: Edgar LUNGU reelected president in the first round; percent of vote - Edgar LUNGU (PF) 50.4%, Hakainde HICHILEMA (UPND) 47.6%, other 2.0%

Legislative branch:
description: unicameral National Assembly (164 seats; 156 members directly elected in single-seat constituencies by simple majority vote in 2 rounds if needed, and 8 appointed by the president; members serve 5-year terms); note - 6 additional electoral seats were added for the 11 August 2016 election, up from 150 electoral seats in the 2011 election
elections: last held on 11 August 2016 (next to be held in 2021)
election results: percent of vote by party - PF 42%, UPND 41.7%, MMD 2.7%, FDD 2.2%, other 1.9%,independent 9.5%; seats by party - PF 80, UPND 58, MMD 3, FDD 1, independent 14

Judicial branch:
highest courts: Supreme Court (consists of the chief justice and deputy chief justice, and at least 11 judges); Constitutional Court (consists of the court president, vice-president, and 11 judges); note - the Constitutional Court began operation in June 2016
judge selection and term of office: Supreme Court and Constitutional Court judges appointed by the president upon the advice of the 9-member Judicial Service Commission headed by the chief justice, and ratified by the National Assembly; judges normally serve until age 65

subordinate courts: Court of Appeal; High Court; Industrial Relations Court; subordinate courts 3 levels, based on upper limit of money involved); Small Claims Court; local courts (2 grades, based on upper limit of money involved)

Political parties and leaders:
Alliance for Democracy and Development or ADD [Charles MILUPI]
Forum for Democracy and Development or FDD [Edith NAWAKWI]
Movement for Multiparty Democracy or MMD [Felix MUTATI]
Patriotic Front or PF [Edgar LUNGU]
United Party for National Development or UPND [Hakainde HICHILEMA]

International organization participation:
ACP, AfDB, AU, C, COMESA, EITI (compliant country), FAO, G-77, IAEA, IBRD, ICAO, ICCt, ICRM, IDA, IFAD, IFC, IFRCS, ILO, IMF, Interpol, IOC, IOM, IPU, ISO (correspondent), ITSO, ITU, ITUC (NGOs), MIGA, MONUSCO, NAM, OPCW, PCA, SADC, UN, UNAMID, UNCTAD, UNESCO, UNHCR, UNIDO, UNISFA, UNMIL, UNMISS, UNOCI, UNWTO, UPU, WCO, WHO, WIPO, WMO, WTO

Diplomatic representation in the US:
chief of mission: Ambassador Ngosa SIMBYAKULA (since 29 November 2017)
chancery: 2200 R Street NW, Washington, DC 20008
telephone: [1] (202) 265-9717 through 9719
FAX: [1] (202) 332-0826

Diplomatic representation from the US:
chief of mission: Ambassador Daniel L. FOOTE (since December 2017)
embassy: Eastern end of Kabulonga Road, Ibex Hill, Lusaka
mailing address: P. O. Box 320065, Lusaka
telephone: [260] 211-357-000
FAX: [260] 211-357-224

Flag description:
green field with a panel of three vertical bands of red (hoist side), black, and orange below a soaring orange eagle, on the outer edge of the flag; green stands for the country's natural resources and vegetation, red symbolizes the struggle for freedom, black the people of Zambia, and orange the country's mineral wealth; the eagle represents the people's ability to rise above the nation's problems

National symbol(s):
African fish eagle; national colors: green, red, black, orange

National anthem:
name: "Lumbanyeni Zambia" (Stand and Sing of Zambia, Proud and Free)
lyrics/music: multiple/Enoch Mankayi SONTONGA
note: adopted 1964; the melody, from the popular song "God Bless Africa," is the same as that of Tanzania but with different lyrics; the melody is also incorporated into South Africa's anthem

ECONOMY

Zambia had one of the world's fastest growing economies for the ten years up to 2014, with real GDP growth averaging roughly 6.7% per annum, though growth slowed during the period 2015 to 2017, due to falling copper prices, reduced power generation, and depreciation of the kwacha. Zambia's lack of economic diversification and dependency on copper as its sole major export makes it vulnerable to fluctuations in the world commodities market and prices turned downward in 2015 due to declining demand from China; Zambia was overtaken by the Democratic Republic of Congo as Africa's largest copper producer. GDP growth picked up in 2017 as mineral prices rose.

Despite recent strong economic growth and its status as a lower middle-income country, widespread and extreme rural poverty and high unemployment levels remain significant problems, made worse by a high birth rate, a relatively high HIV/AIDS burden, by market-distorting agricultural and energy policies, and growing government debt. Zambia raised $7 billion from international investors by issuing separate sovereign bonds in 2012, 2014, and 2015. Concurrently, it issued over $4 billion in domestic debt and agreed to Chinese-financed infrastructure projects, significantly increasing the country's public debt burden to more than 60% of GDP. The government has considered refinancing $3 billion worth of Eurobonds and significant Chinese loans to cut debt servicing costs.

GDP (purchasing power parity):

$68.93 billion (est.)
$66.66 billion (2016 est.)
$64.25 billion (2015 est.)
note: data are in 2017 dollars
country comparison to the world: 102

GDP (official exchange rate):
$25.71 billion (2017 est.) (2017 est.)

GDP - real growth rate:
3.4% (2017 est.)
3.8% (2016 est.)
2.9% (2015 est.)
country comparison to the world: 103

GDP - per capita (PPP):
$4,000 (2017 est.)
$4,000 (2016 est.)
$4,000 (2015 est.)
note: data are in 2017 dollars
country comparison to the world: 178

Gross national saving:
38.3% of GDP (2017 est.)
37.3% of GDP (2016 est.)
38.9% of GDP (2015 est.)
country comparison to the world: 11

GDP - composition, by end use:
household consumption: 52.6% (2017 est.)

government consumption: 21% (2017 est.)
investment in fixed capital: 27.1% (2017 est.)
investment in inventories: 1.2% (2017 est.)
exports of goods and services: 43% (2017 est.)
imports of goods and services: -44.9% (2017 est.)

GDP - composition, by sector of origin:
agriculture: 7.5% (2017 est.)
industry: 35.3% (2017 est.)
services: 57% (2017 est.)

Agriculture - products:
corn, sorghum, rice, peanuts, sunflower seeds, vegetables, flowers, tobacco, cotton, sugarcane, cassava (manioc, tapioca), coffee; cattle, goats, pigs, poultry, milk, eggs, hides

Industries:
copper mining and processing, emerald mining, construction, foodstuffs, beverages, chemicals, textiles, fertilizer, horticulture

Industrial production growth rate:
4.7% (2017 est.)
country comparison to the world: 62

Labor force:
6.898 million (2017 est.)
country comparison to the world: 68

Labor force - by occupation:
agriculture: 54.8%
industry: 9.9%
services: 35.3% (2017 est.)

Unemployment rate:
15% (2008 est.)
50% (2000 est.)
country comparison to the world: 173

Population below poverty line:
54.4% (2015 est.)

Household income or consumption by percentage share:
lowest 10%: 47.4% (2010)
highest 10%: 47.4% (2010)

Distribution of family income - Gini index:
57.5 (2013)
50.8 (2004)
country comparison to the world: 7

Budget:
revenues: 4.473 billion (2017 est.)
expenditures: 6.357 billion (2017 est.)

Taxes and other revenues:
17.4% (of GDP) (2017 est.)
country comparison to the world: 169

Budget surplus (+) or deficit (-):
-7.3% (of GDP) (2017 est.)
country comparison to the world: 195

Public debt:
63.1% of GDP (2017 est.)
60.7% of GDP (2016 est.)
country comparison to the world: 66

Fiscal year:
calendar year

Inflation rate (consumer prices):
6.6% (2017 est.)
17.9% (2016 est.)
country comparison to the world: 192

Central bank discount rate:
9.1% (31 December 2012)
19% (31 December 2011)
country comparison to the world: 29

Commercial bank prime lending rate:
12.5% (31 December 2017 est.)
15.5% (31 December 2016 est.)
country comparison to the world: 66

Stock of narrow money:
$1.764 billion (31 December 2017 est.)
$1.582 billion (31 December 2016 est.)
country comparison to the world: 137

Stock of broad money:
$1.764 billion (31 December 2017 est.)
$1.582 billion (31 December 2016 est.)
country comparison to the world: 146

Stock of domestic credit
$5.401 billion (31 December 2017 est.)
$4.167 billion (31 December 2016 est.)

country comparison to the world: 129

Market value of publicly traded shares:
$3.004 billion (31 December 2012 est.)
$4.009 billion (31 December 2011 est.)
$2.817 billion (31 December 2010 est.)
country comparison to the world: 93

Current account balance:
-$1.006 billion (2017 est.)
-$934 million (2016 est.)
country comparison to the world: 142

Exports:
$8.216 billion (2017 est.)
$6.514 billion (2016 est.)
country comparison to the world: 98

Exports - partners:
Switzerland 44.8%, China 16.1%, Democratic Republic of the Congo 6.2%, Singapore 6%, South Africa 5.9% (2017)

Exports - commodities:
copper/cobalt, cobalt, electricity; tobacco, flowers, cotton

Imports:
$7.852 billion (2017 est.)
$6.539 billion (2016 est.)
country comparison to the world: 113

Imports - commodities:
machinery, transportation equipment, petroleum products, electricity, fertilizer, foodstuffs, clothing

Imports - partners:
South Africa 28.2%, Democratic Republic of the Congo 20.8%, China 12.9%, Kuwait 5.4%, UAE 4.6% (2017)

Reserves of foreign exchange and gold:
$2.082 billion (31 December 2017 est.)
$2.353 billion (31 December 2016 est.)
country comparison to the world: 121

Debt - external:
$11.66 billion (31 December 2017 est.)
$9.562 billion (31 December 2016 est.)

Exchange rates:
Zambian kwacha (ZMK) per US dollar -

9.2 (2017 est.)
10.3 (2016 est.)
10.3 (2015 est.)
8.6 (2014 est.)
6.2 (2013 est.)

ENERGY

ectricity - production:
11.19 billion kWh
country comparison to the world: 93

Electricity - consumption:
7.96 billion kWh
country comparison to the world: 95

Electricity - exports:
578 million kWh
country comparison to the world: 65

Electricity - imports:
23 million kWh
country comparison to the world: 103

Electricity - installed generating capacity:
1.679 million kW
country comparison to the world: 112

Electricity - from fossil fuels:
0.4% of total installed capacity
country comparison to the world: 206

Electricity - from nuclear fuels:
0% of total installed capacity
country comparison to the world: 209

Electricity - from hydroelectric plants:
99.6% of total installed capacity
country comparison to the world: 5

Electricity - from other renewable sources:
0% of total installed capacity
country comparison to the world: 144

Crude oil - production:
174.6 bbl/day
country comparison to the world: 119

Crude oil - exports:
0 bbl/day
country comparison to the world: 209

Crude oil - imports:
12,500 bbl/day
country comparison to the world: 75

Crude oil - proved reserves:
0 bbl
country comparison to the world: 210

Refined petroleum products - production:
12,900 bbl/day
country comparison to the world: 102

Refined petroleum products - consumption:
19,260 bbl/day
country comparison to the world: 130

Refined petroleum products - exports:
254 bbl/day
country comparison to the world: 116

Refined petroleum products - imports:
1,272 bbl/day
country comparison to the world: 189

Natural gas - production:
0 cu m
country comparison to the world: 212

Natural gas - consumption:
0 cu m
country comparison to the world: 212

Natural gas - exports:
0 cu m

country comparison to the world: 211

Natural gas - imports:
0 cu m
country comparison to the world: 83

Natural gas - proved reserves:
0 cu m
country comparison to the world: 210

Carbon dioxide emissions from consumption of energy:
2.434 million Mt

COMMUNICATIONS

Telephones - main lines in use:
90,100
country comparison to the world: 148

Telephones - mobile cellular:
4.947 million
country comparison to the world: 102

Telephone system:
general assessment: among the best in Sub-Saharan Africa
domestic: high-capacity microwave radio relay connects most larger towns and cities; several cellular telephone services in operation and network coverage is improving; domestic satellite system being installed to improve telephone service in rural areas; Internet service is widely available; very small aperture terminal (VSAT) networks are operated by private firms
international: country code - 260; satellite earth stations - 2 Intelsat (1 Indian Ocean and 1 Atlantic Ocean), 3 owned by Zamtel

Broadcast media:
state-owned Zambia National Broadcasting Corporation (ZNBC) operates 1 TV station and is the principal local-content provider; several private TV stations; multi-channel subscription TV services are available; ZNBC operates 3 radio networks; about 2 dozen private radio stations; relays of at least 2 international broadcasters are accessible in Lusaka and Kitwe

Internet country code:
.zm

Internet hosts:
16,372
country comparison to the world: 123

Internet users:
816,200
country comparison to the world: 105

TRANSPORTATION

Railways:	total: 2,157 km narrow gauge: 2,157 km 1.067-m gauge (13 km double-track) note: the total includes 891 km of the Tanzania-Zambia Railway Authority (TAZARA), which operates 1,860 km of 1.067-m narrow gauge track between Dar es Salaam and Kapiri Mposhi where it connects to the Zambia Railways system; TAZARA is not a part of the Zambia Railways system; Zambia Railways assets are scheduled for concessioning (2001)
Highways:	total: 66,781 km paved: NA km unpaved: NA km
Waterways:	2,250 km note: includes Lake Tanganyika and the Zambezi and Luapula rivers
Pipelines:	crude oil 1,724 km
Ports and harbors:	Mpulungu
Airports:	112
Airports - with paved runways:	total: 13 over 3,047 m: 1 2,438 to 3,047 m: 3 1,524 to 2,437 m: 5 914 to 1,523 m: 3 under 914 m: 1
Airports - with unpaved runways:	total: 99 2,438 to 3,047 m: 1 1,524 to 2,437 m: 2 914 to 1,523 m: 65 under 914 m: 31

MILITARY

Military expenditures:
1.53% of GDP
1.75% of GDP (2015)
1.63% of GDP (2014)
country comparison to the world: 74

Military branches:
Zambian Defense Force (ZDF): Zambia Army, Zambia Air Force, Zambia National Service (support organization) (2015)

Military service age and obligation:
national registration required at age 16; 18-25 years of age for male and female voluntary military service (16 years of age with parental consent); no conscription; Zambian citizenship required; grade 12 certification required; mandatory HIV testing on enlistment; mandatory retirement for officers at age 65 (Army, Air Force) (2012)

TRANSNATIONAL ISSUES

Disputes - international:
in 2004, Zimbabwe dropped objections to plans between Botswana and Zambia to build a bridge over the Zambezi River, thereby de facto recognizing a short, but not clearly delimited, Botswana-Zambia boundary in the river

Refugees and internally displaced persons:
refugees (country of origin): 42,308 (Democratic Republic of the Congo) (refugees and asylum seekers), 5,000 (Burundi) (refugees and asylum seekers) (2018)

Illicit drugs:
transshipment point for moderate amounts of methaqualone, small amounts of heroin, and cocaine bound for southern Africa and possibly Europe; a poorly developed financial infrastructure coupled with a government commitment to combating money laundering make it an unattractive venue for money launderers; major consumer of cannabis

IMPORTANT INFORMATION FOR UNDERSTANDING ZAMBIA

PROFILE

OFFICIAL NAME: Republic of Zambia

Geography
Area: 752,614 sq. km. (290,585 sq. mi.); slightly larger than Texas.
Cities: *Capital*--Lusaka (pop. approx. 1 million).
Other cities: Kitwe, Ndola, Livingstone, Kabwe.
Terrain: Varies; mostly plateau savanna.
Climate: Generally dry and temperate.

People
Nationality: *Noun and adjective*--Zambian(s).
Population: Approx. 11.9 million.
Annual growth rate: 1.6%.
Ethnic groups: More than 70 ethnic groups.
Religions: Christian, indigenous beliefs, Muslim, Hindu.
Languages: English (official), about 70 local languages and dialects, including Bemba, Lozi, Kaonde, Lunda, Luvale, Tonga, and Nyanja.
Education: *No compulsory education; 7 years free education.* Net primary school enrollment: 67%. *Literacy*--women: 60.6%; men: 81.6%.
Health: *Infant mortality rate*--102/1,000. *Life expectancy* (2005)--38.4 years. *HIV prevalence (15-49)*--17%.
Work force: *Agriculture*--75%; *mining and manufacturing*--6%; *services*--19%.

Government
Type: Republic.
Independence: October 24, 1964.
Constitution: 1991 (as amended in 1996).
Branches: *Executive*--president (chief of state and head of government), cabinet. *Legislative*--unicameral National Assembly. Judicial--Supreme Court, high court, magistrate courts, and local courts.
Ruling political party: Movement for Multi-party Democracy (MMD).
Suffrage: Universal adult.
Subdivisions: Nine provinces subdivided into 72 districts.

Economy
Natural resources: Copper, cobalt, zinc, lead, coal, emeralds, gold, silver, uranium, hydroelectric power, fertile land.
Agriculture: *Products*--corn, sorghum, rice, groundnuts, sunflower seeds, vegetables, horticultural products, tobacco, cotton, sugarcane, livestock, coffee, and soybeans.
Industry: *Types*--mining, transport, construction, foodstuffs, beverages, chemicals, and textiles.
Trade (2006): *Exports*--$3.54 billion: copper, cobalt, lead, and zinc, cut vegetables, cotton. *Major markets*--South Africa, United Kingdom, Tanzania, Malawi, Japan. *Imports*--$2.7 billion: crude oil, refined petroleum products, manufactured goods, machinery, transport equipment, foodstuffs. *Major suppliers*--South Africa, China, Tanzania, Zimbabwe.
Major donors: Donors provided $1.1 billion in development assistance to Zambia in 2005/6. The World Bank is Zambia's largest multilateral donor. Other key multilateral donors include the International Monetary Fund (IMF), the European Union, UN agencies, and the African Development Bank. Counting direct bilateral assistance and assistance through multilateral agencies, the U.S. is Zambia's largest country donor.

PEOPLE

Zambia's population comprises more than 70 Bantu-speaking ethnic groups. Some ethnic groups are small, and only two have enough people to constitute at least 10% of the population. Most Zambians are subsistence farmers. The predominant religion is a blend of traditional beliefs and Christianity; Christianity is the official national religion. Expatriates, mostly British (about 15,000) or South African, live mainly in Lusaka and in the Copperbelt in northern Zambia, where they are employed in mines and related activities. Zambia also has a small but economically important Asian population, most of whom are Indians. The country is 44% urban. The HIV/AIDS epidemic is ravaging Zambia. Nearly 1 million Zambians are HIV positive or have AIDS. An estimated 100,000 died in 2004. Over 750,000 Zambian children have been orphaned by HIV/AIDS. Life expectancy at birth is 32.7 years.

HISTORY

The indigenous hunter-gatherer occupants of Zambia began to be displaced or absorbed by more advanced migrating tribes about 2,000 years ago. The major waves of Bantu-speaking immigrants began in the 15th century, with the greatest influx between the late 17th and early 19th centuries. They came primarily from the Luba and Lunda tribes of southern Democratic Republic of Congo and northern Angola but were joined in the 19th century by Ngoni peoples from the south. By the latter part of that century, the various peoples of Zambia were largely established in the areas they currently occupy.

Except for an occasional Portuguese explorer, the area lay untouched by Europeans for centuries. After the mid-19th century, it was penetrated by Western explorers, missionaries, and traders. David Livingstone, in 1855, was the first European to see the magnificent waterfalls on the Zambezi River. He named the falls after Queen Victoria, and the Zambian town near the falls is named after him.

In 1888, Cecil Rhodes, spearheading British commercial and political interests in Central Africa, obtained a mineral rights concession from local chiefs. In the same year, Northern and Southern Rhodesia (now Zambia and Zimbabwe, respectively) were proclaimed a British sphere of influence. Southern Rhodesia was annexed formally and granted self-government in 1923, and the administration of Northern Rhodesia was transferred to the British colonial office in 1924 as a protectorate.

In 1953, both Rhodesias were joined with Nyasaland (now Malawi) to form the Federation of Rhodesia and Nyasaland. Northern Rhodesia was the center of much of the turmoil and crisis that characterized the federation in its last years. At the core of the controversy were insistent African demands for greater participation in government and European fears of losing political control.

A two-stage election held in October and December 1962 resulted in an African majority in the legislative council and an uneasy coalition between the two African nationalist parties. The council passed resolutions calling for Northern Rhodesia's secession from the federation and demanding full internal self-government under a new constitution and a new national assembly based on a broader, more democratic franchise. On December 31, 1963, the federation was dissolved, and Northern Rhodesia became the Republic of Zambia on October 24, 1964.

At independence, despite its considerable mineral wealth, Zambia faced major challenges. Domestically, there were few trained and educated Zambians capable of running the government, and the economy was largely dependent on foreign expertise. Abroad, three of its neighbors--Southern Rhodesia and the Portuguese colonies of Mozambique and Angola--remained under white-dominated rule. Rhodesia's white-ruled government unilaterally declared independence in 1965. In addition, Zambia shared a border with South African-controlled South-West Africa (now Namibia). Zambia's sympathies lay with forces opposing colonial or white-dominated rule, particularly in Southern Rhodesia. During the next decade, it actively supported movements such as the Union for the Total Liberation of Angola (UNITA), the Zimbabwe African People's Union (ZAPU), the African National Congress of South Africa (ANC), and the South-West Africa People's Organization (SWAPO).

Conflicts with Rhodesia resulted in the closing of Zambia's borders with that country and severe problems with international transport and power supply. However, the Kariba hydroelectric station on the Zambezi River provided sufficient capacity to satisfy the country's requirements for electricity. A railroad to the Tanzanian port of Dar es Salaam, built with Chinese assistance, reduced Zambian dependence on railroad lines south to South Africa and west through an increasingly troubled Angola.

By the late 1970s, Mozambique and Angola had attained independence from Portugal. Zimbabwe achieved independence in accordance with the 1979 Lancaster House agreement, but Zambia's problems were not solved. Civil war in the former Portuguese colonies generated refugees and caused continuing transportation problems. The Benguela Railroad, which extended west through Angola, was essentially closed to traffic from Zambia by the late 1970s. Zambia's strong support for the ANC, which had its external headquarters in Lusaka, created security problems as South Africa raided ANC targets in Zambia.

In the mid-1970s, the price of copper, Zambia's principal export, suffered a severe decline worldwide. Zambia turned to foreign and international lenders for relief, but as copper prices remained depressed, it became increasingly difficult to service its growing debt. By the mid-1990s, despite limited debt relief, Zambia's per capita foreign debt remained among the highest in the world.

GOVERNMENT

Zambia became a republic immediately upon attaining independence in October 1964. The constitution promulgated on August 25, 1973, abrogated the original 1964 constitution. The new constitution and the national elections that followed in December 1973 were the final steps in achieving what was called a "one-party participatory democracy."

The 1973 constitution provided for a strong president and a unicameral National Assembly. National policy was formulated by the Central Committee of the United National Independence Party (UNIP), the sole legal party in Zambia. The cabinet executed the central committee's policy.

In accordance with the intention to formalize UNIP supremacy in the new system, the constitution stipulated that the sole candidate in elections for the office of president was the person selected to be the president of UNIP by the party's general conference. The second-ranking person in the Zambian hierarchy was UNIP's secretary general.

In December 1990, at the end of a tumultuous year that included riots in the capital and a coup attempt, President Kenneth Kaunda signed legislation ending UNIP's monopoly on power. Zambia enacted a new constitution in August 1991, which enlarged the National Assembly from 136 members to a maximum of 158 members, established an electoral commission, and allowed for more than one presidential candidate who no longer had to be a member of UNIP. The constitution was amended again in 1996 to set new limits on the presidency (including a retroactive two-term limit, and a requirement that both parents of a candidate be Zambian-born). The National Assembly is comprised of 150 directly elected members, up to eight presidentially-appointed members, and a speaker. Zambia is divided into nine provinces, each administered by an appointed deputy minister who essentially performs the duties of a governor.

The Supreme Court is the highest court and the court of appeal; below it are the high court, magistrate's court, and local courts.

Principal Government Officials

Cabinet of Zambia: February 2015 – present

Portfolio	Incumbent
President Commander-in-chief of the Armed Forces	H.E. Edgar Lungu
Vice President of Zambia	H.E. Inonge Wina
Minister of Agriculture and Livestock	Given Lubinda
Minister of Chiefs and Traditional Affairs	Joseph Katema
Minister of Commerce, Trade and Industry	Margaret Mwanakatwe
Minister of Community Development, Mother and Child Health	Emerine Kabashi
Minister of Defence	Richwell Siamunene[4]
Minister of Education, Science, Vocational Training and Early Education	Michael Kaingu
Minister of Finance	Alexander Chikwanda
Minister of Foreign Affairs	Harry Kalaba
Minister of Gender and Child Development	Nkandu Luo
Minister of Health	Joseph Kasonde
Minister of Home Affairs	Davies Mwila
Minister of Information and Broadcasting Services	Chishimba Kambwili
Minister of Justice	Ngosa Simbyakula
Minister of Labour and Social Security	Fackson Shamenda
Minister of Land, Natural Resources and Environmental Protection	Christbel Ngimbu
Minister of Local Government and Housing	John Phiri
Minister of Mines, Energy and Water Development	Christopher Yaluma
Minister of Tourism and Arts	Jean Kapata
Minister of Transport, Works, Supply and Communications	Yamfwa Mukanga
Minister of Youth and Sports	Vincent Mwale
Attorney General	

Zambia maintains an embassy in the United States at 2419 Massachusetts Avenue, NW, Washington, DC 20008 (tel: 202-265-9717/8/9).

Zambia became a republic immediately upon attaining independence in October 1964. The constitution promulgated on August 25, 1973, abrogated the original 1964 constitution. The new constitution and the national elections that followed in December 1973 were the final steps in achieving what was called a "one-party participatory democracy."

The 1973 constitution provided for a strong president and a unicameral National Assembly. National policy was formulated by the Central Committee of the United National Independence Party (UNIP), the sole legal party in Zambia. The cabinet executed the central committee's policy.

In accordance with the intention to formalize UNIP supremacy in the new system, the constitution stipulated that the sole candidate in elections for the office of president was the person selected to be the president of UNIP by the party's general conference. The second-ranking person in the Zambian hierarchy was UNIP's secretary general.

In December 1990, at the end of a tumultuous year that included riots in the capital and a coup attempt, President Kenneth Kaunda signed legislation ending UNIP's monopoly on power. In response to growing popular demand for multi-party democracy, and after lengthy, difficult negotiations between the Kaunda government and opposition groups, Zambia enacted a new constitution in August 1991. The constitution enlarged the National Assembly from 136 members to a maximum of 158 members, established an electoral commission, and allowed for more than one presidential candidate who no longer had to be a member of UNIP. The constitution was amended again in 1996 to set new limits on the presidency (including a retroactive two-term limit, and a requirement that both parents of a candidate be Zambian-born). The National Assembly is comprised of 150 directly elected members, up to eight presidentially-appointed members, and a speaker. Zambia is divided into nine provinces, each administered by an appointed deputy minister who essentially performs the duties of a governor.

The Supreme Court is the highest court and the court of appeal; below it are the high court, magistrate's court, and local courts.

POLITICAL CONDITIONS

The **politics of Zambia** takes place in a framework of a presidential representative democratic republic, whereby the President of Zambia is head of state, head of government and leader of a multi-party system. Executive power is exercised by the government, while legislative power is vested in both the government and parliament. Formerly Northern Rhodesia, Zambia became a republic immediately upon attaining independence in October 1964.

EDGAR CHAGWA LUNGU 2015 - PRESENT

After being sworn in on the January 25, He has held the office of president after taking over from Guy Scott who was acting president after the passing of 5th republican president Micheal Chiluyfa Sata. So Far His presidency has been criticised with the depreciating kwacha and his drinking problem.[citation needed]. However these economic challenges, in particular the depreciating kwacha, have been attributed to the global fall and depressed commodity prices. Zambia derives over 90% of its export earnings to one commodity: COPPER which has lost about 45% of its value on the international commodity market. Numerous individuals and media have repeatedly failed to prove his drinking problem as his health has improved dramatically since his collapse in his early days as president. On 5th January 2016, Edgar Chagwa Lungu became the first president in Zambia's history to successfully conclude the constitutional issue as proposed by the Zambian people when he assented to the 2015 Constitutional Amendment Bill. This Bill is a result of extensive work which started during the Mwanawasa era (The Mwanakatwe Commission) and was later polished by the Michael Chilufya Sata appointed Technical Committee (the Mwanawasa Constitutional Review Commission was rejected by parliament). As Justice Minister, Edgar Chagwa Lungu released the Draft Constitution in a short period of time and was presented to parliament and it was later decided that non-contentious issues will be debated in parliament while the continuous issues will be subjected to a referendum. He has followed this up, as president, by successfully finalising the long standing Constitutional issue.

The major figure in Zambian politics from 1964 to 1991 was Kenneth Kaunda, who led the campaign for independence and successfully bridged the rivalries among the country's various regions and ethnic groups. Kaunda tried to base government on his philosophy of "humanism," which condemned human exploitation and stressed cooperation among people, but not at the expense of the individual.

Kaunda's political party--the United National Independence Party (UNIP)--was founded in 1959 and was in power under Kaunda's leadership from 1964 to 1991. Before 1972, Zambia had three significant political parties--UNIP, the African National Congress (ANC), and the United Progressive Party (UPP). The ANC drew its strength from western and southern provinces, while the UPP found some support among Bemba-speakers in the Copperbelt and northern provinces. Although not strongly supported in all areas of the country, only UNIP had a nationwide following.

In December 1972, Zambian law established a one-party state, and all other political parties were banned; this was later enshrined in the 1973 constitution. Kaunda, the sole candidate, was elected President in the 1973 elections. Elections also were held for the National Assembly. Only UNIP members were permitted to run, but these seats were sharply contested. President Kaunda's mandate was renewed in December 1978, October 1983, and October 1988 in a "yes" or "no" vote on his candidacy.

Growing opposition to UNIP's monopoly on power led to the rise in 1990 of the Movement for Multiparty Democracy (MMD). The MMD assembled an increasingly impressive group of important Zambians, including prominent UNIP defectors and labor leaders. During the year, President Kaunda agreed to a referendum on the one-party state but, in the face of continued opposition, dropped the referendum and signed a constitutional amendment making Zambia a multi-party state. Zambia's first multi-party elections for parliament and the presidency since the 1960s were held on October 31, 1991. MMD candidate Frederick Chiluba resoundingly carried the presidential election over Kenneth Kaunda with 81% of the vote. To add to the MMD landslide, in the parliamentary elections the MMD won 125 of the 150 elected seats and UNIP the remaining 25. However, UNIP swept the Eastern Province, gathering 19 of its seats there.

By the end of Chiluba's first term as President (1996), the MMD's commitment to political reform had faded in the face of re-election demands. A number of prominent supporters founded opposing parties. Relying on the MMD's overwhelming majority in parliament, President Chiluba in May 1996 pushed through constitutional amendments that eliminated former President Kaunda and other prominent opposition leaders from the 1996 presidential elections. In the presidential and parliamentary elections held in November 1996, Chiluba was re-elected, and the MMD won 131 of the 150 seats in the National Assembly. Kaunda's UNIP party boycotted the parliamentary polls to protest the exclusion of its leader from the presidential race, alleging in addition that the outcome of the election had been predetermined due to a faulty voter registration exercise. Despite the UNIP boycott, the elections took place peacefully, and five presidential and more than 600 parliamentary candidates from 11 parties participated. Afterward, however, several opposition parties and non-governmental organizations declared the elections neither free nor fair. As President Chiluba began his second term in 1997, the opposition continued to reject the results of the election amid international efforts to encourage the MMD and the opposition to resolve their differences through dialogue.

Early in 2001, supporters of President Chiluba mounted a campaign to amend the constitution to enable Chiluba to seek a third term of office. Civil society, opposition parties, and many members of the ruling party exerted sufficient pressure on Chiluba to force him to back away from any attempt at a third term.

Presidential, parliamentary, and local government elections were held on December 27, 2001. Eleven parties contested the elections. The elections encountered numerous administrative problems. Opposition parties alleged that serious irregularities occurred. Nevertheless, MMD presidential candidate Levy Mwanawasa, having garnered a plurality of the vote (29%), was declared the victor by a narrow margin, and he was sworn into office on January 2, 2002. Three parties submitted petitions to the Supreme Court, challenging the election results, but the court ruled against the petitioners in February 2005. Opposition parties won a majority of parliamentary seats in the December 2001 election, but subsequent by-elections gave the ruling MMD a majority in parliament.

During his first months in office, President Mwanawasa encouraged the Zambian Anticorruption Commission to aggressively pursue its mandate. In July 2002, in a speech before the Zambian National Assembly, President Mwanawasa provided details on a number of corruption allegations targeting former President Chiluba, and called for parliament to consider lifting Chiluba's immunity from prosecution. Mwanawasa appointed a special Task Force to investigate and prosecute corrupt officials. Zambian courts are now hearing cases involving corruption charges against Chiluba and numerous officials from his regime.

During his first term in office, President Mwanawasa appointed an Electoral Reform Technical Committee (ERTC) and a Constitutional Reform Committee (CRC) to make recommendations for reforms. The ERTC submitted its final report to the President in August 2005. Voter registration began on October 31, 2005 and continued through

December 31, 2005. The CRC presented its final report and a draft constitution in December 2005. In February 2006 the government agreed to allow the formation of a Constituent Assembly to consider and adopt the draft constitution, subject to certain conditions. However, to date, a Constituent Assembly has not been formed. The Government of Zambia introduced very limited legislative changes to electoral procedures in mid-2006.

On July 25, 2006, President Mwanawasa dissolved parliament and his cabinet and set September 28, 2006 as the date for presidential, parliamentary, and local government elections. Mwanawasa won the September 2006 election with 1,177,846 votes, while the Patriotic Front's Michael Sata came in second with 804,748 votes. The head of a three-party alliance, Hakainde Hichilema, placed third. In parliamentary elections, the ruling MMD party won a slim majority of seats. International observers commended the overall conduct of the elections, but noted some anomalies.

ECONOMY

Rank	105th
Currency	Zambian kwacha (ZMK)
Fiscal year	calendar year
Trade organisations	WTO, SADC, COMESA
	Statistics
GDP	$24.36 billion
GDP growth	7.3%
GDP per capita	$1700
GDP by sector	agriculture: 20.4%, industry: 32.2%, services: 46.4%
Inflation (CPI)	6.6%
Population below poverty line	60%
Labour force	5.956 million
Labour force by occupation	agriculture: 85%, industry: 6%, services: 9%
Unemployment	14%
Main industries	copper mining and processing, construction, foodstuffs, beverages, chemicals, textiles, fertilizer, horticulture
Ease-of-doing-business rank	84th)
	External
Exports	$8.589 billion f.o.b.
Export goods	copper/cobalt 64%, cobalt, electricity; tobacco, flowers, cotton
Main export partners	China 42.2% South Africa 7.2% DR Congo 7.2% South Korea 5.3% India 4.5% Egypt 4.5% United Arab Emirates 4.4%
Imports	$7.361 billion f.o.b.
Import goods	machinery, transportation equipment, petroleum products, electricity, fertilizer; foodstuffs, clothing
Main import partners	South Africa 36.2% DR Congo 21.3% China 10.1% Kuwait 5.7% (2012 est.)

	Public finances
Public debt	$4.137 billion
Revenues	$4.256 billion
Expenses	$5.256 billion
Economic aid	recipient: $640.6 million
Credit rating	B+ (Domestic) B+ (Foreign) B+ (T&C Assessment) (Standard & Poor's)

Zambia is one of Sub-Saharan Africa's most highly urbanized countries. About one-half of the country's 11.5 million people are concentrated in a few urban zones strung along the major transportation corridors, while rural areas are under-populated. Unemployment and underemployment are serious problems. National GDP has actually doubled since independence, but due in large part to high birth rates and AIDS per capita annual incomes are currently at about two-thirds of their levels at independence. This low GDP per capita, which stands at $1400, places the country among the world's poorest nations. Social indicators continue to decline, particularly in measurements of life expectancy at birth (about 50 years) and maternal and infant mortality (85 per 1,000 live births). The high population growth rate of 2.3% per annum makes it difficult for per capita income to increase. The country's rate of economic growth cannot support rapid population growth or the strain which HIV/AIDS-related issues (i.e., rising medical costs, street children, and decline in worker productivity) places on government resources.

For the first time since 1989 Zambia's economic growth reached the 6%-7% mark(in 2007) needed to reduce poverty significantly. Copper output has increased steadily since 2004, due to higher copper prices and the opening of new mines. The maize harvest was again good in 2005, helping boost GDP and agricultural exports. Cooperation continues with international bodies on programs to reduce poverty, including a new lending arrangement with the IMF in the second quarter of 2004. A tighter monetary policy will help cut inflation, but Zambia still has a serious problem with high public debt.

Zambia was ranked the 127th safest investment destination in the world in the March 2011 Euromoney Country Risk rankings

Over 70% of Zambians live in poverty. Per capita annual incomes are currently at about one-half their levels at independence and, at $627, place the country among the world's poorest nations. Social indicators continue to decline, particularly in measurements of life expectancy at birth (about 38 years) and maternal mortality (729 per 100,000 pregnancies). The country's rate of economic growth cannot support rapid population growth or the strain which HIV/AIDS related issues (i.e., rising medical costs, decline in worker productivity) place on government resources. Zambia is also one of Sub-Saharan Africa's most highly urbanized countries. Almost one-half of the country's 10 million people are concentrated in a few urban zones strung along the major transportation corridors, while rural areas are underpopulated. Unemployment and underemployment are serious problems.

HIV/AIDS is the nation's greatest challenge, with 16% prevalence among the adult population. HIV/AIDS will continue to ravage Zambian economic, political, cultural, and social development for the foreseeable future.

Once a middle-income country, Zambia began to slide into poverty in the 1970s when copper prices declined on world markets. The socialist government made up for falling revenue by increasing borrowing. After democratic multi-party elections, the Chiluba government (1991-2001) came to power in November 1991 committed to an economic reform program. The government was successful in some areas, such as privatization of most of the parastatals, maintenance of positive real interest rates, the elimination of exchange controls, and endorsement of free market principles. Corruption grew dramatically under the Chiluba government. Zambia has yet to address effectively issues such as reducing the size of the public sector and improving Zambia's social sector delivery systems.

Zambia's total foreign debt stood at about $7 billion when Zambia reached the Highly Indebted Poor Countries Initiative (HIPC) completion point in April 2005. In December 2005, the U.S. and Zambian Governments signed an agreement for cancellation of $280 million in bilateral debt. Once debt cancellation under HIPC is completed, almost $6 billion in debt will be eliminated.

The IMF conducts periodic economic reviews under a three-year Poverty Reduction and Growth Facility. In November 2006, the Fund commended Zambia's macroeconomic stability and continued fiscal discipline, but noted lags in the implementation of some reform measures. In 2006, the rate of inflation dropped into single digits for the first time in recent history. The Zambian economy has historically been based on the copper-mining industry. Output of copper had fallen, however, to a low of 228,000 metric tons in 1998, after a 30-year decline in output due to lack of investment, low copper prices, and uncertainty over privatization. Following privatization of the industry, copper production rebounded, reaching almost 400,000 metric tons in 2004 and 440,000 metric tons in 2005. Improvements in the world copper market have magnified the effect of this volume increase on revenues and foreign exchange earnings.

The Zambian Government is pursuing an economic diversification program to reduce the economy's reliance on the copper industry. This initiative seeks to exploit other components of Zambia's rich resource base by promoting agriculture, tourism, gemstone mining, and hydro power.

DEFENSE

The Zambian Defense Force (ZDF) consists of the army, the air force, and Zambian National Service (ZNS). The ZNS, while operating under the Ministry of Defense, is responsible primarily for public works projects. The ZDF is designed primarily for internal defense. The HIV/AIDS epidemic has hit the ZDF especially hard.

The ZDF contributes to African Union and United Nations peacekeeping operations in Africa, and in 2005 became a partner in the African Contingency Operations and Training Assistance (ACOTA) program.

FOREIGN RELATIONS

Zambia is a member of the Non-Aligned Movement (NAM), the African Union, the Southern African Development Community (SADC), and the Common Market for Eastern and Southern Africa (COMESA), which is headquartered in Lusaka.

President Kaunda was a persistent and visible advocate of change in Southern Africa, supporting liberation movements in Angola, Mozambique, Namibia, Southern Rhodesia (Zimbabwe), and South Africa. Many of these organizations were based in Zambia during the 1970s and 1980s.

President Chiluba assumed a somewhat higher profile internationally in the mid- and late 1990s. His government played a constructive regional role sponsoring Angola peace talks that led to the 1994 Lusaka Protocols. Zambia has provided troops to UN peacekeeping initiatives in Mozambique, Rwanda, Angola, and Sierra Leone. Zambia was the first African state to cooperate with the International Tribunal investigation of the 1994 genocide in Rwanda.

In 1998, Zambia took the lead in efforts to establish a cease-fire in the Democratic Republic of Congo. Zambia was active in the Congolese peace effort after the signing of a cease-fire agreement in Lusaka in July and August 1999, although activity diminished considerably after the Joint Military Commission tasked with implementing the ceasefire relocated to Kinshasa in September 2001.

U.S.-ZAMBIAN RELATIONS

The United States and Zambia enjoy warm relations. The United States works closely with the Zambian Government to defeat the HIV/AIDS pandemic that is ravaging Zambia, to promote economic growth and development, and to effect political reform needed to strengthen the nation's emerging democratic institutions. The United States is also supporting the government's efforts to root out corruption. Zambia is a beneficiary of the African Growth and Opportunity Act (AGOA). Total U.S. Government assistance obligated for Zambia in 2006 was approximately $268 million. These funds provided a variety of technical assistance and other support that is managed by the Department of State, U.S. Agency for International Development, Millennium Challenge Account (MCA) Threshold Program, Centers for Disease Control, Department of Treasury, Department of Defense, and Peace Corps. The majority of assistance was provided through the President's Emergency Plan for AIDS Relief (PEPFAR), in support of the fight against HIV/AIDS.

In addition to supporting development projects, the United States has provided considerable emergency food aid during periods of drought through the World Food Program (WFP) and is a major contributor to refugee programs in Zambia through the UN High Commission for Refugees and other agencies.

U.S. Agency for International Development (USAID)

USAID administered more than $141 million in obligated funding for 2006. This included the management of over $70 million for PEPFAR and $22 million for the MCA assistance to Zambia to fight corruption, reduce administrative barriers, and make customs clearance more efficient, to improve trade. During 2006, USAID focused on the following programs in addition to PEPFAR and MCA:

- Increased private sector competitiveness;
- Improved quality of basic education for more school-aged children;

- Improved health status of Zambians; and
- Reduced impact of HIV/AIDS through a multi-sectoral response.

Peace Corps
A country agreement inviting the Peace Corps to work in Zambia was signed by the United States and Zambia on September 14, 1993. The first group of volunteers was sworn in on April 7, 1994. In 2007, the Peace Corps program in Zambia continues to increase understanding between Zambians and Americans. More than 160 two-year Volunteers and as many as 10 extension and Crisis Corps Volunteers promote sustainable development through their activities in agricultural and natural resource management, health and sanitation, rural education, and humanitarian assistance. Volunteers are working in eight of Zambia's nine provinces building local capacity to manage family fish farms, to promote food security and positive resource management practices near forest reserves, to implement health reforms at the village level, to promote and support rural education, and to extend HIV/AIDS education and prevention efforts through full participation in PEPFAR. Volunteers live primarily in rural villages in remote parts of the country without running water, electricity, or other amenities. New trainees undertake training in local language, culture, and the relevant technical specialty for 9-12 weeks at a center in the Chongwe district of Lusaka province.

Principal U.S. Officials
chief of mission: Ambassador Daniel L. FOOTE (since December 2017)
Deputy Chief of Mission--Michael Koplovsky
Public Affairs Officer--Christopher Wurst
Political/Economic Section Chief--Jill Derderian
Consular Officer--Malia Heroux
Defense Attaché--Lt. Col. David Dougherty
Centers for Disease Control and Prevention--Dr. Marc Bulterys
USAID Mission Director--Melissa Wells
Peace Corps Director--Cynthia Threlkeld
The U.S. Embassy in Zambia is at the corner of Independence and United Nations Avenues (P.O. Box 31617), Lusaka (tel: 260-1- 250955; fax 260-1-252225).

TRAVEL AND BUSINESS INFORMATION

The U.S. Department of State's Consular Information Program advises Americans traveling and residing abroad through Consular Information Sheets, Public Announcements, and Travel Warnings. **Consular Information Sheets** exist for all countries and include information on entry and exit requirements, currency regulations, health conditions, safety and security, crime, political disturbances, and the addresses of the U.S. embassies and consulates abroad. **Public Announcements** are issued to disseminate information quickly about terrorist threats and other relatively short-term conditions overseas that pose significant risks to the security of American travelers. **Travel Warnings** are issued when the State Department recommends that Americans avoid travel to a certain country because the situation is dangerous or unstable.
For the latest security information, Americans living and traveling abroad should regularly monitor the Department's Bureau of Consular Affairs Internet web site at http://www.travel.state.gov, where the current Worldwide Caution, Public Announcements, and Travel Warnings can be found. Consular Affairs Publications, which contain information on obtaining passports and planning a safe trip abroad, are

also available at http://www.travel.state.gov. For additional information on international travel, see http://www.usa.gov/Citizen/Topics/Travel/International.shtml.

The Department of State encourages all U.S citizens traveling or residing abroad to register via the State Department's travel registration website or at the nearest U.S. embassy or consulate abroad. Registration will make your presence and whereabouts known in case it is necessary to contact you in an emergency and will enable you to receive up-to-date information on security conditions.

Emergency information concerning Americans traveling abroad may be obtained by calling 1-888-407-4747 toll free in the U.S. and Canada or the regular toll line 1-202-501-4444 for callers outside the U.S. and Canada.

The National Passport Information Center (NPIC) is the U.S. Department of State's single, centralized public contact center for U.S. passport information. Telephone: 1-877-4USA-PPT (1-877-487-2778). Customer service representatives and operators for TDD/TTY are available Monday-Friday, 7:00 a.m. to 12:00 midnight, Eastern Time, excluding federal holidays.
Travelers can check the latest health information with the U.S. Centers for Disease Control and Prevention in Atlanta, Georgia. A hotline at 877-FYI-TRIP (877-394-8747) and a web site at http://wwwn.cdc.gov/travel/default.aspx give the most recent health advisories, immunization recommendations or requirements, and advice on food and drinking water safety for regions and countries. A booklet entitled "Health Information for International Travel" (HHS publication number CDC-95-8280) is available from the U.S. Government Printing Office, Washington, DC 20402, tel. (202) 512-1800.

ZAMBIA LEGAL SYSTEM BASICS

The Zambian legal system is based primarily on the English common law tradition. Zambia is overly reliant on the colonial legal system (many of the government's inefficiencies can be traced to its decision to adhere to a system that is ill-fitted for post-colonial rule). For instance, English law is used as a gap filler in all aspects of law from procedure, to contract, to legislative acts. Moreover, the system is structured in the same manner as it was during colonial rule and recognizes traditional customary law only if it is not "repugnant" to "civilized" ideas of justice. Further still, judges and lawyers continue to wear the antiquated dress of judges in the 19th century – especially complicated robes and white-haired wigs – while these customs have been phased out in most of the rest of the world, including England where they originated.

Like the American and South African legal systems (which were heavily influenced by the British tradition), Zambia has a hybrid common law system with a legal authority hierarchy as follows: 1) constitutional law 2) statutory law 3) common law 4) customary law and 5) authoritative texts (which are merely persuasive and not binding).

The Zambian constitution is the highest law of the land and provides for, essentially, the structure of government and the protection of the Zambian people's rights. The constitution is broken into parts and articles. Article five provides for citizenship, while articles 12 through 21 provide for the rights to life, personal liberty, a fair hearing, freedom of conscience and religion, expression, assembly, and protections from slavery, inhuman treatment, deprivation of property, against arbitrary search.

Zambia lies between the Democratic Republic of Congo to the north, Tanzania to the north-east, Malawi to the east, Mozambique, Zimbabwe, Botswana, and Namibia to the south, and Angola to the west. The country measures approximately 752,618 sq km with a population of approximately 11 862 740. The country's leadership is democratic.

Zambia's population comprises more than 70 Bantu-speaking ethnic groups. Some ethnic groups are small, and only two have enough people to constitute at least 10% of the population. Most Zambians are subsistence farmers. The predominant religion is a blend of traditional beliefs and Christianity; Christianity is the official national religion. Expatriates, a majority of whom are British (about 15,000) and South African, live mainly in Lusaka and in the Copper belt in northern Zambia, where they are employed in mines and related activities. Zambia also has a small but economically important Asian population, most of whom are Indians.

The indigenous hunter-gatherer occupants of Zambia began to be displaced or absorbed by more advanced migrating tribes about 2,000 years ago. The major waves of Bantu-speaking immigrants began in the 15th century, with the greatest influx between the late 17th and early 19th centuries. They came primarily from the Luba and Lunda tribes of southern Democratic Republic of Congo and northern Angola but were joined in the 19th century by Ngoni peoples from the south. By the latter part of that century, the various peoples of Zambia were largely established in the areas they currently occupy.

Except for an occasional Portuguese explorer, the area lay untouched by Europeans for centuries. After the mid-19th century, it was penetrated by Western explorers, missionaries, and traders. David Livingstone, in 1855, was the first European to see the magnificent waterfalls on the Zambezi River. He named the falls after Queen Victoria, and the Zambian town near the falls is named after him.

In 1888, Cecil Rhodes, spearheading British commercial and political interests in Central Africa, obtained mineral rights concession from local chiefs. In the same year, Northern and Southern Rhodesia (now Zambia and Zimbabwe, respectively) were proclaimed a British sphere of influence. Southern Rhodesia was annexed formally and granted self-government in 1923, and the administration of Northern Rhodesia was transferred to the British colonial office in 1924 as a protectorate. In 1953, both Rhodesias were joined with Nyasaland (now Malawi) to form the Federation of Rhodesia and Nyasaland. Northern Rhodesia was the center of much of the turmoil and crisis that characterized the federation in its last years. At the core of the controversy were insistent African demands for greater participation in government and European fears of losing political control.

A two-stage election held in October and December of 1962 resulted in an African majority in the legislative council and an uneasy coalition between the two African nationalist parties. The council passed resolutions calling for Northern Rhodesia's secession from the federation and demanding full internal self-government under a new constitution and a new national assembly based on a broader, more democratic franchise. On December 31, 1963, the federation was dissolved, and Northern Rhodesia became the Republic of Zambia on October 24, 1964.

At independence, despite its considerable mineral wealth, Zambia faced major challenges. Domestically, there were few trained and educated Zambians capable of running the government, and the economy was largely dependent on foreign expertise. Abroad, three of its neighbors--Southern Rhodesia and the Portuguese colonies of Mozambique and Angola--remained under white-dominated rule. Rhodesia's white-ruled government unilaterally declared independence in 1965. In addition, Zambia shared a border with South African-controlled South-West Africa (now Namibia). Zambia's sympathies lay with forces opposing colonial or white-dominated rule, particularly in Southern Rhodesia. During the next decade, it actively supported movements such as the Union for the Total Liberation of Angola (UNITA), the Zimbabwe African People's Union (ZAPU), the African National Congress of South Africa (ANC), and the South-West Africa People's Organization (SWAPO).

Conflicts with Rhodesia resulted in the closing of Zambia's borders with that country and severe problems with international transport and power supply. However, the Kariba hydroelectric station on the Zambezi River provided sufficient capacity to satisfy the country's requirements for electricity. A railroad to the Tanzanian port of Dar es Salaam, built with Chinese assistance, reduced Zambian dependence on railroad lines south to South Africa and west through an increasingly troubled Angola.

By the late 1970s, Mozambique and Angola had attained independence from Portugal. Zimbabwe achieved independence in accordance with the 1979 Lancaster House agreement, but Zambia's problems were not solved. Civil war in the former Portuguese colonies generated refugees and caused continuing transportation problems.

The Benguela Railroad, which extended west through Angola, was essentially closed to traffic from Zambia by the late 1970s. Zambia's strong support for the ANC, which had its external headquarters in Lusaka, created security problems as South Africa raided ANC targets in Zambia. In the mid-1970s, the price of copper, Zambia's principal export, suffered a severe decline worldwide. Zambia turned to foreign and international lenders for relief, but as copper prices remained depressed, it became increasingly difficult to service its growing debt. In response to growing popular demand, and after lengthy, difficult negotiations between the Kaunda government and opposition groups, Zambia enacted a new constitution in 1991 and shortly thereafter became a multi-party democracy. Kaunda's successor, Frederick Chiluba, made efforts to liberalize the economy and privatize industry, but allegations of massive corruption characterized the latter part of his administration. By the mid-1990s, despite limited debt relief, Zambia's per capita foreign debt remained among the highest in the world.

Although poverty continues to be a significant problem in Zambia, its economy has stabilized, attaining single-digit inflation in 2006-2007, real GDP growth, decreasing interest rates, and increasing levels of trade. Much of its growth is due to foreign investment in Zambia's mining sector and higher copper prices on the world market. In 2005, Zambia qualified for debt relief under the Heavily Indebted Poor Countries (HIPC) initiative, consisting of approximately U.S. $6 billion in debt relief.

GOVERNMENT

Zambia became a republic immediately upon attaining independence in October 1964. The constitution promulgated on August 25, 1973, abrogated the original 1964 constitution. The new constitution and the national elections that followed in December 1973 were the final steps in achieving what was called a "one-party participatory democracy." The 1973 constitution provided for a strong president and a unicameral National Assembly. National policy was formulated by the Central Committee of the United National Independence Party (UNIP), the sole legal party in Zambia. The cabinet executed the central committee's policy. In accordance with the intention to formalize UNIP supremacy in the new system, the constitution stipulated that the sole candidate in elections for the office of president was the person selected to be the president of UNIP by the party's general conference. The second-ranking person in the Zambian hierarchy was UNIP's secretary general.

In December 1990, at the end of a tumultuous year that included riots in the capital and a coup attempt, President Kenneth Kaunda signed legislation ending UNIP's monopoly on power. Zambia enacted a new constitution in August 1991, which enlarged the National Assembly from 136 members to a maximum of 158 members, established an electoral commission, and allowed for more than one presidential candidate who no longer had to be a member of UNIP. The first multi-party elections in November 1991 resulted in the victory of the Movement for Multi-Party Democracy (MMD) and the election of President Frederick Chiluba, a former trade Unionist. The present Constitution dates from June 1996. While similar to the 1991 Constitution, it contains amended provisions regarding the qualifications of presidential candidates and grants the President and the National Assembly increased powers in respect of their relationship with the judiciary. The May 1996 amendment set new limits on the presidency (including a retroactive two-term limit, and a requirement that both parents of a candidate be Zambians-by birth or descent). This amendment had the direct effect of excluding former President Kaunda, whose parents were Malawian, from standing in the presidential elections. The UNIP boycotted the November 1996 elections that confirmed the government of MMD and President Chiluba. Executive power is vested in the President, who is elected directly by universal suffrage for a term of five years and may be re-elected only once. The President is the Head of State and the Commander-in-Chief.

On 2 August 1991, the adoption of a new Constitution introduced a multi-party system, thereby ending the monopoly of Kaunda's United National Independence Party (UNIP). The President appoints the Ministers of his Cabinet from among the members of the National Assembly, and they are collectively answerable to the National Assembly. The President has the power to declare a state of emergency and to dissolve the National Assembly. Article 45 of the Constitution provides for the office of the Vice-President, who is appointed from among the members of the National Assembly and performs such functions as are assigned to him by the President of the Republic. Legislative power is vested in the Parliament, which consists of the President and the National Assembly. The National Assembly is composed of 150 members elected by universal, direct suffrage, with not more than eight members nominated by the President, and the Speaker, nominated by the members of the National Assembly. Traditional chiefs are not qualified to be elected as members of the Parliament. Legislation passed by the National Assembly must be assented to by the President in order to become law. Members of the Parliament form parliamentary committees with the mandate to consider specific matters or bills.

The Constitution also provides for a House of Chiefs, an advisory body composed of 27 chiefs from the various provinces. 401 Zambia *–Attacks on Justice, eleventh edition* International Commission of Jurists .The country is divided into nine provinces, including the capital of Lusaka, each of which is administered by a centrally appointed Provincial Secretary and a partially elected Provincial Council. The provinces are subdivided into 55 districts, each administered by a centrally appointed Governor and a partially elected District Council. Presidential and parliamentary elections are to be held on 27 December 2001.

At the beginning of 2001 President Chiluba had seemed eager to amend the Constitution in order to seek a third term, but on 8 May 2001, following pressure from the opposition, international donors and even by members of his own cabinet, Chiluba announced that he would not stand for an unconstitutional third term in office. In the meantime, more than 20 dissident members of the ruling MMD party including the country's Vice-President and eight ministers have been expelled from the Parliament. In May 2001, an impeachment petition was filed against President Chiluba before the House Speaker of the National Assembly. The petitioners, mostly MMD parliamentarians, obtained 65 signatures, enough to compel the Speaker to convene parliament to hear charges of gross misconduct against President Chiluba, who had come under intense criticism for corruption in his government. On 30 May 2001, the Parliament postponed the debate on the impeachment motion.

In December 1990, at the end of a tumultuous year that included riots in the capital and a coup attempt, President Kaunda signed legislation ending UNIP's monopoly on power. In response to growing popular demand for multi-party democracy, and after lengthy, difficult negotiations between the Kaunda government and opposition groups, Zambia enacted a new constitution in August 1991. The constitution enlarged the National Assembly from 136 members to a maximum of 158 members, establishing an electoral commission, and allowed for more than one presidential candidate who no longer had to be members of UNIP. The constitution was amended again in 1996 to set new limits on the presidency (including a retroactive two term limit, and a requirement that both parents of a candidate be Zambian-born.) The National Assembly is comprised of 150 directly elected members, up to 8 presidentially appointed members and a speaker. Zambia is divided into nine provinces, each administered by an appointed governor.

FOREIGN RELATIONS

Zambia is a member of the Non-Aligned Movement (NAM), the African Union, the Southern African Development Community (SADC), and the Common Market for Eastern and Southern Africa (COMESA), which is headquartered in Lusaka. President Kaunda was a persistent and visible advocate of change in southern Africa, supporting liberation movements in Angola, Mozambique, Namibia, Southern Rhodesia (Zimbabwe), and South Africa. Many of these liberation organizations were based in Zambia during the 1970s and 1980s. President Chiluba assumed a visible international role in the mid- and late 1990s. His government sponsored Angola's peace talks that led to the 1994 Lusaka Protocols. Zambia provided troops to UN peacekeeping initiatives in Mozambique, Rwanda, Angola, and Sierra Leone. Zambia was the first African state to cooperate with the International Tribunal investigation of the 1994 genocide in Rwanda.

In 1998, Zambia took the lead in efforts to establish a cease-fire in Democratic Republic of the Congo. After the signing of a cease-fire agreement in Lusaka in July and August 1999, Zambia was active in supporting the Congolese peace effort, although activity diminished considerably after the Joint Military Commission tasked with implementing the ceasefire relocated to Kinshasa in September 2001.

During President Mwanawasa's administration, Zambia contributed troops to support UN peacekeeping operations in southern Sudan. During his tenure as SADC Chair, President Mwanawasa brought the issue of Zimbabwe to the fore in the SADC, taking a lead role in pressuring President Mugabe for reforms in his country. Zambia's history of stability and its commitment to regional peace has made it a haven for large numbers of refugees. Currently, Zambia hosts approximately 87,000 refugees (down from a high of 203,000 in 2002), including roughly 51,000 Congolese, 27,000 Angolans, and 9,000 other nationalities (mainly Rwandans, Burundians, and Somalis). In recent years, Zambia has made serious efforts to repatriate many of these refugees, including organized repatriation for 74,000 Angolan and 17,000 Congolese refugees.

ECONOMY

About two-thirds of Zambians live in poverty. Per capita annual incomes are well below their levels at independence and, at $852, place the country among the world's poorest nations. Life expectancy at birth is about 51 years, and maternal mortality is 649 per

100,000 pregnancies. The country's rate of economic growth cannot support rapid population growth or the strain which HIV & AIDS-related issues (i.e., rising medical costs, decline in worker productivity) place on government resources. Zambia is also one of Sub-Saharan Africa's most highly urbanized countries. Over one-third of the country's 12.9 million people are concentrated in a few urban zones strung along the major transportation corridors, while rural areas are under-populated. Unemployment and underemployment are serious problems. HIV & AIDS is the nation's greatest challenge, with 14.3% prevalence among the adult population.

HIV & AIDS will continue to ravage Zambian economic, political, cultural, and social development for the foreseeable future. Once a middle-income country, Zambia began to slide into poverty in the 1970s when copper prices declined on world markets. The socialist government made up for falling revenue by increasing borrowing. After democratic multi-party elections, the Chiluba government (1991-2001) came to power in November 1991 committed to an economic reform program. The government was successful in some areas, such as privatization of most of the parastatals, maintenance of positive real interest rates, the elimination of exchange controls, and endorsement of free market principles. Corruption grew dramatically under the Chiluba government. Zambia has yet to address effectively issues such as reducing the size of the public sector and improving Zambia's social sector delivery systems.

For 30 years, copper production declined steadily from a 1973 high of 700,000 metric tons to a 2000 low of 226,192 metric tons. The decline was the result of poor management of state-owned mines and lack of investment. With the privatization of the mines in April 2000, the downward trend in production and exports was reversed as a result of investments in plant rehabilitation, expansion, increased exploration, and high copper prices on the international market. Copper production rose to 535,000 metric tons in 2007, but slumping copper prices in late 2008 put significant pressure on the mining companies and government revenue. Zambia experienced positive economic growth for the ninth consecutive year in 2007 with a GDP of U.S. $10.9 billion and a real growth rate of 6% (according to preliminary IMF estimates). The rate of inflation dropped from 30% in 2000 to single-digit inflation of 8.9% by December 2007 due to fiscal and monetary discipline and the growth of the domestic food supply.

Year-on-year inflation grew to double digits in late 2008, due to rising fuel and food prices. In April 2005, the International Monetary Fund (IMF) and the World Bank's International Development Association (IDA) provided Zambia significant debt service relief and debt forgiveness under the Heavily Indebted Poor Countries (HIPC) initiative. Zambia was the 17th country to reach the HIPC completion point and has benefited from approximately U.S. $6 billion in debt relief. In July 2005, the G-8 agreed on a proposal to cancel 100% of outstanding debt of eligible HIPC countries to the IMF, African Development Fund, and IDA. Zambia is among the beneficiaries of this additional multilateral debt relief.

Zambia also completed a Poverty Reduction and Growth Facility (PRGF) arrangement with the IMF for the period 2008-2011. The Zambian Government is pursuing an economic diversification program to reduce the economy's reliance on the copper industry. This initiative seeks to exploit other components of Zambia's rich resource base by promoting agriculture, tourism, gemstone mining, and hydropower. The government is also seeking to create an environment that encourages entrepreneurship and private-sector led growth. Zambia's economy has been affected by the global economic crisis and the fall in world copper prices. High inflation, currency volatility, rising unemployment, and restricted access to capital are likely to dampen Zambia's economic performance in 2009.

SOURCES OF LAW

Zambia does not have a single code containing its laws. These are drawn from a variety of sources. The following are sources of law in Zambia:

- Constitution
- Legislation
- Common Law
- Judicial precedent
- Customary Law
- Authoritative texts

Constitution of Zambia

The constitution was adopted in 1991 and was amended in 1996. It abrogates the 1973 constitution, which allowed, as stated above, only one political party. More political parties were allowed to participate as enshrined by the new constitution.

Legislation

Legislation in Zambia is contained in statute books that are available in most libraries. The Ministry of Justice Law library offer legislation. The government website is also helpful in as far as legislation is concerned. Constitutionally, legislation refers to laws that have been passed by parliament and have been assented to by the President. Subsidiary legislation refers to laws passed by other bodies to which parliament have validly delegated such legislative powers. These include government gazettes and municipal bye-laws, *inter alia.*

In Zambia the legislative vests in the National assembly and is assented to by the President. Parliament can confer power on any authority to create binding laws. Currently parliament consists of one House; the National assembly. In terms of the constitution, legislation brought through parliament has to be scrutinized by the National assembly before it goes for assent to the President (article 78(2)). A bill shall not become law unless the President has assented to it and signed it in token of that assent (article 78). By virtue of Article 54(2) (a), the Attorney General is charged with drafting and signing all bills presented before parliament. The Attorney General may delegate functions to the Solicitor General (article 55(5) (b)). Laws made by the National Assembly and assented to by the president shall be styled "Acts" and the words of enactment shall be "Enacted by the Parliament of Zambia" (article 78(8)).

Precedent

Precedent forms part of the law of Zambia. Decisions of superior courts of record are therefore binding to lower courts. Decisions from South African courts are only persuasive, and courts refer to them in formulating their decisions. Decisions from similar jurisdiction can also be cited for their persuasive value. Magistrates' courts decisions do not become precedent since these are lower courts. They are however bound by decisions of the High Court and the Supreme Court of Appeal. Precedent assists in consistency in legal interpretation and application of the law. It has also been justified for bringing certainty and uniformity to the law. However, precedent has been blamed for causing rigidity of legal systems, preventing development of the law.

Authoritative texts

Written works of eminent authors have persuasive value in the courts of Zambia. These include writings of the old authorities as well as contemporary writers from similar jurisdictions.

INTERNATIONAL LAW

Zambia is signatory to many international instruments. Although the country is quick to ratify, implementation is often slow or never materialises. Zambia belongs to the dualist tradition, thus views international law and domestic law as two separate legal systems. Hence domestication of international law by an Act of Parliament is necessary before international law can be applied. This of course excludes customary international law which is binding on all states. The Attorney General is mandated by article 54(2) (b) to draft and peruse treaties and agreements the government of Zambia is party to.

THE JUSTICE SYSTEM OF ZAMBIA

At the apex of the Zambian justice system is the Supreme Court which is the final court of appeal on all matters. It has a supervisory and review jurisdiction over all courts of Zambia. The Supreme Court has appellate jurisdiction for all legal and constitutional disputes. The High Court, which holds regular sessions in all nine provincial capitals, has authority to hear criminal and civil cases and appeals from lower courts. The Industrial Relations court deals exclusively with industrial and labour matters. There is also a Land Tribunal and Revenues Appeals Tribunal. Magistrate courts have original jurisdiction in some criminal and civil cases; local, or customary, courts handle most civil and petty criminal cases in rural areas.

Local courts employ the principles of customary law, which vary widely throughout the country. Lawyers are barred from participating in proceedings in such courts, and there are few formal rules of procedure. Presiding judges, who usually are prominent local citizens, have substantial power to invoke customary law, render judgments regarding marriages, divorces, inheritances, other civil proceedings, and rule on minor criminal matters. Judgments often are not in accordance with the Penal Code. For example, they tend to discriminate against women in matters of inheritance.

The Constitution and the Judiciary

Judicial power exclusively vests in the judiciary in terms of Article 91(2) of the Constitution. Article 91 (3) of the Constitution further provides that justice shall be administered in accordance with the provisions of an Act of Parliament which shall be independent and subject on. Article 91(1) provides that the judiciary shall consist of

the Supreme Court of Judicature comprising:

(a) The Supreme Court, and

(b) The High Court

(c) Such other courts as may be prescribed by an Act of Parliament.

Chapter outline of the constitution

The constitution of Zambia is the supreme law and if any other law inconsistent with the constitution that other law shall, to the extent of its inconsistency, be void (article1(3)). Therefore Zambia has a constitutional supremacy.

The constitution was adopted in 1991 after consultations with the citizens of Zambia. It was amended in 1996. It repealed the constitution of Zambia Act, 1973. It purports to be an autochthonous document. The constitution set out clearly the state structure, bill of rights, the separate arms of government as well as other administrative organs such as the public service commission.

Constitutional clauses analysis:

Fundamental rights and freedoms Article11

Protection of right to life Article 11(a), Article 12

Protection of right to personal liberty Article13

Protection from slavery Article 14

Protection from inhuman or degrading treatment Article 15

Protection from deprivation of property Article16

Right to a fair hearing Article 18(1)

Protection against arbitrary search or entry Article 17(1)

Protection of freedom of conscience and religion Article 19

Protection of freedom of expression Article 20

Protection of freedom of assembly and association Article 21

Rights of child
Article 24

Enforcement of protective provisions Article 28

National Sovereignty and the state

Zambia is defined as a unitary sovereign, multiparty and democratic state. (This part sets out that all power resides in the people who shall exercise their sovereignty through the democratic institutions of the state). This part also establishes the Public Seal. The supremacy of the constitution is set out in this part. The constitution also sets out the anthem and the National Emblem.

Citizenship

Citizenship is the state of belonging. Citizenship guarantees rights of nationality and all other rights from being a national of a particular country. Amongst other inherent rights is the ability to pass on to natural and adopted children since they cannot obtain their independent citizens at that stage. This part talks about acquisition and loss of acquisition. Citizenship in Zambia can be by way of descent, operation of the law or birth, marriage or by registration.

Most notable is the fact that either the mother or the father or both can confer citizenship on children (Article 5). Article 9 provides for the establishment of the Citizenship Board, which deals with any matters pertaining registration as citizens and powers of parliament in making provisions for acquisition of citizenship of Zambia by persons who are not eligible to become citizens of Zambia.

Protection of Fundamental Rights and Freedom of the Individual

Part three is concerned with the promotion and protection of fundamental human rights and freedom of the individual.

Protection of the right to life

Zambia still retains the death penalty, whilst Article 12(1) states that no person shall be deprived of life, it permits the use of death penalty in the execution of the sentence of a curt in respect of criminal offence which that person has been convicted. This is not enough to ensure the full guarantee of the right to life. The right to life, as guaranteed by the second protocol to the International Covenant on Civil and political Rights aiming at the abolition of the death penalty, and the African Charter on Human and Peoples Rights. Imposition of the death penalty itself is not only a violation of the right to life, but also the ultimate form of cruel, inhuman or degrading punishment or treatment.

Protection of the right to personal liberty

The protection guaranteed in the international standards is missing or not fully recognized and entrenched in this constitution. For example International standards of fair trial provide that anyone arrested or detained must be notified at the time of the arrest of the reasons of their arrest or detention and their right, including their right to counsel. This information is essential to allow detained persons to challenge the lawfulness of their arrest or detention and, if they are charged, to start the preparation of their defense. It is essential against arbitrary arrest and detention, to ensure that no detainee is held incommunicado detention, or in a place other than an official detention centre or prison or held in any manner intended to frustrate proper and prompt access to the detainee by legal representatives, doctors or next of kin. Finally, it is not clear why this part on the protection of the right to personal liberty should include exceptions allowing for orders requiring a person to remain within a specific area or prohibiting that person from being within such an area as envisaged by article 16(1)(i).

Protection of Women's rights

The Zambian Constitution is silent on the issue of women's equal participation in electoral politics. Moreover, no provision of the Zambian Constitution ensures substantive equality between women and men, though Article 11 does include a blanket non-discrimination clause that guarantees everyone the enjoyment of fundamental rights and freedoms regardless of "race, place of origin, political opinions, colour, creed, sex or marital status" (emphasis added). Article 23 of the Constitution further guarantees that, except for certain limitations, "A law shall not make any provision that is discriminatory either of itself or in its effect."

Article 23(4) of the Zambian Constitution allows discrimination in the area of customary Law, family law and other areas such as adoption, marriage, divorce and inheritance. Article 11(1) recognizes and declares every person in Zambia to be entitled to the fundamental rights and freedoms of the individual, whatever "his sex". However, the same article states that the entitlement of these rights and freedoms are subject to limitations contained in this related to Fundamental Rights and Freedoms. Linked to Article 23(4), this means that discrimination against women in areas related to property and inheritance rights is allowed. Article 16 provides for protection against deprivation of property, which may only be carried out under an Act of Parliament providing for payment of adequate compensation.

The right of persons of with disabilities

There is no specific provision in the Zambian constitution that stipulates the rights of persons with disabilities. Article 23 proscribes discrimination in any form against any person and could be used to govern the rights of the disabled. Persons with disabilities should have their rights protected and guaranteed. However, Zambia has a specific legislation on the rights of disabled persons. It is contained in the Handicapped Persons Act of 1968 as amended. The Zambian statute establishes a Council of the disabled, which provides for voluntary registration of disabled persons and of associations that maintain their welfare. A commissioner of the disabled is responsible for the administration of the Act.

The Executive

Article 33(1) states that there shall be a president of the Republic of Zambia who shall be the head of state and of the government and the Commander-in-chief of the defense force. Article 33(2) clearly states that the executive power of the Republic of Zambia shall vest in the president and, subject to the other provisions of this constitution; shall be exercised by him either directly or through officers subordinates to him. In line with the doctrine of separation of powers Article 33(2) emphasizes that exercise of executive power by the president shall be in accordance with the constitution. This serves to curtail any excess on the use of such power. The constitution further provides for the appointment of the Vice-President, ministers and their deputies.

The Attorney general

The attorney General (AG) plays the role of the legal advisor to the government, hence the relationship between the office of the AG and the ministry of justice. The AG is not part of the cabinet per se but works closely with the executive. Article 54(1) of the constitution which is the provision creating this office provides that the AG shall be appointed by the president. It further spells out the qualifications of the persons to be appointed. The AG is the Principal legal advisor to the government and an ex-officio member of cabinet. The AG represents the government in courts or any other legal proceedings to which government is a party.

Government also makes use of the office of the Solicitor General (SL) who shall be appointed by the president as per Article 55(1). The SL may exercise any power or duty imposed on the AG when the AG is unable to act owing to illness or absence and in any case where the AG has authorized the AG.

Apart from the AG's office and the SL's office government also makes use of the office of the Director of Public Prosecutions (DPP), mainly in criminal matters. Article 56(1) set up this office and provides for the appointment of the DPP. The DPP is appointed by the President subject to ratification by the National Assembly, and qualification for appointment to this office is the same as that for a judge of the High Court with experience biased on criminal law, (Article 56(2)).

Article 56(3) provides that the DPP shall have power in any case which he considers it proper to do so, to;

(a) Institute and undertake criminal proceedings against any person in any court, other than a court martial, in respect of any offence alleged to have been committed by that person;

(b) Take over and continue any such criminal proceedings as have been instituted or undertaken by any other person or authority;

(c) To discontinue, at any stage before judgment is delivered, any such criminal proceedings instituted or undertaken by himself or any other person or authority.

The DPP in person or by delegation to subordinate officers has the power to institute and undertake criminal proceedings against any person before any court. This office can take over and continue or discontinue any criminal proceedings instituted by any person or authority, at any stage before judgment is delivered. Although individuals can prosecute (that is institute criminal proceedings) at the private instance. The drawback of provisions allowing for prosecution at the private instance is that the DPP's office never really gets to totally relinquish its powers to prosecute. Article 56(3) (b) of the constitution acts as a drawback clause that can easily be open to abuse, to frustrate any attempts at private prosecutions. Notwithstanding the issue of a *nolle prosequi*, the DPP's office can still intercept private prosecution proceedings and take over in its capacity as a public prosecutor: thus effectively excluding the person or authority that initiated the proceedings. The DPP's office need not give reasons for such move, save that it is proper to do so.

Further, after rejoining the fray, the DPP's office may then exercise its powers under paragraph (c) to terminate any criminal proceedings, whether started by the office at the public instance or any person at private instance.

It is submitted that this vicious cycle is open to abuse. In effect it means that prosecution can only be undertaken by the DPP and no other individual or authority.

The Legislature

The constitution portrays the government in Zambia as a multi-party and democratic Sovereign State. The constitution further provides that parliament shall consist of the President and the National Assembly. In terms of Article 63(2) membership to the National Assembly is through ordinary elections and being voted into parliament. The elected members shall not exceed one hundred and fifty members (150), not more than eight (8) nominated members and the speaker of the national assembly. Since Zambia is a multi-party democracy members of parliament represent their respective political parties. The constitution is silent on the issue of Women's equal participation in electoral politics.

The Judicature

The constitution provides that the judicature shall be autonomous and shall be administered in accordance with the provisions of an Act of parliament. The judicature shall be independent and subject to only the constitution. The judiciary shall consist of superior court of judicature comprising of;

- Supreme Court
- High Court
- Industrial Court
- Subordinate Courts
- The Local Courts
- Such other courts as may be prescribed by act of parliament.

The judiciary has jurisdiction in all matters civil and criminal, including matters relating to the constitution, and such other jurisdiction as by law conferred on it. The superior courts are courts of record and have power to commit for contempt to themselves and all such powers as were vested in a superior court of record immediately before the commencement of the constitution.

Infringement on judicial independence

The constitution gives very wide powers to the head of state to appoint judicial officers. The president appoints the chief justice and the deputy chief justice. According to article

93(1) the chief justice and deputy chief justice shall subject to ratification by the national assembly, be appointed by the president. Article 93(2) gives the president the power to appoint judges of the Supreme Court. Article 95(1) states that puisne judges shall subject to ratification by national assembly be appointed by the president on the advice of judicial services commission. Furthermore, the president with the advice of the JSC appoints the chairman and deputy chairman of the industrial court. Section 96(1) states that any position appointed under article 93 to act as a judge of the Supreme Court shall continue to act for the period of that person's appointment is marked by the president.

Judges and other judicial officers ought to be hired on full time basis to ensure that they enjoy security of the tenure to enable them to carry out their duties in a competence fashion without fear or favour. Judges on contract are under pressure particularly when their contracts are about to end. This is contrary article 91(2) which promotes judicial independence and frowns upon infringement on this independence by other organs of government. Appointment of judges on acting or contract basis is detrimental to judicial independence since such judges are put in a state of suspense regarding whether they would be confirmed or not. In such a situation the judge may find himself / herself trying to please those with power to confirm him/ her by deciding cases in their favour. The involvement of the head of state in the process of appointing judges intimidates against an independent judiciary. Due to this fact such appointment can not be free of political considerations. The constitution still rests arguably judicial powers on the president. In a situation where the appointing body is politically influenced one cannot hope for independent judiciary. People seeking judicial appointments might be lobby appointed. Thus such people would feel a sense of obligation to the executive and be inclined to favour the executive in the adjudicatory process.

Judicial tenure and remuneration

Article 98(1) provides a position holding the offices of a judge of the Supreme Court or the office of a judge of the high court shall vacate that office on attaining the age of 65 years. Provided that the president –(a) may appoint a judge of the supreme court, who has attained that age to continue in office for such further period, not exceeding seven years as the president may determine. Judges along with other specified officers such as attorney general, investigators- general solicitor- general director of public prosecutions are paid from the general revenues of the republic. Such salaries and or allowances may be presented by or under an act of parliament. Article 119(3) provides that the salary payable to the holder of any holder of office shall not be uttered to his disadvantage after his appointment. Note article 96.

Removal of judges from office

According to Article 98(2) a judge of the Supreme Court, high court chairman of deputy chairman of the industrial relations court may be removed from office only for inability to perform the functions of his office whether arising from infirmity of body or mind, incompetence or misbehavior and shall not be so removed except in accordance with the provisions of this article. Article 98(3) provides for the establishment of a tribunal which will investigate the case of a judge before removal in which the tribunal consists of a chairman and not less than the other members who hold or have held high judicial office. This tribunal can be biased in the sense that the judge whose perpetual removal has been influenced by the political motives can collude to remove him from offices in order to gain favour from the executive. The tribunal after a proper inquiry represents the matter to the president and advices the president whether the judge ought to be removed from office for inability or incompetence or for misbehavior for which the president has an obligation to remove such judge from office. Article 98 gives so much power on the president to remove and suspend judge and this compromises the independence of judiciary as narrated by article 91(2).

The Supreme Court

Article 92 establishes the supreme court of Zambia, which shall consist of: the chief justice, the deputy chief justice, seven Supreme Court judges or such greater number as may be prescribed by an act of parliament. The Supreme Court is a superior court of record.

The High Court

Article 97 establishes the high court of Zambia which shall have, except as to the proceedings in which the industrial relations court has exclusive jurisdiction under the industrial relations (act no.27 of 1993), unlimited or original jurisdiction to hear and determine any civil or criminal proceedings under any law and such jurisdiction and powers as may be conferred on it by this constitution or any other law. The high court shall be divided into such divisions as may be determined by an act of parliament 94(2). The chief justice shall be such an ex-offices judge of the high court (3). The other judges of the high court shall be such number of puisne judges as maybe prescribed by parliament.

Article 94(6) provides that the high court shall be a superior court of record. The high court has jurisdiction to supervise any civil or criminal proceedings before any subordinate court or any court martial and may such order issues such as writs and give such direction as it may consider appropriate for the purposes of ensuring that question as is duly administered by such court.

Specialist courts in Zambia

Apart from the Supreme Court and the High Court which are ordinary courts, Zambia also has specialist courts set up to deal with particular matters. These are creatures of statute, with limited jurisdiction as set out in the legislation establishing them. The Industrial Court and Local courts are examples of specialist courts in Zambia.

The Local Courts

The local courts play an important part in the settlement of disputes of the majority of the majority of the population the customary law itself is in a state of flux. The main thrust of the law governing the operation of the Local Courts, contained in Chapter 29 o the Laws of Zambia, is the administration of customary law. In reality the Local Courts are the focal point of varied societal claims. Customary law is the ambiguous expression in which are hidden many legal claims. It can be safely asserted that Local Courts are the clearing grounds for simple torts, contracts, and petty crimes. But the main workload of the courts is the law relating to non-statutory marriages. Divorce, reconciliation, custody of children, payment of mabolo or lobola, persons who die without a will-these are areas which affect the legal rights of the majority of the population. The effective handling of these disputes and their fair and just resolution assure stability in the community.

There is no uniform formal educational qualification for adjudicators of local courts. They bring important innovation in the administration of community justice derived in part from their practical understanding of the workings of a post-traditional society. These justices are often fluent in more than four local languages.

Small Claims Courts

There is on the Zambian statute books the Small Claims Court Act. The objective of the Act is to provide for the establishment, of Small Claims Courts to be situated in areas to be designated by the Chief Justice. The Small Claims Courts adopt arbitration as a mode of resolving disputes. The choice of this mode of dispute resolution is questionable because arbitration is typically adjudicative and is quite formal. Mediation would probably have been a more apt mode of resolving disputes in the Small Claims Courts. The tragedy of the Small Claims Court legislation is that although the legislation has been on the statute books for over a decade, the Small Claims Courts have not yet been operationalized. However the idea of Small Claim Courts is a very good one. It depends on involvement of legal practitioners of 5 year standing with more personnel allocated to them. The Small Claims Court could utilize existing infrastructure such as school buildings, community halls and several others. If the existing mechanisms of resolving disputes in both rural and urban areas are adopted but also adapted to suit the needs of the poor the small claims court could work most effectively. Rules that normally apply to formalized courts should be more flexible to enable the poor.

The Legal Aid Board

The Legal Aid Act 70 was enacted on 20th November 1967. The objective of the Act is to provide for legal aid in civil and criminal matters and causes to persons whose means are inadequate to enable them to engage practitioners to represent them. The Directorate of Legal Aid Board operated as a department within the Ministry of Legal Affairs and consequently enjoyed limited autonomy. However, by the Legal Aid (Amendment) Act the Legal Aid department was transformed into a Legal Aid Board. The Legal Aid Board comprised the following part-time members appointed by the Minister: 73

(a) A person qualified to be a Judge of the High Court who shall be the Chairperson;

(b) A representative of the Law Association of Zambia;

(c) The Permanent Secretary in the Ministry responsible for legal affairs;

(d) A representative of the Ministry responsible for Home Affairs;

(e) The Director who shall be an ex officio member;

(f) A representative of a non-governmental organization active in the promotion of human rights; and

g) One other person

Furthermore, the Legal Aid (Amendment) Act defined the functions of the Board as being to:

(a) Manage and administer the Legal Aid Fund; and

(b) To carry out any other activities relating to the provision for legal aid which are necessary or conducive to the performance of its functions under the Act. There was however a proviso placed on this function, namely, that the Board would not be responsible for the supervision and administration of the Directorate. It is difficult to fathom the intention of the legislature in this respect because it is usual for boards of corporate bodies to superintend secretariats or directorates. A further amendment was made to Legal Aid legislation in 2005. By the Legal Aid (Amendment) Act, the Legal Aid Board was re-constituted as a body corporate, with perpetual succession and legal capacity to sue and to be sued. The composition of the Board was enlarged to include representatives from the Ministries responsible for finance and national planning; community development and social welfare; labour and sport and child development.

Furthermore, the functions of the board were reformulated and enlarged. The functions of the Board are to:

(a) Administer and manage the Legal Aid Fund;

(b) Facilitate the representation of persons granted legal aid under the Act;

(c) Assign practitioners to persons granted legal aid under the Act;

(d) Advise the Minister on policies relating to the provision of legal aid and implement

Government policies relating to the same; and

(e) Undertake such other activities relating to the provision of legal aid and which are conducive or incidental to the performance of its functions under the Act.

Although the Legal Aid Board has been established as a body corporate, it has not been delinked from the Ministry of Justice. The Ministry still recruits, disciplines and determines the conditions of service for legal aid personnel. The Ministry is also still responsible for mobilizing and disbursing resources to the Board. The de-linkage is important in order to establish an independent body that can effectively plan for expansion, hiring and retention of staff as well as mobilize resources from either Government or cooperating partners. The formality surrounding the Legal Aid Board still makes it difficult for the ordinary person to easily approach the Board.

The Legal Aid Board has offices in Lusaka, Kitwe, Ndola, Kabwe and Livingstone. It has on its establishment a total of twenty-one lawyers, out of an establishment of thirty four. 79 the lawyers for the Board are faced with crashing case loads. Apart from facing a critical shortage of staff, the Board has inadequate transport and operational tend to suffer. In view of the preceding constraints, the Board tends to limit the grant of legal aid to accused persons facing serious criminal cases mostly in the High Court. The Board therefore handles a very limited number of civil cases. The woes of the Board are also worsened by the fact that the Board is unable to attract and retain lawyers due to the poor conditions of service. The failure to decentralize the Board and its myriad of administrative and logistical problems has resulted in denying many indigent persons especially in rural areas legal aid.

Law reports

Zambia has a law report series known as the Zambia Law Reports (ZLR). These Law reports are available online and they are obtainable at the high court. The statutes of Zambia are available online and are listed by name. Supreme Court, High Court, Industrial Relations Court, Land Tribunal, Revenue Tribunal rulings are also found online. The 'Zambian Law Journal' is found at the school of Law in the University of Zambia. The 'Laws of Zambia' is a 1996 compilation of 26 Volumes containing all the laws and the entire respective various Republican Constitutions since independence. Volume 1 Contains the Index of the Laws of Zambia. The Laws are in read only PDF format. Zambia law Reports can also be obtained at the University of Pretoria. There is also 'Zambia Law Reports Consolidated Index' containing the cumulative indexes of cases reported, cases referred to, legislation referred to, and subject matter from 1963 to 1978 Published in 1984, Council of Law Reporting, and High Court for Zambia (Lusaka, Zambia).

The Zambia Legal Information Institute (ZamLII) was established by the Law School of the University of Zambia in 1996, in partnership with Zamnet. It has received important start-up assistance from the Legal Information Institute of Cornell Law School. The Institute's aim is to improve access to judgments, statutes and other legal materials of the Republic of Zambia both within Zambia and elsewhere and to connect lawyers, judges, academics, students and others within Zambia with the growing collection of legal information available around the globe via the Internet.

ZamLII provides on-line research of Zambian and foreign legal information and general information about Zambia. Our collection of legal information in Zambia includes The Constitution of the Greater Republic of Zambia, rules and selected decisions of the courts, selected acts,legal commentary, a legal directory, and finally, information about the University of Zambia School of Law. ZamLII also provides links toforeign legal information in and outside of Africa. You can also find general information about Zambia through our link with Zamnet.

Government Gazettes

The government of Zambia publishes a gazette that contains all relevant announcements and enactment or amendments of laws and regulations. It incorporates various government decisions, and once they feature in the Gazette, government decisions are deemed and laws and regulations are deemed to have been published and validly promulgated.

Gazettes are used by both the government and ordinary citizens to convey information to the public. The following are some of the normal uses of gazettes:

- Notices to creditors and debtors in administration of estates.
- Publication of amendments to existing laws, regulations and rules.
- Publications of newly enacted laws, regulations and rules.

- Invitation for tenders from government departments.
- Insurance of trading licenses for companies.
- Publication of title deeds and deed of transfer in respect of property.

POLITICAL PARTIES

Significant political developments have occurred in Zambia since the 2001 tripartite elections. After having had two previous elections in 1991 and 1996, the 2001 elections produced a multiparty Parliament for the first time since Zambia's independence in 1964. These elections seem to signal that the country has moved from a dominant one party political system to a competitive multi-party system. Despite these positive political developments, political parties and the party system in Zambia still remain relatively undeveloped. This trend in Zambian political culture may be partly due to the short time period in which political parties have had to organize, a lack of organizational funds, and a host of legal and political obstacles that have exacerbated political party fragmentation. Political parties play a vital and indispensable role in modern political systems and are the raison d'être of a multiparty system.

To its credit Zambia has been deemed an "oasis of peace" in Africa since its independence. Although the country experienced one-party rule for 27 years, there was not the degree of repression and social anarchy that characterized many other African countries. Because of this unique attribute, Zambia's political transition in 1991 was peaceful; Zambia successfully held presidential and parliamentary elections in 1996 and 2001. Despite disputes over the election results in 1996 and 2001, the country has been able to utilize constitutional provisions to resolve political differences.

The MMD government was elected in 1991 and within six months of assuming office; fragmentation began to surface within the ruling party. Several MPs resigned in the fracas. In 1993, several former cabinet ministers and notable MPs left MMD to form the National Party. Although several MPs successfully won their seats on the NP ticket, the party atrophied and failed to offer a serious challenge to the MMD government. Due to continued dissatisfaction with MMD, two other parties, the Zambia Democratic Congress (ZDC) and the Agenda for Zambia (AZ) were formed in 1995 and 1996 respectively.

Faced by a perceived threat from the political opposition, by 1996 the MMD government orchestrated a constitutional amendment to preclude the strongest challenger, UNIP's Kenneth Kaunda, from competing in the 1996 elections. Traditional tribal chiefs were also barred from standing as candidates. In a backlash attempt by supporters of UNIP, the 1996 elections were widely boycotted by civil society representatives, and supporters of UNIP, resulting in a consolidation of MMD's dominance in Parliament. That year, the MMD increased its parliamentary seats from 125 to 131, while the political opposition remained largely fragmented. Both parties were led by individuals who held senior positions in the first MMD National Executive Committee and were ministers in Chiluba's first cabinet.

With the combined opposition parties winning only nine seats and the independent candidates having won ten seats, this parliamentary result followed serious irregularities in the electoral process. The alleged irregularities included poor management of the voter registration process, resulting in a massive reduction in voters eligible to participate in the elections. The overwhelming evidence of widespread vote rigging and other forms of electoral fraud in the 1996 elections led to the elections result being challenged in the Courts.

Amid popular contestation, Chiluba announced in May 2001 that he would not seek a third presidential term on the MMD ticket. In late August 2001, Levy Mwanawasa emerged as the party's choice for its presidential candidate. The election date was announced at the end of November, in the middle of the rainy season and well after the MMD had commenced its election campaign. At the dissolution of Parliament, prior to the election, MMD held 89 seats as compared to 131 when elected in 1991. The opposition UPND, NP and UNIP held twenty seats in sum. Forty seats in Parliament were vacant. After a split within the MMD, forty seats that were occupied by that party were left vacant, as several MP's who left the government either joined the opposition or formed other parties.

The 2001 tripartite elections were also widely regarded as flawed by both domestic and international observers. There were serious doubts as to whether the results reflected the will of the people. The final results released by the Electoral Commission of Zambia indicated that about 70% of the registered electorate cast their votes for president. Of these votes the MMD party received 28.69%, while the UPND receiving 26.76%, a difference of 30,000 votes. Expressed as a percentage of registered voters, the MMD received less than 20% of the vote, which makes it the only party to win the government with such a narrow margin of victory since independence, in spite of allegations against the party over vote rigging and other alleged abuses of electoral fraud.

The 2001 elections seem to highlight the risks associated with transitioning from a dominant single party system to a non-authoritarian competitive party system. Of the seven political parties in Parliament, no party had an absolute majority. The MMD won less than 50 % of the seats (46%), while the UPND had just about a third (33%). Combined, MMD and UPND shared about 80% of seats in Parliament. Together, UNIP and FDD accounted for 17% of the seats while the remaining three opposition parties shared 5% of the seats. At the local government level, opposition parties controlled key city and municipal councils in about six provinces.

Movement for Multiparty Democracy (MMD)

The MMD originally formed during a planned referendum in July 1991 as a pressure group to campaign for the restoration of a multiparty system to contest the ruling party UNIP. In January 1991, MMD transformed itself into a political party with diverse representation, including trade unions, commercial farmers, the clergy, students, academics, businesspersons and former UNIP politicians. Under the leadership of the former Zambia Congress of Trade Unions (ZCTU) chairman-general, Frederick Chiluba, the party united around a cohesive platform to remove UNIP from power. As MMD consolidated power in 1991 and 1996 elections, with the party leadership garnering the majority vote, there were fears that the country was regressing back to a one-party state. As Although legislation severed the formal links between the party and government, MMD's priority position in government allowed it to use the incumbency to access state resources, especially during election campaigns. As a result of discord within the party over governance issues, between 1993 and 1996 the party experienced several defections and resignations leading to the formation of rival political parties.

In 2001, the MMD had an organizational presence in every province within the country. Consequently the party could boast of national structures and coverage and it held regular elections for its national leaders. However, as the 2001 elections drew nearer, the party was faced with the prospect of defeat, triggered by the desire of President Chiluba to run for a third term in office. As public pressure against the third term mounted and senior party leaders began denouncing the action, the party began to lose its popularity. Eventually, the president declared he would not seek a third term and the MMD went on to win its third mandate. However, MMD's electoral performance was very poor -having gained less than 30% of the national vote and winning less than three seats in four provinces. This was perhaps the lowest mandate won by any ruling party in Zambia since independence and posed serious challenges to the new leadership.

The MMD manifesto is based on the promotion of a free market economy and good governance. Since 1991 the party has implemented a very ambitious economic reform program. It has liberalized the economy and removed most of the controls that characterized the Zambian economy in the Second Republic. These policies have produced a serious social impact, which has contributed to deterioration in living standards and a high incidence of poverty. The party faces a number of challenges, as has been reflected in the party's declining representation in Parliament, considering that since the 2001 elections the MMD no longer commands an absolute majority.

The United Party for National Development

United Party for National Development (UPND) was formed the UPND in 1998. The party was established on a social democratic platform of providing free health and educational services to the Zambian people. It also articulated a commitment to providing agricultural subsidies to rural farmers to increase agricultural production. The UPND's performance in local government and parliamentary elections between 1998 and 2000 made it the main opposition party to the MMD.

The party won more than 60 local council seats in the 1998 local government elections and six parliamentary by-elections in Southern, Western and Central provinces. It also controlled one council in Northwestern province. Although the party claimed an organizational presence in almost all of Zambia's nine provinces, it was better organized in Central, Northwestern, Southern and Western provinces.

UPND finished second to the MMD presidential candidate in the 2001 elections. The party won the majority of local government seats in Western, Central, Northwestern, Southern and Lusaka provinces. With these 49 seats UPND was the second largest party in Parliament. Historically, UPND has strong ties to other opposition parties, with which it contested the results of the 2001 election in the Supreme Court. The party has encountered serious leadership and organizational challenges, including its level of dependency on the patronage of its party president. Although the party's national leadership is representative of all the ethnic groups, the electorate perceives it as a regional or ethnic party. Additionally, the party has had difficulty asserting itself as the main opposition party in the country. Without recognition as the official opposition, on account of falling short of the threshold of 53 seats, the party has been unable to systematically challenge government policy in Parliament and to initiate legislation. Notwithstanding these shortcomings, UPND has been internally cohesive and self-confident, as evidenced by very few defections among the senior leadership. Additionally, it is the only political party that successfully expelled its MP for accepting a ministerial appointment in the MMD government.

United National Independence Party (UNIP)

UNIP is the oldest African political party in Zambia. It was established in 1959. It was briefly involved governmentwiththeANCbetween1962-1964and it was the governing party in Zambia from 1964-1991.The leader of the party until 1992 was former President Kenneth Kaunda, who was the first president of the independent country of Zambia. He voluntarily stepped down in favour of Kebby Musokotwane, but returned to the party in 1995 to increase the party's chances of defeating the MMD in 1996. Kaunda was excluded from running on the party's ticket in 1996 due to a controversial constitutional amendment passed by the ruling MMD, which barred persons whose parents were not born in Zambia from contesting the presidency.

Between 1992 and 1998 UNIP suffered harassment under the government's rule, including arrests and detentions over allegations that the party conspired to overthrow the Government. The most controversial of these alleged conspiracy acts were the "Zero Option" and "Black Mamba" "plots" that resulted in a number of UNIP leaders being detained, including the party's vice president Chief Inyambo Yeta. Additionally, UNIP president Kenneth Kaunda was detained in connection with an alleged coup attempt to overthrow the MMD government in December 1997.

Although the party can legitimately claim to have countrywide organizational structures, the party has experienced serious organizational problems since leaving office in 1991. During the one-party era prior to 1991, UNIP benefited from the use of public funds because there was no distinction between the ruling party's purse and the government as evidenced by the fact that party officials were paid from the public treasury, the party used government vehicles and the State financed party offices. Since leaving office, UNIP has had to rely upon its own resources and properties, which has translated into a diminution of the party's organizational capacity. The Central Committee that was formerly full-time is now part-time and a number of staff have been laid off or have not been paid for a significant period of time. Due to financial problems the party has not been able to hold important party meetings.

In addition to organizational problems, the party has also experienced serious leadership problems since 1992. Internal bickering and factionalism has led to frequent leadership turnover, suspensions and sometimes expulsions. The influence of the party's founder and former president Kenneth Kaunda may have had a negative impact on party organization and membership morale, as the party seems to be divided between two camps between supporters of the former president, and those who want fresh leadership without formal ties to Kaunda.

A leadership crisis in 2000 led to the ouster of party president Francis Nkhoma and his replacement by Kaunda's son and UNIP's secretary general, Tilyenji Kaunda, who later contested the 2001 presidential elections. There are concerns within the party over Tilyenji Kaunda's leadership ability, as he is perceived to be directing the affairs of the party from outside the country and lacking necessary organizational experience. UNIP espouses a distinct social-democratic ideology that calls for more state- involvement in the economy and the provision of state resources for social services. However, the perceived failure of its past policies, coupled with its serious leadership problems have contributed to the party's failure to offer a formidable opposition to the ruling MMD.

Forum for Democracy and Development (FDD)

This party was formed in July 2001 by senior party and government officials who were expelled from the MMD for opposing a third term of the country's president. The original founders included the former Vice President of Zambia, Christon Tembo, cabinet ministers, deputy ministers and MPs. In September 2001 Tembo was elected as the party's first president, with a similar manifesto as the MMD. In the 2001 elections the FDD won 12 MP seats in Lusaka and Eastern provinces. It also gained control of the Lusaka City Council. Additionally, its candidate in presidential elections finished third, managing to win 13% of the national vote. Additionally, the party fielded the largest number of councilors and MPs and won the mayoral ticket. Unsatisfied with the results, however, the FDD have joined in collaboration with other parties to contest the 2001 elections results in the Supreme Court. The party has an organizational presence in all nine provinces of the country. Although relatively well organized, lately a significant number of FDD party members have defected to the MMD government. Recently three of its MPs were appointed to governmental ministerial positions without party consultation. While the party supports a Government of National Unity (GNU), as it has sought to negotiate its involvement in the MMD government with the President to date it has been unable to reach a workable partnership.

Heritage Party (HP)

Godfrey Miyanda, former Zambian Vice President from 1994 to 1997 founded the HP. Like other opposition parties, the HP was formed in protest of the government's bid for a third presidential term. HP is committed to promoting integrity in public office, transparency and greater public accountability. The party's leader is a central force in the party's operation. Although the party contested the 2001 elections and finished fifth with about 8% of the national vote, it obtained only four MPs in the most recent elections. Since those elections two of these MPs have defected to the ruling party, while the remaining two HP MPs have both been appointed to Deputy Ministerial positions in the MMD government party approval. The party views this action as "poaching" and because there is no expulsion clause in the HP constitution, it has not challenged with the "erring" MPs. Currently HP is one of the parties challenging the election of the country's president in the Supreme Court

Zambia Republican Party (ZRP)

Many former MMD members claim that their only quarrel with the MMD was Chiluba's desire to run for a third term. This explains why a number of FDD members and officials have gravitated back to the MMD after Levy Mwanasa was elected President. The ZRP was formed in early 2001 through an alliance of four parties including the Republican Party. The ZRP presidential candidate in the 2001 elections did not perform well finishing sixth with less than five percent (4.8%) of the national vote. Although the party did win one Parliamentary seat in Lusaka Province, the MP has since been appointed by the government as Cabinet Minister. The party's policy direction does not differ fundamentally from the MMD. ZRP supports a free-market economy based on private entrepreneurship, good incentives to the private sector and a Government that is responsive and responsible to the citizens.

Patriotic Front (PF)

In September 2001 Michael Sata, a former Cabinet Minister and the MMD National Secretary, formed the PF. It was the last of the parties to be formed as a result of MMD succession problems. The party was organized quickly to contest the 2001 elections and consequently it did not perform well. The PF secured under 4% (3.3%) of the national vote and won only one MP seat. The party's main policy platform is the reduction in taxes and prudence in the management of public resources. The party's leader is a central force in the party's operation. However, the main problem the party faces is a public perception that its leader supported Chiluba's third term bid and was at the forefront of prosecuting those opposed to it through suspensions and expulsions. The are other political parties which have contested parliamentary seats and they include National Citizens Coalition (NCC), Social Democratic Party (SDP), Zambia Alliance for Progress (ZAP), National Leadership for Development (NLD) and the NCC (National Citizens Coalition).

Civil society

Zambia has a variety of non-governmental organizations working on issues of human rights and related fields. Despite the euphoria over the defeat of President-since-independence, Kenneth Kaunda's, United National Independence Party (UNIP) in Zambia's first ever multi-party elections, it has become clear that elections did not herald an end to the prominence of human rights issues in the political life of the country. The then ruling Movement for Multiparty Democracy (MMD has been beset by political scandal, defection, corruption and allegations of involvement in the traffic of illegal drugs. The new government has also demonstrated a certain degree of intolerance by declaring a state of emergency and detaining several opponents, following claims of a coup plot hatched by members of UNIP. At the same time, law enforcement agencies for the most part remain fixated on their erstwhile methods of operation, which were, to say the least, not human rights-sensitive. The press is often targeted for harassment.

Human rights organizations (HROs) in Zambia are, in the main, faced with extending the experience they gained in the monitoring of elections and civic education to other areas of human rights work. While the elections were an issue around which it was fairly easy to galvanize interest and attention, there is a need to aggressively promote knowledge of human rights among the general populace--broadly described as "apathetic". Some prominent cases from the past regime, such as the detention-without-trial of Katiza Cebekhulu (the key witness in the trial of Winnie Mandela, who was spirited away from South Africa in order not to give testimony expected to be potentially damaging), have been passed over to the new government, but the government has done little to address the concerns expressed by human rights groups about them. Torture is reported to take place on a regular basis. In addition, there have been reports of a number of incidents where police have detained the relatives of their intended victims, in order to flush them out of hiding--the case of opposition UNIP member, William Banda, being the most prominent. The new HROs that have come into existence are largely believed to be "elitist", and need to cooperate more effectively with the press and others involved in the human rights struggle.

Centre for Human Rights and Democracy (CHRD)

The Centre for Human Rights and Democracy (CHRD) has yet to make a significant impact on the human rights scene in Zambia, although it runs an office for *pro bono* counseling on legal and human rights matters. The Centre faced initial problems with registration, as the authorities suspected their motives. Although the registration matters were overcome, it continues to encounter problems with government obstruction of receipt of external funding granted to the organization. The Centre is nevertheless looking around for alternatives, and intends to organize a paralegal training course to be conducted in June 1994.

Christian Council of Zambia (CCZ)

The Christian Council of Zambia (CCZ) was part of the group that was active in the Foundation for Democratic Process (FODEP), but it has, in general, adopted a low profile with respect to advocacy on human rights issues in Zambia. Instead it deals with questions such as refugees and relief, some gender questions, ethics, development and unemployment. This activity is all conducted under the auspices of the Social Justice Committee of the CCZ.

Foundation for Democratic Process (FODEP)

Initially begun as a monitoring group prior to the 1991 general elections, FODEP is an umbrella organization comprised of several church groups, women's organizations, the Law Association and the Press Association. Today, FODEP has broadened its mandate to cover civic education for the purposes of enhancing the general awareness of the population. Drawing on its experience in the elections, FODEP intends to focus on civil and political rights at the local level, and to involve parliamentary and other elected representatives in the dissemination of knowledge and information about these rights.

Human Rights Committee of the Law Association of Zambia (LAZ)

The Law Association of Zambia (LAZ), a statutory body recognized by law in 1973, established a Human Rights Committee to function under its auspices. The Committee was heavily involved in civic education around the elections and produced a number of programs for the broadcast media on elections and civic rights. The Committee transcribed the notes from these seminars and circulated them as a further mechanism of sensitization. In conjunction with the Catholic Secretariat, it has also designed a program for the conduct of simultaneous seminars on human rights in all the provincial centres of the country, as a starting-point for the sensitization of the broad populace on general human rights issues. A series of seminars for the police force have also been designed, the first to commence in Lusaka. As a major human rights actor, the Committee has received several reports on police violence and prison conditions, and attempts to ensure that these issues are expeditiously addressed.

Inter-African Network for Human Rights (AFRONET)

AFRONET is billed as an organization designed to promote coordination and networking among African HROs. As yet, it has only begun to meet with various organizations within Zambia and to publicize its operations outside the country. Although it has observer status at the African Commission on Human and Peoples' Rights, it still has a long way to go, both in the conceptualization of its precise goals and programs, and in raising the consciousness of HROs throughout the continent on the need for coordination and networking. Its programs focus on communication, the promotion of good governance and sustainable development, human rights, and the interaction of law and society.

Legal Resources Foundation (LRF)

The Legal Resources Foundation (LRF) was established as a company limited by guarantee, in order to obviate the possibility of the authorities' exercising their powers to ban a society under the provisions of the Societies Act. The idea of the LRF was conceived in 1991 prior to the meeting of the Commonwealth Heads of Government (CHOGUM) in Harare. LRF has several objectives, including the promotion of an interest in human rights; the development of law (through the publication of cases, law reports and a monthly newsletter); and reform of the law. So far, however, LRF has not commenced operations and has yet to formulate specific programs to actualize its objectives.

National Women's Lobby Group

Established on July 20, 1991, the National Women's Lobby Group (WLG) is a pressure group established to pursue the rights of women, children and minorities, especially in relation to the policy-making bodies in the country. It is headed by a Secretary General, who is presently assisted only by a secretary. WLG is composed of a number of women's NGOs and its approach is broad in ambit. It is involved in networking and is a resource base for information and policies about women. It also lobbies the President and informs the electorate about issues of women's rights. WLG has developed a three-year plan by which it will work towards a core budget to cover training in human rights and, especially, in lobbying and outreach.

Office of Social Education of the Zambian Episcopal Conference (ZEC)

Often working in collaboration with the other church groups in Zambia (the Christian Council and the Evangelical Fellowship); the Zambian Episcopal Conference (ZEC) has been more public and active in the arena of human rights, especially in the issuance of public statements or pastoral letters, than have its counterparts. ZEC statements have covered issues such as structural adjustment and its impact on human rights, a review of the Constitution, and problems with the transition to the third (present) republic. The ZEC has embarked on an active program of encouraging the formation of Justice and Peace Committees at the local level, building on the model of the Zimbabwean experience. To this end, it has conducted a total of five seminars over the past two years in order to sensitize its members on the spirituality of justice and peace, and the need for respect for human rights. The attendees at these seminars have then proceeded out into the countryside, and sought to disseminate the information they have culled to the broader populace. The results have varied, but are a significant beginning for a process that will invariably take some time to gel. Individual Justice and Peace Committees also identify areas of specific concern to their local communities. Among the issues that have been addressed are: the treatment of prisoners on remand, the payment and condition of domestic workers at large and within church institutions, the issue of allocation of places in schools, and the effect of the structural adjustment program. A national Justice and Peace Committee/Commission is yet to be established.

Women's Rights Committee of the Law Association of Zambia (WRC)

Established in 1988 as part of the LAZ, the Women's Rights Committee (WRC) gained impetus after the passing of the Intestate Succession Act. Following this, WRC established a National Legal Aid Clinic for Women in November 1990, which has been run in the main by volunteer lawyers. A full-time Coordinator for the Clinic was appointed in 1991, and continues to be assisted by volunteers. The clinic still has problems of recognition and has not been formally registered, but utilizes the framework of the Citizen's Advice Bureau of the LAZ in order to appear in court. The WRC functions like a private law firm and the majority of its cases are on inheritance, divorce, and custody and maintenance matters. The clientele are mainly the unemployed who are charged only a nominal fee.

Zambia Civic Education Association (ZCEA)

The Zambia Civic Education Association (ZCEA) initially commenced as a program of UNIP--the former ruling political party--as a mechanism in its "revival campaign" to meet the challenges following the general election, but the party was not extremely responsive to its overtures. Consequently, the group has attempted to distance itself from any direct political affiliation and claims to be wholly independent. The ZCEA is under the organizational control of a Chair, who is the only full-time worker, while all its programs are implemented by volunteers. One of its first actions was to inaugurate what it calls "clinics", which are held every Saturday and Sunday, where ZCEA holds public information sessions, discussing the role of public officers, human rights education and issues such as health, hygiene and the environment, as the most "basic needs" of the community. The group has also targeted the police and attempted to implement a community-policing scheme in at least one area of peri-urban Lusaka. This has been approached as a pilot project, and an attempt has been made to deal with common problems in the relationship between police and the community. The scheme has also addressed conditions at the stations, related to the cells, women prisoners, and so on. The ZCEA has also designed a "right to shelter" project in Mapoloto Township.

National Assembly

The National Assembly is comprised of 150 directly elected members, up to eight presidentially-appointed members, and a speaker. Zambia is divided into nine provinces, each administered by an appointed deputy minister who essentially performs the duties of a governor. The Supreme Court is the highest court and the court of appeal; below it are the high court, magistrate's court, and local courts.

Voting in Parliament

Voting is done through simple majority. There are no reserved seats or quotas for women, ethnic minorities or other categories. Vacancies arising between general elections are filled through by-elections. Voting is not compulsory.

Voting is open to all people above 18 years and eligibility to stand for parliamentary is 21 years, of Zambian citizenship (including naturalized citizens), and resident in the country at the time of election. Also eligible are people who are able to speak and read in the official language of Zambia, as well as citizens overseas, who are not civil servants.

Disqualified are people who pay allegiance to a foreign State, insanity, sentence of death or imprisonment, conviction of a corrupt or illegal practice within five years preceding the elections, persons found guilty of such practice upon the trial of an election petition, lawful custody, persons who are not in possession of a national registration card, insanity, undischarged bankrupts, sentence of death or imprisonment, restriction in movement or detention pursuant to certain laws, etc.

ZAMBIA CRIMINAL JUSTICE SYSTEM: STRATEGIC INFORMATION AND DEVELOPMENTS

BASIC INFORMATION

The Penal Code is that principalsource of criminal law in Zambia. Also there are a number of other Acts which are important in that they deal with particular types of crimes. The most important of these is the Road and Road Traffic Act (Chapter 766 of the Laws of Zambia) which covers the whole range of road traffic offences and which resulted in 110,891 convictions in 1975.[3] This was more than the convictions under the Penal Code itself, although most of the road traffic cases involved minor infractions.

The English common law was an important source, Section 2(1) of the Penal Code provides that nothing in the Code affects the liability, trial or punishment of a person for an offence against the common law. However, the preserva-tion of common law offences must be considered in the light of Section 20(8) of the Constitution of Zambia (chapter I of the Laws of Zambia) which states:

Since the re-introduction of multi-party democracy in Zambia in 1991, some progress has been registered in the governance system of the country, including its criminal justice system. However, many challenges remain across Zambia's criminal justice institutions, and these inhibit the efficient and effective delivery of justice to its citizens.

One overarching structural problem centres on the uneasy coexistence of common and customary law. This gives rise to a troublesome paradox whereby the constitutionally recognised legal system is known and accessed by the few while the many - mostly rural people – only know, understand and access customary law.

With regard to customary law, an important provision is to be found in the Local Courts Act (chapter 54 of the Laws of Zambia). Section 12(2) states:

Practically any offence may be dealt with by a local court as an offence under such law notwithstanding that a similar offence may be constituted by the Penal Code or by any other written law. Such local court shall not impose any punishment for such offence in excess of the maximum permitted by the Penal Code or by such other written law for such similar offence.

For example, once a marriage is contracted under the Marriage Act, the provisions of the Penal Code and Marriage Act apply.[7] The provisions of section 12(2) of the Local Courts Act do not apply to the higher courts. In *R* v *Ndhlovu** the accused was charged in the High Court of Northern Rhodesia with the minder of his wife. It appeared that during an argument between the accused and the deceased, the latter used a 'foul and abusive expression' which according to customary law amounted to a sufficient insult to warrant the chastisement of the wife by the husband.

CRIME AND PUNISHMENT

The High Court refused to consider this evidence and emphasised that the law on which criminal cases are to be decided in the High Court is that to be found in the Penal Code and related statutes.

Notwithstanding the replacement of the common law by the Penal Code, the relationship between English and Zambian criminal law has always been close and the change to the Code did not fundamentally change the criminal law. Indeed, the English secretary of state for the colonies in referring to the Code in 1929 stated:

Officers will find it easier to apply a code which employs to terms and principles with which they are familiar in England.[9]

The general rule of construction of the new Code was stated in the Code itself as follows:

The Penal Code shall be interpreted in accordance with the principles of legal interpretation obtaining in England [and expressions used in it shall be presumed, so far as is consistent with their con-text, and except as may be otherwise expressly provided, to be used with the meaning attaching to them in English criminal law and shall be construed in accordance therewith."][10]

The part in square brackets has now been removed by the Penal Code Amendment Act 1972,[11]—a provision which will be considered later.

The rationale for the interpretation section (as it will be referred to hereafter) was considered by the Court of Appeal in *D.P.P. v Chirwa.*[12,] Doyle, Ag. C. J. giving the judgment of the court stated:[13]

The Penal Code is a codification of a large portion of the criminal law in England for application to Zambia. It does not follow that in all cases the legislature intended entirely to follow the English law, both statute and case, but substantially it did so intend. It is therefore not strange that [the interpretation section] was introduced. It was in the nature of a slip rule to cover the fallibility of draftsmen.

The following punishments may be inflicted by a court:

(a) Death;

(b) Imprisonment;

(c) Corporal punishment;

(d) Fine; (e) Payment of com-pensation;

(f) Finding security to keep the peace and be of good behaviour; or to come up for judgment;

(g) Forfeiture;

(h) Deportation; (i) Any other punishment provided by this code or by any other law.

(i) there are two important sentences to be considered.

The first is the probation order (under the Probation of Offenders Act, Chapter 147 of the Laws of Zambia), which empowers a court to require an offender to be under the supervision of a probation officer for a specified period. This is considered later. The suspended sentence gives the court the power to suspend a sentence upon conviction for the majority of offences. This is also considered later in this section.

The death sentence

Capital punishment is mandatory for both murder[33] and treason[34] and for certain types of piracy.[35] By virtue of section 12 of the Penal Code Amendment Act (Number 2) of 1974, the penalty for aggravated robbery is death: (i) where a firearm was used,[36] or (ii) where the offensive weapon or instrument used is not a firearm and grievous harm is done to any person in the course of the offence.[37] Unless otherwise directed the sentence of death is carried out by hanging.[38]

The death sentence cannot be passed: (i) if the person convicted of a capital offence was under the age of 18 years at the time of the commission of the offence;[39] or (ii) if a female convicted of a capital offence is pregnant. In this case she must be sentenced to be imprisoned for life.[40]

The prerogative of mercy vests in the president and gives him the power to commute the death sentence or to issue a pardon.[41] By virtue of section 61 of the Constitution of Zambia (chapter I of the Laws of Zambia), an advisory committee on the prerogative of mercy is established and all cases in which a sentence of death has been passed are referred to it. The recommendation of the committee is to be based on the record of the case together with any recommendations or observations, which the judge, who confirmed the sentence, may think fit to make.[42] As a result each case is decided upon its own particular facts and explains the reason why the method of dealing with persons sentenced to death may vary from year to year. Table III illustrates this point.

IMPRISONMENT

Zambia has a territorial control for the Zambia Prisons. The new Prisons Act was passed in 1965 and has came into operation on the 31st October, 1966. The Act is based upon the Minimum Standard Rules which were agreed upon by the First United Nations Congress on the Prevention of Crime and Treatment of Offenders.

All prisoners are classified at the time of admission into the prison system and the different categories are kept separate as far as possible. Section 60(i) of the Prisons Act states that "male and female prisoners shall be kept apart and confined in separate prisons or in separate parts of the same prison, in such a maimer as to prevent, as far as is practicable, their seeing or communicating with each other". Sub-section two further divides prisoners and states:

JUVENILE OFFENDERS

The sentencing of juveniles is considered in detail later. However, with regard to imprisonment, no person under the age of sixteen years may be so sentenced,[48] and a person between sixteen and nineteen years of age may only be sentenced to imprisonment if he cannot be suitably dealt with in any other manner.[49] The sentencing of a juvenile offender to imprisonment should be undertaken only in the last resort. As Silungwe C. J., stated in the Supreme Court in *Mvula:* The object of the Juveniles Act is that as far as possible juveniles should not be sent to prison, because if they come into contact with adult hardened criminals, the chances are that they will become hardened criminals.

A SUSPENDED SENTENCE

Section 16 of the Criminal Procedure Code 5S gives any court the power to pass sentence on a convicted person but order that the whole or part of such sentence be suspended for a period not exceeding three years. This provision applies to all offences save those which are expressly excluded by the Criminal Procedure Code. These, in general, relate to the most serious criminal offences.[54] The court is empowered to attach conditions to the order. These may relate, for example, to compensation being paid by the offender to the victim, or to the requirement that the offender refrain from committing further offences of the type for which he was convicted. Failure to comply with any condition renders the offender liable to have the original sentence implemented.

The main reason for the use of the suspended sentence has been said by Doyle C. J., in *Mbanga*[5*] "to be in order to ensure that an offender behaves himself in future." There are no figures readily available as to the use of the suspended sentence but in view of the high rate of imprisonment (see Table II above) it would appear that relatively few sentences are being suspended.

FINES AND COMPENSATION

The imposition of fines is by far the most frequent sentence passed by the courts, (see Table II above) and account for almost 60% of all sentences in cases of offences against the Penal Code. The powers of the court as regards the imposition of fines is found in section 28 of the* Penal Code. This section states that when a fine is imposed under any written law, then in the absence of any express provisions relating thereto, the amount of the fine which may be imposed is unlimited but must not be excessive, provided no sum is expressed to which the fine might extend. The section also lays down the length of imprisonment which may be ordered by a court in respect of the non-payment of the fine.[60] In the case of juvenile offenders, the offender and/or his parent or guardian may be ordered to pay a fine.[61] However, no parent or guardian may be ordered to pay a fine in such a case unless the court is satisfied that the parent or guardian has conduced to the commission of the offence by neglecting to exercise due control over the juvenile.[62]

A person who has been convicted of any offence other than one punishable by death, may be ordered to pay compensation if it appears: (a) that some person has suffered material or personal injury in consequence of the offence committed; and (b) that substantial compensation is, in the opinion of the court, recoverable by that person from the offender by a civil suit.[63] Such compensation shall not exceed fifty kwacha.[64] However in most cases of theft and related offences,[65] compensation may be ordered to any bona fide purchaser of stolen property who has restored such property to the person entitled to it.[66] There is little evidence from the statistics to indicate a wide use of compensation orders by the higher courts—in contrast to the local courts where it is a common order. This may well be due to the different approaches of the courts as to how such cases should be dealt with—a matter that was discussed earlier.

CORPORAL PUNISHMENT

Section 27 of the Penal Code restricts the use of caning to

(i) male offenders over 21 years of age who have been convicted of either certain named offences (which generally cover sexual offences or offences involving violence), or property offences where it is expedient in the interests of the community to do so; and

(ii) male offenders who have been convicted of any offence punishable by imprisonment for under a term of three months or more. Caning is often used as an alternative to a prison sentence in juvenile cases. No female may be caned. A maximum of twelve strokes may be awarded against a person under 19 years or less and a maximum of 24 strokes in other cases.

DEPORTATION

Section 33(i) of the Penal Code (as amended)[78] states that any court which sentences a person to imprisonment may in addition recommend that such person be deported if: (i) he is not a citizen of Zambia; and (ii) he has committed any offence referred to in the sub-section.

This recommendation must be sent to the High Court for approval. An interesting provision is to be found in section 34 of the Penal Code. This states that where a person is convicted before the High Court of a felony, the High Court may, in addition, to or in lieu of any other punishment, recommend to the president that such person be deported to such part of Zambia as the president shall direct. Deportation may also be recommended to the president in cases where a person has failed to find security for his peace and good behaviour and in cases where the conduct of a person is dangerous to peace and good order in any part of Zambia. A subordinate court is given the same powers as the High Court in this matter but the decision must be reported to the High Court which has the power to revise the decision.[79]

COURT STRUCTURE

The constitution of Zambia states that the court system is autonomous and administered in accordance with the provisions of an Act of parliament. The judicature shall be independent and subject to only the constitution.

The judiciary comprising of;

- **Supreme Court**
- **High Court**

- **Industrial Court**
- **Subordinate Courts**
- **The Local Courts**
- Such other courts as may be prescribed by act of parliament.

The judiciary has jurisdiction in all matters civil and criminal, including matters relating to the constitution, and such other jurisdiction as by law conferred on it. The superior courts are courts of record and have power to commit for contempt to themselves and all such powers as were vested in a superior court of record immediately before the commencement of the constitution.

The constitution gives very wide powers to the head of state to appoint judicial officers. The president appoints the chief justice and the deputy chief justice. According to article 93(1) the chief justice and deputy chief justice shall subject to ratification by the national assembly, be appointed by the president. Article 93(2) gives the president the power to appoint judges of the Supreme Court. Article 95(1) states that puisne judges shall subject to ratification by national assembly be appointed by the president on the advice of judicial services commission. Furthermore, the president with the advice of the JSC appoints the chairman and deputy chairman of the industrial court. Section 96(1) states that any position appointed under article 93 to act as a judge of the Supreme Court shall continue to act for the period of that person's appointment is marked by the president.

Judges and other judicial officers ought to be hired on full time basis to ensure that they enjoy security of the tenure to enable them to carry out their duties in a competence fashion without fear or favour. Judges on contract are under pressure particularly when their contracts are about to end. This is contrary article 91(2) which promotes judicial independence and frowns upon infringement on this independence by other organs of government. Appointment of judges on acting or contract basis is detrimental to judicial independence since such judges are put in a state of suspense regarding whether they would be confirmed or not. In such a situation the judge may find himself / herself trying to please those with power to confirm him/ her by deciding cases in their favour. The involvement of the head of state in the process of appointing judges intimidates against an independent judiciary. Due to this fact such appointment can not be free of political considerations. The constitution still rests arguably judicial powers on the president. In a situation where the appointing body is politically influenced one cannot hope for independent judiciary. People seeking judicial appointments might be lobby appointed. Thus such people would feel a sense of obligation to the executive and be inclined to favour the executive in the adjudicatory process.

Article 98(1) provides a position holding the offices of a judge of the Supreme Court or the office of a judge of the high court shall vacate that office on attaining the age of 65 years. Provided that the president –(a) may appoint a judge of the supreme court, who has attained that age to continue in office for such further period, not exceeding seven years as the president may determine. Judges along with other specified officers such as attorney general, investigators- general solicitor- general director of public prosecutions are paid from the general revenues of the republic. Such salaries and or allowances may be presented by or under an act of parliament. Article 119(3) provides that the salary payable to the holder of any holder of office shall not be uttered to his disadvantage after his appointment. Note article 96.

REMOVAL OF JUDGES

According to Article 98(2) a judge of the Supreme Court, high court chairman of deputy chairman of the industrial relations court may be removed from office only for inability to perform the functions of his office whether arising from infirmity of body or mind, incompetence or misbehavior and shall not be so removed except in accordance with the provisions of this article. Article 98(3) provides for the establishment of a tribunal which will investigate the case of a judge before removal in which the tribunal consists of a chairman and not less than the other members who hold or have held high judicial office. This tribunal can be biased in the sense that the judge whose perpetual removal has been influenced by the political motives can collude to remove him from offices in order to gain favour from the executive. The tribunal after a proper inquiry represents the matter to the president and advices the president whether the judge ought to be removed from office for inability or incompetence or for misbehavior for which the president has an obligation to remove such judge from office. Article 98 gives so much power on the president to remove and suspend judge and this compromises the independence of judiciary as narrated by article 91(2).

CONSTITUTIONAL COURT

The establishment of the Constitutional Court is prescribed in clause 127 of the Constitution of Zambia.

127. There is established the Constitutional Court which consists of—

(a) the President of the Constitutional Court;

(b) the Deputy President of the Constitutional Court; and

(c) eleven other judges or a higher number of judges, as prescribed.

128. (1) Subject to Article 28, the Constitutional Court has original and final jurisdiction to hear—

(a) a matter relating to the interpretation of this Constitution;

(b) a matter relating to a violation or contravention of this Constitution;

(c) a matter relating to the President, Vice-President or an election of a President;

(d) appeals relating to election of Members of Parliament and councillors; and

(e)whether or not a matter falls within the jurisdiction of the Constitutional Court.

(2) Subject to Article 28 (2), where a question relating to this Constitution arises in a court, the person presiding in that court shall refer the question to the Constitutional Court.

(3) Subject to Article 28, a person who alleges that—

(a) an Act of Parliament or statutory instrument;

(b) an action, measure or decision taken under law; or

(c) an act, omission, measure or decision by a person or an authority; contravenes this Constitution, may petition the Constitutional Court for redress.

(4) A decision of the Constitutional Court is not appealable to the Supreme Court.

129. (1) The Constitutional Court shall be constituted by an uneven number of not less than three judges, except when hearing an interlocutory matter.

(2) The Constitutional Court shall be constituted by one judge when hearing an interlocutory matter.

(3) The full bench of the Constitutional Court shall be constituted by an uneven number of not less than five judges.

(4) The Constitutional Court shall be presided over by—

(a) the President of the Constitutional Court;

(b) in the absence of the President of the Constitutional Court, the Deputy-President of the Constitutional Court; and

(c) in the absence of the Deputy-President of the Constitutional

Court, the most senior

SUPREME COURT

Article 92 establishes the supreme court of Zambia, which shall consist of: the chief justice, the deputy chief justice, seven Supreme Court judges or such greater number as may be prescribed by an act of parliament. The Supreme Court is a superior court of record.

The Supreme Court of Zambia is the final Court of appeal and it has such jurisdiction and powers as conferred on it by the Constitution and any other law.

Establishment, Jurisdiction and sittings of Superior Courts:-

124. There is established the Supreme Court which consists

of—

(a) the Chief Justice;

(b) the Deputy Chief Justice; and

(c) eleven other judges or a higher number of judges, as prescribed.

125. (1) Subject to Article 128, the Supreme Court is the final court of appeal.

(2) The Supreme Court has—

(a) appellate jurisdiction to hear appeals from the Court of

Appeal; and

(b) jurisdiction conferred on it by other laws.

(3) The Supreme Court is bound by its decisions, except in the interest of justice and development of jurisprudence.

126. (1) The Supreme Court shall be constituted by an uneven number of not less than three judges, except when hearing an interlocutory matter.

(2) The Supreme Court shall be constituted by one judge when hearing an interlocutory matter.

COURT OF APPEAL

The establishment of the Court of Appeal is prescribed in clause 130 of the Constitution of Zambia.

130. There is established the Court of Appeal which consists of such number of judges as prescribed.

131. (1) The Court of Appeal has jurisdiction to hear appeals from—

(a) the High Court;

(b) other courts, except for matters under the exclusive jurisdiction of the Constitutional Court; and

(c) quasi-judicial bodies, except a local government elections tribunal.

(2) An appeal from a decision of the Court of Appeal shall be made to the Supreme Court with leave of the Court of Appeal

132. (1) The Court of Appeal shall be constituted by an uneven number of not less than three judges, except when hearing an appealing an interlocutory matter.

(2) The Court of Appeal shall be constituted by one judge when hearing an interlocutory matter

HIGH COURT

Article 97 establishes the high court of Zambia which shall have, except as to the proceedings in which the industrial relations court has exclusive jurisdiction under the industrial relations (act no.27 of 1993), unlimited or original jurisdiction to hear and determine any civil or criminal proceedings under any law and such jurisdiction and powers as may be conferred on it by this constitution or any other law. The high court shall be divided into such divisions as may be determined by an act of parliament 94(2). The chief justice shall be such an ex-offices judge of the high court (3). The other judges of the high court shall be such number of puisne judges as maybe prescribed by parliament.

Article 94(6) provides that the high court shall be a superior court of record. The high court has jurisdiction to supervise any civil or criminal proceedings before any subordinate court or any court martial and may such order issues such as writs and give such direction as it may consider appropriate for the purposes of ensuring that question as is duly administered by such court.

The High Court of Zambia.

133. (1) There is established the High Court which consists

of—

(a) the Chief Justice, as an ex-officio judge; and

(b) such number of judges as prescribed.

(2) There are established, as divisions of the High Court, the

Industrial Relations Court, Commercial Court, Family Court and

Children's Court.

(3) The Chief Justice may constitute, by statutory instrument,

specialised courts of the High Court to hear specific matters.

(4) The composition of courts specified in clauses (2) and (3) shall be prescribed.

134. The High Court has, subject to Article 128—

(a) unlimited and original jurisdiction in civil and criminal matters;

(b) appellate and supervisory jurisdiction, as prescribed; and

(c) jurisdiction to review decisions, as prescribed.

135. The High Court shall be constituted by one judge or such other number of judges as the Chief Justice may determine.

SUBBORDINATE COURTS

The Constitution of the republic of Zambia provides for the establishment of various courts. With reference to the Subordinate Courts; Chapter 28 of the Laws of Zambia provides for the creation of Subordinate Courts in all the districts in Zambia. These are the lower courts and the courts of the first instance.

Section 3 of the Subordinate Courts Act establishes the classes of courts which are subordinate to the High court as follows:

A Subordinate Court of the first class to be presided over by a

– Principal Resident Magistrate who is mandated to handle a case of NOT more than K30,000.00

– Senior Resident Magistrate mandated to handle a case of NOT more than K25,000.00

– Resident Magistrate mandated to handle a case of NOT more than K20,000.00

– Magistrate of the First Class mandated to handle a case of NOT more than K10,000.00

A Subordinate Court of the second class to be presided over by a Magistrate of the second class mandated to handle a case of NOT more than K8,000.00

A Subordinate Court of the third class to be presided over by a Magistrate of the third class mandated to handle a case of NOT more than K4,000.00

Section 4 of the Subordinate Courts Act states that the appointment of Magistrates shall be made by the Judicial Service Commission acting in the name and on behalf of the president. Section 7 of the Subordinate Court Act grants all magistrates equal power, autonomy and jurisdiction.

Subordinate Courts are Courts of record and the jurisdiction vested in these courts shall be exercised (so far as regards practice and procedure) in the manner provided by the Subordinate court Act and the Criminal Procedure Code, Cap 89 of the Laws of Zambia. Subordinates Courts are also courts of first instance and they decide all matters as provided for by the Act except for offences of treason, murder, aggravated robbery, election petitions and all matters that involve the interpretation of the Constitution.

According to Section 7 of the Criminal Procedure Code Chapter 88 of the Laws of Zambia, a Subordinate Court of the first, second or third Class may try any offence under any written laws of Zambia and pass any sentence but;

A Subordinate Court presided over by the Principle Resident Magistrate and Senior Resident Magistrate cannot pass a sentence of imprisonment of more than 9 years;

A Resident Magistrate cannot pass a sentence of imprisonment of more than 7 years;

A Magistrate Class 1 cannot pass a sentence of imprisonment of more than 5 years;

A Subordinate Court presided over by a Magistrate of second and third Class cannot pass a sentence of imprisonment of more than 3 years.

However, under Section 8 of the Criminal Procedure Code, a Court of any class may promote reconciliation between the parties to facilitate the settlement in an amicable way in less serious offences like assaults and offences of personal or private nature.

Appeals Appeals from Subordinate Courts go to the High Court.

SPECIALIST COURTS

Apart from the Supreme Court and the High Court which are ordinary courts, Zambia also has specialist courts set up to deal with particular matters. These are creatures of statute, with limited jurisdiction as set out in the legislation establishing them. The Industrial Court and Local courts are examples of specialist courts in Zambia.

LOCAL COURTS

The local courts play an important part in the settlement of disputes of the majority of the majority of the population the customary law itself is in a state of flux. The main thrust of the law governing the operation of the Local Courts, contained in Chapter 29 o the Laws of Zambia, is the administration of customary law. In reality the Local Courts are the focal point of varied societal claims. Customary law is the ambiguous expression in which are hidden many legal claims. It can be safely asserted that Local Courts are the clearing grounds for simple torts, contracts, and petty crimes. But the main workload of the courts is the law relating to non-statutory marriages. Divorce, reconciliation, custody of children, payment of mabolo or lobola, persons who die without a will-these are areas which affect the legal rights of the majority of the population. The effective handling of these disputes and their fair and just resolution assure stability in the community.

There is no uniform formal educational qualification for adjudicators of local courts. They bring important innovation in the administration of community justice derived in part from their practical understanding of the workings of a post-traditional society. These justices are often fluent in more than four local languages.

SMALL CLAIMS COURTS

There is on the Zambian statute books the Small Claims Court Act. The objective of the Act is to provide for the establishment, of Small Claims Courts to be situated in areas to be designated by the Chief Justice. The Small Claims Courts adopt arbitration as a mode of resolving disputes. The choice of this mode of dispute resolution is questionable because arbitration is typically adjudicative and is quite formal. Mediation would probably have been a more apt mode of resolving disputes in the Small Claims Courts. The tragedy of the Small Claims Court legislation is that although the legislation has been on the statute books for over a decade, the Small Claims Courts have not yet been operationalized. However the idea of Small Claim Courts is a very good one. It depends on involvement of legal practitioners of 5 year standing with more personnel allocated to them. The Small Claims Court could utilize existing infrastructure such as school buildings, community halls and several others If the existing mechanisms of resolving disputes in both rural and urban areas are adopted but also adapted to suit the needs of the poor the small claims court could work most effectively. Rules that normally apply to formalized courts should be more flexible to enable the poor.

1. Who may institute a claim?

Anyone except registered entities such as companies, corporation or associations.

A person under the age of 21 must be assisted by his/her parents or legal guardians.

2. Against whom may a claim be instituted?

Against anyone, including companies, corporations or municipalities or other entities.

3. What matters are excluded from the jurisdiction of the Small Claims Court?

Claims that exceed the limit of K 20,000.

Claims for damages in respect of defamation, malicious, prosecution, wrongful imprisonment, wrongful arrest, adultery and seduction.

Claims concerning the validity of a will

Claims concerning the status of a person in respect of his medical capacity.

Claims made under customer law.

Claims in which specific performance is sought without an alternative claim for payment of damages.

Claims against foreign states and consular officers.

4. Are you compelled to institute your case in the small claims court?

No, you may choose whether you want to institute the claim in the small claims court or any other competent court or any other court such as the Subordinate court.

5. Legal representation and assistance in the preparation of your claim.

Representation by an Advocate is not allowed. You may however, at your own cost obtain prior advice from an Advocate.

The clerk of court will assist you free of charge to prepare your claims.

6. Interpreter

Any Zambian language may be used in the court. Arrangements with an interpreter must be made with the court clerk before hand if evidence is to be given in any language other than English.

7. How do I commerce an action in a small claims court?

An action in the small claims court will be instituted by issuing a letter of demand first. The letter of demand will be addressed to the defendant setting out your claim. This letter of demand will be served you upon the defendant and an expiry date of fourteen (14) days if he/she does not respond favorably; you will then be entitled to issue a notice of claim.The clerk of court will assist you to prepare both the letter of demand and notice of claim and then advise you how best to effect service.

What to take to the clerk of court:

Contract, letter, document or other proof upon which your claim is based or that has regard thereto.

The defendant's full name and address (home and business address, if available.)What re the duties of the clerk of court?

He / She will inform you of the date and time for the hearing of the case.

He /she will issue the notice of claim and hand it to you for service.What do you do with the notice of claim?

You should serve the notice of claim on the defendant in person. Try to get an acknowledgement of receipt by having the defendant sign and date a copy of the notice of claim.

OR

You can request the clerk of court to instruct the sheriff to effect the service on your behalf at a fee. What do you do then?

Where the sheriff has undertaken the service, you must check with the court if the sheriff has filed a certificate of service with the court. After that, obtain a hearing date from the court. Keep the contract, letter, document or other proof upon which your claim is based at hand. Inform your witness of the date and time the case will be heard and arrange for them to be present in court at the appointed date and time.What do you do when you receive a notice of a claim?

You should immediately see the clerk of court for assistance in responding to it.

The clerk of court will assist you to complete the notice of defence or admission of claim.

If you have a counterclaim, he/she will assist you in completing the notice in respect of your counterclaim.

He/she will examine the documents you are intends relying upon for your defense or counterclaim and advise you on which ones to come with to court.

He / she will advise you of the hearing date.

8. Possible to steps by the defendant after receipt of the notice of claim.

He/she may comply with the plaintiff's claim by offering to the settle the claim.

He/she may deliver a written statement, containing the nature of his defense, and/or his/her counterclaim and particulars of the grounds on which it is based, to the clerk of court and send a copy thereof the plaintiffs

9. What do you do if the defendant has satisfied your claim in the meantime?

Supply him with a written receipt

Inform the clerk of court immediately that your claim has been satisfied and you no longer wish to proceed with the case.

10. What do you do on the appointed date and time of hearing?

You must appear at court in person at the appointed.

Ensure that you have with you all the documents upon which your claim is based.

Ensure that all your witnesses are present

Ensure that you have written proof that the notice of claim was served on the opposing party.

11. Who will preside over the court?

The small claims court will be presided over by commissioners. These persons are qualified lawyers and have practiced law for a period of not less than five years.

12. The hearing

The court proceedings are informal and simple

No Advocate may appear on your behalf. You will present you case in court

The commissioner of court will request you state your case.

State facts as concisely as possible.

Answer the questions of the commissioner and submit your supporting documents.

No cross examination between the parties is allowed. With the commissioner's permission you may however, put a few questions to the defendant and vice-versa.

Listen attentively to the defendant's explanation and once he has finished talking, bring the attention of the commissioner to any facts which in your opinion he has not presented correctly. After the commissioner has heard you, the defendant and any witness that may be present, he/she will pass judgment.

13. Review

No appeal may be filed against a judgment or order of the court.

The judgment may be referred to a panel of three (3) commissioners for a review if good cause is shown.

14. Steps following judgment

In case judgment is given against you

The judgment of the court is final, unless some ground for review exists. Settle any order for costs that the court might make against you. The only possible costs can be those that the opposing part may have incurred in respect of fees for the sheriff and filing documents.

In case Judgment is given in your favour

The defendant will pay you the amount of the judgment within the period of payment stipulated in judgment if he has the money available. Give him/her a receipt for the amount immediately. In case the defendant cannot comply with the judgment forthwith the court ability will investigate his/her financial position and his/her to settle the judgment debt and costs and make an order that he pays by monthly installments.

If the judgment debtor fails to comply with the judgment or order of the court. If the judgment debtor fails to comply with the judgment or order of the court and you want to enforce the judgment or order concerned, you will be at liberty to file a writ of execution instructing the sheriff to seize his property.

LOCAL COURTS

The Local Courts are established by Article 91(1)(e) of the Constitution of Zambia, Chapter 1 of the Laws of Zambia. The Local Courts are recognized and established by the Local Courts Act, Cap 29 of the Laws of Zambia. Local Courts have different grades, exercising jurisdiction only within the limits prescribed for such grade.

Provided that no Local Court shall be given jurisdiction:

to determine civil claims other than matrimonial or inheritance claims of a value greater than one hundred and twenty fee units

to impose a fine exceeding forty penalty units or

to order probation or imprisonment for a period exceeding two years.

Section 8 of the Local Courts Act states that Local Courts shall have and may exercise within the territorial limits set out such jurisdiction as may be prescribed for the grade of court. Grade A are mandated to handle Cases of up to K3,060.00 while Grade B Local Courts are mandated to handle Cases of up to K2,500.00.

Local Courts, subject to section 12 of the Local Courts Act administer-

African Customary law applicable to any matter before it so far as such law is not repugnant to natural justice or morality or incompatible with the provisions of any written law;

the provisions of all by-laws and regulations made under the provisions of the Local Government Act Cap and is force is the area of jurisdiction of such local courts and

the provisions of any written law which such Local Court is to administer under the provisions of section thirteen.

Under Section 11 of the Act no Local Court shall have jurisdiction to try any case in which a person is charged with an offence in consequence of which death is alleged to have occurred or which is punishable by death.

Appeals

Appeals from Local Courts against any judgement or older go to the Subordinate Court.

THE ADMINISTRATION OF JUDICATURE

According to Section 3(1) of the Judicature Administration Act Chapter 24 of the Laws of Zambia, The President, on recommendation of the Judicial Service Commission, appoints a Chief Administrator who is responsible for the day to day running of the Judicature and the implementation of resolutions of the Judicial Service Commission.

The Chief Administrator :-

is the Controlling Officer regarding the expenditure of the Judicature within the meaning of the Finance (Control and Management) Act Chapter 347 Of the Laws of Zambia.

Keeps books of accounts and other records in relation to the accounts of the Judicature.

Prepares and submits financial reports concerning the activities of the Judicature to the President.

APPOINTMENT OF JUDGES

Clause140 states that, The President shall, on the recommendation of the Judicial Service Commission and subject to ratification by the National Assembly, appoint the—

(a) Chief Justice;

(b) Deputy Chief Justice;

(c) President of the Constitutional Court;

(d) Deputy President of the Constitutional Court; and

(e) other judges.

Under clause 141, a person qualifies for appointment as a judge if that person is of proven integrity and has been a legal practitioner, in the case of the—

(a) Supreme Court, for at least fifteen years;

(b) Constitutional Court, for at least fifteen years and has specialised training or experience in human rights or constitutional law;

(c) Court of Appeal, for at least twelve years; or

(d) High Court, for at least ten years.

A person appointed as judge to a specialised court shall have the relevant expertise, as prescribed.

The Chief Justice and President of the Constitutional Court shall hold office for not more than ten years and may, thereafter, continue as a judge of the Supreme Court or Constitutional Court provided they are under the age of 75 years.

THE JUDICIAL SERVICE COMMISSION

Article 219 of the Constitution of the Republic of Zambia provides for the establishment of the Judicial Service Commission.

The Service Commissions Act No 10. Of 2016 provides for the composition of the Judicial Service Commission as follows:

5. (1) The Judicial Service Commission consists of—

(a) the Chairperson, appointed by the President and who is a person who holds or qualifies to hold high judicial office or has held high judicial office;

(b) a judge nominated by the Chief Justice;

(c) the Attorney-General, with the Solicitor-General as the alternate;

(d) the Permanent Secretary responsible for public service management;

(e) a magistrate nominated by the Chief Justice;

(f) a representative of the Law Association of Zambia nominated by that Association and appointed by the President;

(g) the Dean of a Law School of a public higher education institution, nominated by the Minister responsible for justice;

and (h) one member appointed by the President.

(2) The Vice-Chairperson of the Commission shall be elected by the members from amongst themselves, except that the members referred to in paragraphs (b), (c) and (e) of subsection (1) shall not be appointed or elected as Vice-Chairperson

The current membership of the Judicial Service Commission is as follows:

Hon. Mr. Justice Mathew MSW Ngulube (Rtd) – Chairperson

Hon. Mr. Justice Bobby Bwalya (Rtd)-Vice Chairperson (Nominated by His Excellency the Republican President)

The Hon. Deputy Chief Justice, Hon. Mr. Justice Marvin S Mwanamwambwa – Member (Nominated by the Hon. Chief Justice)

Mr. Likando Kalaluka SC, Attorney General and Mr. Abraham Mwansa SC, Solicitor General as the alternate member

Mr. Boniface Chimbwali – Member (Permanent Secretary, Public Service Management Division)

Mr. Kenneth Mulife- Member (Magistrate nominated by the Hon. Chief Justice

Mr. Louise Mukande SC – Member (Nominated representative of the Law Association of Zambia and appointee of His Excellency the Republican President)

Mr. Fredrick Mudenda, Outgoing member (Former Dean, University of Zambia School of Law)

Mr. Charles Kafunda (Secretary)

ZAMBIA CRIME & SAFETY REPORT[1]

CRIME AND SAFETY SITUATION

U.S. Embassy Lusaka does not assume responsibility for the professional ability or integrity of the persons or firms appearing in this report. The American Citizens' Services unit (ACS) cannot recommend a particular individual or location, and assumes no responsibility for the quality of service provided.

The U.S. Department of State has assessed Lusaka as being a **HIGH**-threat location for crime directed at or affecting official U.S. government interests.

Please review OSAC's Zambia-specific page for original OSAC reporting, consular messages, and contact information, some of which may be available only to private-sector representatives with an OSAC password.

CRIME THREATS

Criminality continues to affect ordinary citizens, diplomats, and visitors alike. The use of firearms and edged weapons during the commission of many crimes is common, and visitors are advised not to resist if confronted.

The most commonly reported crimes against Westerners in Lusaka are non-violent confrontations characterized as crimes of opportunity (theft of unattended possessions in public places or hotel rooms, confidence scams). Pickpockets operate in crowded markets and on public transportation, and visitors have reported snatch attacks of bags and smartphones on busy city streets as well as smash-and-grabs of valuables from idle vehicles in traffic and from parked cars. Other crimes, including thefts, violent attacks, including home invasions/robberies, and sexual assaults have occurred on many occasions in 2017. Victims are often followed from banks, nightclubs, and ATMs and robbed at gunpoint, on the street, or upon arrival at their residence. Walking alone is not advisable in the downtown areas, lower socio-economic/informal settlement areas, public parks, and other poorly-illuminated areas—especially at night.

In Lusaka's poorer neighborhoods (Chalala, Bauleni, Kalingalinga, Chibolya, Chainda), groups of criminals commit crimes that go uninvestigated due to a lack of police resources. These criminal gangs often go on to victimize residents, including foreigners, in wealthier neighborhoods. While Zambian citizens are more often the victims of residential crimes, burglary and theft also occur in the more affluent neighborhoods where Americans reside—despite countermeasures. Americans and other foreigners are viewed as especially lucrative targets to thieves, often for no other reason than their perceived wealth.

Crime is not confined to late night hours. Robberies involving the use of firearms occurred in Lusaka during daylight hours and in populated areas in 2017; including a fatal knife attack in the vicinity of the U.S. Embassy. Carjackings are uncommon.

In 2017, two Americans reported theft of money and property from locked hotel rooms. It was determined that these crimes were inside jobs perpetrated by hotel employees and house-keeping staff. No hotel -- even upscale establishments -- in Zambia is immune. Even the small safes provided by the hotel are vulnerable and should not be trusted for high value items.

[1] U.S. Department of State

The occurrence of credit card theft and fraud is low in comparison to the U.S. and South Africa. Zambia is generally a cash economy; however, credit card terminals exist in major shops, hotels, most supermarkets, and some restaurants. Travelers are reminded to enable PIN codes for all transactions and check credit card statements shortly after the transaction occurs. For more information, please review OSAC's Report, "The Overseas Traveler's Guide to ATM Skimmers & Fraud."

Money laundering is present to facilitate other criminal activities throughout Zambia.

CYBERSECURITY ISSUES

Cybercrime is not yet a major problem in Zambia. This is likely due to a relatively low rate of personal computer ownership and internet penetration. The latter is estimated at 30%.

Advance-fee fraud schemes are prevalent throughout Africa, including in Zambia, and pose a danger of grave financial loss. These scams begin with unsolicited communication (usually e-mails) from strangers who promise quick financial gain, often by transferring large sums of money or valuables out of the country, but then require a series of "advance fees," such as fees for legal documents or taxes, to be paid. The final payoff does not exist; the purpose of the scam is simply to collect the advance fees.

A common variation is the scammer's claim to be a refugee or émigré of a prominent family or a relative of a present or former political leader who needs assistance in transferring large sums of cash.

Still other variations appear to be legitimate business deals that require advance payments on contracts. Sometimes victims are convinced to provide bank account and credit card information and financial authorization that is used to drain their accounts, incur large debts against their credit, and take their life savings.

Another common scam in Zambia is the "black money" or "wash wash" scam in which con artists attempt to fraudulently obtain money from a victim by persuading him/her that piles of banknote-sized paper in a trunk or a safe are actually U.S. currency notes that have been dyed to avoid detection by authorities. The victim is persuaded to pay fees and purchase chemicals to remove the dye, with the promise of a share in the proceeds.

The best way to avoid becoming a victim of any scheme is common sense. Any unsolicited business proposal should be thoroughly researched before committing any funds, providing any goods or services, or undertaking any travel. It is virtually impossible to recover money lost through these scams.

TRANSPORTATION-SAFETY SITUATION

For more information, please review OSAC's Report, "Security in Transit: Airplanes, Public Transport, and Overnights."

ROAD SAFETY AND ROAD CONDITIONS

Road safety is an even more significant threat to persons residing in or visiting Zambia than crime. Vehicle travel is extremely hazardous under normal conditions but particularly at night and during inclement weather. Zambia has an average of 50 fatalities per 100,000 residents (by comparison, the highest metropolitan rate in the U.S. is 17.8 fatalities per 100,000 residents). In 2017, approximately 1,400 traffic deaths were recorded by the Zambia Police Service. However, evidence collected by the WHO suggests that Zambia's road deaths are underreported by almost

200%. If true, this puts the highway death toll at more than 6,000. Approximately 55% of fatal accidents occur during hours of darkness, according to the Zambia Road Transport and Safety Agency.

Defensive driving is a must. Local drivers often exhibit little regard for pedestrians, other motorists' right-of-way, bicycle traffic, speed limits, or general safe driving practices. Traffic laws are routinely ignored by many local drivers, who often possess poor driving skills and/or training. Pedestrian deaths are a major problem, given that virtually all streets and roads lack sidewalks or overhead lighting. Traffic moves on the left side, so it is essential to look *right* before crossing the street on foot or pulling on to a road in a vehicle. Often, stop signs are stolen by individuals seeking to recycle the materials for profit, so approach intersections with caution. Drunk drivers are a major concern. There are no emergency services for stranded or injured drivers, and auto accident victims are vulnerable to theft by those pretending to be helpful. Road conditions are even worse in outlying or rural areas. This is especially true during the rainy season (December-April) when roads deteriorate at a rapid rate, causing extensive potholes and other road hazards.

Impromptu roadblocks set up by local security forces are commonplace and may or may not be officially sanctioned. Drivers stopped at these roadblocks may be subjected to a road permit, insurance, and/or safety inspection of their vehicles. Police may check for required road safety equipment (reflective triangles, fire extinguisher, and first aid kit) and test the vehicle's lights and brakes. Those who do not have the required equipment or otherwise fail the inspection may be fined.

A visitor must have a valid driver's license and be in Zambia for less than 90 days. Rental car companies are becoming common, and most vehicle rates include a driver. For more information on self-driving, please review OSAC's Report "Driving Overseas: Best Practices."

PUBLIC TRANSPORTATION CONDITIONS

Operators of many small passenger vans drive aggressively, dangerously passing on road shoulders or in opposing traffic lanes. Public mini-buses should be avoided, as they are normally overcrowded and poorly maintained. Many vehicles are in poor mechanical condition with worn tires and broken/missing tail, brake, and head lights. Official taxi cabs are generally considered safe but some lack seat belts. Cabs found at the major hotels tend to be more reliable. To avoid confrontation or fleecing, rates should be negotiated with the driver prior to embarkation. Do not share taxis with strangers. If you are going to be in Zambia for a few days, it is possible to work out an arrangement with most taxi drivers for daily transportation for the duration of your visit. Ensure that you obtain the driver's name, telephone number, national registration card number, and license plate.

TERRORISM THREAT

The U.S. Department of State has assessed Lusaka as being a **LOW**-threat location for terrorist activity directed at or affecting official U.S. government interests.

Local, Regional, and International Terrorism Threats/Concerns

The government of the Republic of Zambia (GRZ) is sensitive to the threat of terrorism and is engaged with international partners to combat this issue. However, visitors should carefully consider attendance of any large public gatherings that could become attractive targets for terrorists. The GRZ is not a state sponsor of terrorist activities and does not permit foreign fighters to transit the country. However, transnational terrorism is a concern throughout Africa, as increased law enforcement and anti-terrorism activities in the Horn of Africa have the potential to force terrorist organizations to seek targets in areas outside their traditional sphere of operations.

POLITICAL, ECONOMIC, RELIGIOUS, AND ETHNIC VIOLENCE

The U.S. Department of State has assessed Lusaka as being a **MEDIUM**-threat location for political violence directed at or affecting official U.S. government interests.

Zambia held a general election in August 2016, in which President Edgar Lungu won re-election to a five-year term by garnering more than 50% of votes, narrowly defeating rival Hakainde Hichilema by just under 3%. Although the results were deemed credible, media coverage, police actions, and legal restrictions heavily favored the ruling party and prevented the election from being genuinely fair. The pre-election and post-election periods were marred by limits on press freedom and political party intolerance resulting in sporadic violence across the country. In the campaign period preceding the election, police officers frequently harassed opposition supporters and denied free assembly. Police regularly arrested opposition candidate supporters indiscriminately and dispersed public gatherings with lethal force; however, they allowed ruling party gatherings to proceed in general or failed to interdict PF supporters aiming to disrupt opposition rallies. Tensions between the ruling and main opposition party remain, amid efforts by international actors to bring about dialogue and necessary reforms.

CIVIL UNREST

Spontaneous demonstrations take place throughout the country. Police often exacerbate tense situations. Police have continued the trend of supporting ruling party events and attempting to thwart opposition or civil society events critical of the government. Visitors are cautioned to avoid any large crowds, demonstrations, or political activities. Visitors should also stay current with local events, and be aware of their surroundings when traveling in Zambia.

POST-SPECIFIC CONCERNS

CRITICAL INFRASTRUCTURE

Only 31% of the country is connected to the national power grid.

Water resource mismanagement and deteriorating infrastructure have had negative impacts on Zambia's hydro power-dependent generation capacity causing blackouts.

Zambia's telecommunications and internet infrastructure is substandard and of limited availability outside of urban areas and large towns. Approximately 75% of the Zambian population has access to cell phones but less than 1% has landlines. This makes telephonic communication difficult, dependent upon coverage areas, and prone to cell tower or system overloading.

PERSONAL IDENTITY CONCERNS

Zambia presents a challenging environment for individuals with physical disabilities.

Although there have been no incidents with LGBTQI members of the U.S. citizen community, police have attempted to arrest openly gay citizens, including foreigners. Traditional cultural norms and conservative tendencies permeate Zambian society and, as a result, there is often LGBTQI intolerance.

Gender-based violence also continues to be a significant problem in Zambia.

DRUG-RELATED CRIMES

Possession of more than 0.5 grams of an illegal substance can constitute drug trafficking in Zambia.

The Zambian Drug Enforcement Commission has detained a number of U.S. citizens for possession of antihistamines and other over-the-counter medications, which contained small quantities of diphenhydramine, an ingredient that is on Zambia's list of controlled substances. U.S. citizens have been charged with drug-trafficking offenses, had their passports confiscated, and have been fined or jailed. While government officials have told the Embassy that carrying certain over-the-counter medications with a doctor's prescription is permitted, U.S. citizens visiting Zambia should consider leaving such medications behind. For more information, please refer to OSAC's Report, "Traveling with Medications."

POLICE RESPONSE

The majority of Zambia's police units do not compare to a U.S. police force in terms of capability, responsiveness, discipline, or professionalism. The Zambia Police Service is almost solely a reactive force and demonstrates rather poor proactive law enforcement techniques or initiative to deter or investigate crime. Police often lack equipment, resources, training, and personnel to respond to calls for assistance or other emergencies. Police response times can be long, if at all. Lack of adequate transportation is often cited as an excuse for slow response.

Most crimes go unreported and/or are not investigated at all. The police have a poor record of solving serious crimes, and few are ever brought to trial. Inadequate legislation results in the lack of prosecution or large numbers of acquittals. Corruption occurs at all levels, resulting in an ineffective legal and justice system. Vigilantism is present, as the critically under-funded and ill-equipped police have a poor rate of investigative closure and prosecution for crimes.

Low pay and morale create an environment in which bribes of even a few dollars can make allegations disappear. Attempt to cooperate and follow the instructions of police at checkpoints to avoid problems. It is not recommended to pay bribes, comply with requests for a "gift," or pay on-the-spot fines. If an officer persists, comply with instructions, identify yourself as a U.S. citizen, obtain the officer's name and badge number, and politely ask to speak with a supervisor and/or request to be taken to police headquarters for further processing. An official receipt will be issued for all legitimate fines associated with traffic law violations.

How to Handle Incidents of Police Detention or Harassment

Zambian police officers are required to notify the U.S. Embassy when an American citizen has been arrested; however, they consistently fail to do so. If arrested, be certain to assert this right and demand to speak with a representative from the U.S. Embassy by calling +260 (0) 211-357-000, or if after normal business hours +260 (0) 966 864-030.

CRIME VICTIM ASSISTANCE

Zambia Police Service: 991 or 112 on local phones

POLICE/SECURITY AGENCIES

The major law enforcement agencies are the Zambia Police Service (a nationwide police force responsible for traditional policing and investigations), Immigration, Customs, the Drug Enforcement Commission, the Anti-Corruption Commission, and the Department of National Parks and Wildlife.

There is no dedicated "Border Patrol." Border security is performed by whichever law enforcement agency may have a presence at the border at any given time.

MEDICAL EMERGENCIES

Medical facilities fall critically short of U.S. standards in terms of cleanliness and quality of treatment. Many lack adequate equipment or properly trained staff and possess limited to non-existent screening and testing capabilities. Trauma care is extremely limited, and local hospitals should only be used in the event of an extreme medical emergency. Misdiagnosis, unreliable treatment, and improper use of drugs are often reported.

Many medications are in short supply, of inferior quality, or are fraudulent. When traveling with prescription medications, U.S. citizens should carry a doctor's prescription and ensure that the medication is in its original bottle. Visitors should bring their own supply of medications as the quality of medications in Zambia is inconsistent, and counterfeit drugs are a problem. In the event medications are needed, such as over-the-counter medication, antibiotics, allergy remedies, or malaria prophylaxis, travelers may contact the U.S. Embassy's American Citizen Services (ACS) Unit to receive general information about reliable pharmacies.

Visitors with serious health concerns or who are on blood thinners (with the exception of aspirin) are discouraged from traveling to Zambia.

CONTACT INFORMATION FOR AVAILABLE MEDICAL SERVICES

For medical assistance, please refer to the Embassy's Medical Assistance page.

Insurance Guidance

Most health care facilities require patients to pay before being admitted or provided treatment and require them to settle the bill in full with cash prior to being discharged. A majority of medical facilities accept debit/credit cards, but some only accept cash. Foreigners are commonly charged a higher rate than local residents for most medical services.

All travelers to Zambia are advised to purchase insurance to cover medical evacuation in case of a serious accident, injury, or illness. Medical evacuation can cost thousands of dollars, depending on the severity of the situation, so all travelers should ensure their policies provide sufficient coverage.

ZAMBIA PENAL CODE

PART I-GENERAL PROVISIONS

CHAPTER I PRELIMINARY

1. This Act may be cited as the Penal Code Act.

Short title Cap. 87

2. Except as hereinafter expressly provided, nothing in this Code shall affect-

(*a*) the liability, trial or punishment of a person for an offence against the common law or against any other law in force in Zambia other than this Code; or

(*b*) the liability of a person to be tried or punished for an offence under the provisions of any law in force in Zambia relating to the jurisdiction of the local courts in respect of acts done beyond the ordinary jurisdiction of such courts; or

(*c*) the power of any court to punish a person for contempt of such court; or

(*d*) the liability or trial of a person, or the punishment of a person under any sentence passed or to be passed, in respect of any act done or commenced before the commencement of this Code; or

(*e*) any power of the President to grant any pardon or to remit or commute in whole or in part or to respite the execution of any sentence passed or to be passed; or

(*f*) any written law for the time being in force for the government of the Defence Force or the Zambia Police Force:

Saving of certain laws

Provided that if a person does an act which is punishable under this Code and is also punishable under another Act or Statute of any of the kinds mentioned in this section, he shall not be punished for that act both under that Act or Statute and also under this Code.

(*As amended by No.* 10 *of* 1935 *and S.I. No.* 63 *of* 1964 *and No 12 of 2000*)

CHAPTER II INTERPRETATION

3. This Code shall be interpreted in accordance with the principles of legal interpretation obtaining in England.

(*No.* 5 *of* 1972)

General rule of interpretation

4. Unless the context otherwise requires-

Interpretation

" community service" means form of punishment as a condition of suspension of a sentence of imprisonment requiring an offender tyo perform unpaid work within the community where the offender resides for the period specified in the order for community service"

"dwelling-house" includes any building or structure or part of a building or structure or any tent, or caravan or vessel which is for the time being kept by the owner or occupier for the residence therein of himself, his family or servants or any of them, and it is immaterial that it is from time to time uninhabited; a building or structure adjacent to or occupied with a dwelling-house is deemed to be part of the dwelling-house if there is a communication between such building or structure and the dwelling-house, either immediate or by means of a covered and enclosed passage leading from the one to the other, but not otherwise;

"explosive" or "explosive substance" means-

(*a*) nitro-glycerine, dynamite, gun-cotton, blasting powders, gunpowder, fulminate of mercury or other metals, and every other substance or mixture, whether similar to those enumerated herein or not, used with a view to producing a practical effect by explosion; and

(*b*) any detonating, igniter or safety fuse, or article of like nature, any detonator, and every adaption or preparation of an explosive as herein defined;

"felony" means an offence which is declared by law to be a felony or, if not declared to be a misdemeanour, is punishable, without proof of previous conviction, with death, or with imprisonment with hard labour for three years or more;

"grevious harm" means any harm which endangers life or which amounts to a maim or which seriously or permanently injures health or which is likely so to injure health, or which extends to permanent disfigurement, or to any permanent or serious injury to any external or internal organ, member or sense;

"harm" means any bodily hurt, disease or disorder whether permanent or temporary;

"judicial proceeding" includes any proceeding had or taken in or before any court, tribunal, commission of inquiry, or person in which evidence may be taken on oath,

"knowingly", used in connection with any term denoting uttering or using, implies knowledge of the character of the thing uttered or used;

"local authority" means a city council, municipal council, town council, district council;

"maim" means the destruction or permanent disabling of any external or internal organ, member or sense;

"misdemeanour" means any offence which is not a felony;

"money" includes bank notes, currency notes, bank drafts, cheques and other similar orders, warrants or requests for the payment of money;

"night" or "night-time" means the interval between seven o'clock in the evening and six o'clock in the morning;

"offensive weapon" means any article made or adapted for use for causing or threatening injury to the person, or intended by the person in question for such use, and includes any knife, spear, arrow, stone, axe, axe handle, stick or similar article;

"owner" and other like terms, when used with reference to property, include corporations of all kinds and any other association of persons capable of owning property, and also when so used include the President;

"person employed in the public service" means any person holding any of the following offices or performing the duty thereof, whether as a deputy or otherwise, namely:

(*a*) any public office; or

(*b*) any office to which a person is appointed or nominated by Act or Statute; or

(*c*) any civil office, the power of appointing to which or removing from which is vested in any person or persons holding an office of any kind included in either of the two last preceding paragraphs of this definition; or

(*d*) any office of arbitrator or umpire in any proceeding or matter submitted to arbitration by order or with the sanction of any court, or in pursuance of any Act;

and the said term further includes-

(i) a member of a commission of inquiry appointed under or in pursuance of any Act;

(ii) any person employed to execute any process of a court;

(iii) all persons belonging to the Defence Force;

(iv) all persons in the employment of any department of the Government, or a person in the employ of any corporation, body or board, including an institution of higher learning, in which the Government has a majority or controlling interest or any director of any such corporation, body or board;

(v) a person acting as a minister of religion of whatsoever denomination in so far as he performs functions in respect of the notification of intending marriage or in respect of the solemnisation of marriage, or in respect of the making or keeping of any register or certificate of marriage, birth, baptism, death or burial, but not in any other respect;

(vi) a councillor of, or a person in the employ of a local authority;

(vii) a person in the employ of a local authority;

"petroleum" has the meaning assigned to it by section *two* of the Petroleum Act,

"possession", "be in possession of" or "have in possession"-

(*a*) includes not only having in one's own personal possession, but also knowingly having anything in the actual possession or custody of any other person, or having anything in any place (whether belonging to, or occupied by oneself or not) for the use or benefit of oneself or of any other person;

(*b*) if there are two or more persons and any one or more of them with the knowledge and consent of the rest has or have anything in his or their custody or possession, it shall be deemed and taken to be in the custody and possession of each and all of them;

"property" includes any description of real and personal property, money, debts, and legacies, and all deeds and instruments relating to or evidencing the title or right to any property, or giving a right to recover or receive any money or goods, and also includes not only such property as has been originally in the possession or under the control of any person, but also any property into or for which the same has been converted or exchanged, and anything acquired by such conversion or exchange, whether immediately or otherwise;

"public" refers not only to all persons within Zambia, but also to such indeterminate persons as may happen to be affected by the conduct in respect to which such expression is used;

"public place" or "public premises" includes any public way and any building, place or conveyance to which for the time being the public are entitled or permitted to have access, either without any condition or upon condition of making any payment, and any building or place which is for the time being used for any public or religious meetings, or assembly or as an open court;

"public way" includes any highway, market place, square, street, bridge or other way which is lawfully used by the public;

"publicly" when applied to acts done means either-

(*a*) that they are so done in any public place as to be seen by any person whether such person be or be not in a public place; or

(*b*) that they are so done in any place, not being a public place, as to be likely to be seen by any person in a public place;

"the State" means the Sovereign Republic of Zambia;

"Statute" means any British Act and includes any orders, rules, regulations, by-laws, or other subsidiary legislation made or passed under the authority of any Statute;

"utter" includes using or dealing with and attempting to use or deal with and attempting to induce any person to use, deal with or act upon the thing in question;

"valuable security" includes any document which is the property of any person, and which is evidence of the ownership of any property or of the right to recover or receive any property;

"vessel" includes a ship, a boat and every other kind of vessel used in navigation either on the sea or in inland waters, and includes aircraft;

"wound" means any incision or puncture which divides or pierces any exterior membrane of the body, and any membrane is exterior for the purpose of this definition which can be touched without dividing or piercing any other membrane.

(*As amended by No.* 26 *of* 1940, *No.* 29 *of* 1948, *No.* 53 *of* 1957, *Nos.* 7 *and*34 *of* 1960, *G.N. No.* 268 *of* 1964, *S.I. No.* 63 *of* 1964, *Nos.* 69 *and* 76 *of* 1965, 35 *of* 1973 *No.* 20 *of* 1966, *Nos.* 25 *and* 36 *of* 1969, *No.* 5 *of* 1972, *No.* 29 *of*1974, *and No.* 3 *of* 1990

CHAPTER III APPLICATION OF THIS CODE

5. The jurisdiction of the courts of Zambia for the purposes of this Code extends to every place within Zambia.

Extent of jurisdiction of local courts

6. (1) Subject to subsection (3), a citizen of Zambia who does any act outside Zambia which, if wholly done within Zambia, would be an offence against this Code, may be tried and punished under this Code in the same manner as if such act had been wholly done within Zambia.

Liability for offences committed outside the jurisdiction, or partly within and partly beyond the jurisdiction

(2) When an act which, if wholly done within Zambia, would be an offence against this Code, is done partly within and partly outside Zambia, any person who within Zambia does any part of such act may be tried and punished under this Code as if such act had been wholly done within Zambia.

(3) Nothing in subsection (1) shall render any person liable to be tried and punished under this Code in respect of any act done outside Zambia which, if wholly done within Zambia, would be an offence against this Code if such person has been convicted and punished outside Zambia in respect of the same act, but, save as aforesaid, any such conviction shall, for the purposes of any law including this Code, be deemed to be a conviction for the said offence against this Code.

(*No.* 39 *of* 1970)

CHAPTER IV GENERAL RULES AS TO CRIMINAL RESPONSIBILITY

7. Ignorance of the law does not afford any excuse for any act or omission which would otherwise constitute an offence unless know-ledge of the law by the offender is expressly declared to be an element of the offence.

Ignorance of law

8. A person is not criminally responsible in respect of an offence relating to property, if the act done or omitted to be done by him with respect to the property was done in the exercise of an honest claim of right and without intention to defraud.

Bona fide claim of right

9. (1) Subject to the express provisions of this Code relating to negligent acts and omissions, a person is not criminally responsible for an act or omission which occurs independently of the exercise of his will, or for an event which occurs by accident.

Intention and motive

(2) Unless the intention to cause a particular result is expressly declared to be an element of the offence constituted, in whole or part, by an act or omission, the result intended to be caused by an act or omission is immaterial.

(3) Unless otherwise expressly declared, the motive by which a person is induced to do or omit to do an act, or to form an intention, is immaterial so far as regards criminal responsibility.

10. A person who does or omits to do an act under an honest and reasonable, but mistaken, belief in the existence of any state of things is not criminally responsible for the act or omission to any greater extent than if the real state of things had been such as he believed to exist. The operation of this rule may be excluded by the express or implied provisions of the law relating to the subject.

Mistake of fact

11. Every person is presumed to be of sound mind, and to have been of sound mind at any time which comes in question, until the contrary is proved.

Presumption of sanity

12. A person is not criminally responsible for an act or omission if at the time of doing the act or making the omission he is, through any disease affecting his mind, incapable of understanding what he is doing, or of knowing that he ought not to do the act or make the omission. But a person may be criminally responsible for an act or omission, although his mind is affected by disease, if such disease does not in fact produce upon his mind one or other of the effects above mentioned in reference to that act or omission.

Insanity

12A. (1) Where a person kills or is a party to the killing of another, he shall not be convicted of murder if he was suffering from such abnormality of mind (whether arising from a condition of arrested or retarded development of mind or any inherent causes or is induced by disease or injury) which has substantially impaired his mental responsibility for his acts or omissions in doing or being party to the killing.

Defence of diminished responsibility

(2) The provisions of subsection (2) of section *thirteen* shall apply with necessary modifications to the defence of diminished responsibility under this section:

Provided that the transient effect of intoxication as described in that subsection shall be deemed not to amount to disease or injury for purposes of this section.

(3) On a charge of murder, it shall be for the defence to prove the defence of diminished responsibility and the burden of proof shall be on a balance of probabilities.

(4) Where the defence of diminished responsibility is proved in accordance with this section, a person charged with murder shall be liable to be convicted of manslaughter or any other offence which is less than murder.

(*As amended by Act No.* 3 *of* 1990)

13. (1) Save as provided in this section, intoxication shall not constitute a defence to any criminal charge.

Intoxication

(2) Intoxication shall be a defence to any criminal charge if, by reason thereof, the person charged at the time of the act or omission complained of did not know that such act or omission was wrong or did not know what he was doing and-

(*a*) the state of intoxication was caused without his consent by the malicious or negligent act of another person; or

(*b*) the person charged was by reason of intoxication insane, temporarily or otherwise, at the time of such act or omission.

(3) Where the defence under subsection (2) is established, then in a case falling under paragraph (*a*) thereof the accused person shall be discharged, and in a case falling under paragraph (*b*) the provisions of section *one hundred and sixty-seven* of the Criminal Procedure Code relating to insanity shall apply.

(4) Intoxication shall be taken into account for the purpose of determining whether the person charged had formed any intention, specific or otherwise, in the absence of which he would not be guilty of the offence.

(5) For the purposes of this section, "intoxication" shall be deemed to include a state produced by narcotics or drugs.

(*No.* 10 *of* 1935 *as amended by No.* 3 *of* 1936)

14. (1) A person under the age of eight years is not criminally responsible for any act or omission.

Immature age

(2) A person under the age of twelve years is not criminally responsible for an act or omission, unless it is proved that at the time of doing the act or making the omission he had capacity to know that he ought not to do the act or make the omission.

(3) A male person under the age of twelve years is presumed to be incapable of having carnal knowledge.

(*As amended by No.* 20 *of* 1953)

15. Except as expressly provided by this Code, a judicial officer is not criminally responsible for anything done or omitted to be done by him in the exercise of his judicial functions, although the act done is in excess of his judicial authority or although he is bound to do the act omitted to be done.

Judicial officers

16. (1) Except as provided in this section, a person shall not be guilty of an offence if he does or omits to do any act under duress or coercion.

Defence of duress or coercion

(2) For the purpose of this section a person shall be regarded as having done or omitted to do any act under duress if he was induced to do or omit to do the act by any threat of death or grievous harm to himself or another and if at the time when he did or omitted to do the act he believed (whether or not on reasonable grounds)-

(*a*) that the harm threatened was death or grievous injury;

(*b*) that the threat would be carried out-

(i) immediately; or

(ii) before he could have any real opportunity to seek official protection,

if he did not do or omit to do the act in question; and

(*c*) that there was no way of avoiding or preventing the harm threatened.

(3) In this section "official protection" means the protection of the police or any authority managing any prison or other custodial institution, or any other authority concerned with the maintenance of law and order.

(*As amended by Act No.* 13 *of* 1990)

17. Subject to any other provisions of this Code or any other law for the time being in force, a person shall not be criminally responsible for the use of force in repelling an unlawful attack upon his person or property, or the person or property of any other person, if the means he uses and the degree of force he employs in doing so are no more than is necessary in the circumstances to repel the unlawful attack.

(*As amended by Act* 3 *of* 1990)

Defence of person or property

8. Where any person is charged with a criminal offence arising out of the arrest, or attempted arrest, by him of a person who forcibly resists such arrest or attempts to evade being arrested, the court shall, in considering whether the means used were necessary or the degree of force used was reasonable for the apprehension of such person, have regard to the gravity of the offence which had been, or was being, committed by such person and the circumstances in which such offence had been, or was being, committed by such person.

19. Repealed by Act No. 3 of 1990.

Use of force in effecting arrest

20. A person cannot be punished twice either under the provisions of this Code or under the provisions of any other law for the same act or omission, except in the case where the act or omission is such that by means thereof he causes the death of another person, in which case he may be convicted of the offence of which he is guilty by reason of causing such death, notwithstanding that he has already been convicted of some other offence constituted by the act or omission.

Person not to be punished twice for same offence

CHAPTER V PARTIES TO OFFENCES

21. (1) When an offence is committed, each of the following persons is deemed to have taken part in committing the offence and to be guilty of the offence, and may be charged with actually committing it, that is to say:

Principal offenders

(*a*) every person who actually does the act or makes the omission which constitutes the offence;

(*b*) every person who does or omits to do any act for the purpose of enabling or aiding another person to commit the offence;

(*c*) every person who aids or abets another person in committing the offence;

(*d*) any person who counsels or procures any other person to commit the offence.

(2) In the case of paragraph (*d*) of subsection (1), such person may be charged either with committing the offence or with counselling or procuring its commission. A conviction of counselling or procuring the commission of an offence entails the same consequences in all respects as a conviction of committing the offence. Any person who procures another to do or omit to do any act of such a nature that, if he had himself done the act or made the omission, the act or omission would have constituted an offence on his part, is guilty of an offence of the same kind and is liable to the same punishment, as if he had himself done the act or made the omission; and he may be charged with doing the act or making the omission.

22. When two or more persons form a common intention to prosecute an unlawful purpose in conjunction with one another, and in the prosecution of such purpose an offence is committed of such a nature that its commission was a probable consequence of the prosecution of such purpose, each of them is deemed to have committed the offence.

Offences committed by joint offenders in prosecution of common purpose

23. When a person counsels another to commit an offence, and an offence is actually committed after such counsel by the person to whom it is given, it is immaterial whether the offence actually committed is the same as that counselled or a different one, or whether the offence is committed in the way counselled or in a different way, provided in either case that the facts constituting the offence actually committed are a probable consequence of carrying out the counsel. In either case the person who gave the

counsel is deemed to have counselled the other person to commit the offence actually committed by him.

Counselling another to commit an offence

CHAPTER VI PUNISHMENTS

24. The following punishments may be inflicted by a court:

(*a*) death;

(*b*) imprisonment or an order for community service;

(*c*) Repealed by Act No. 10 of 2003

(*d*) fine;

(*e*) forfeiture;

(*f*) payment of compensation;

(*g*) finding security to keep the peace and be of good behaviour, or to come up for judgment;

(*h*) deportation;

(*i*) any other punishment provided by this Code or by any other law.

(*As amended by No.* 26 *of* 1933 *and No.*26 *of* 1940 and *No 12 of* 2000)

Different kinds of punishment

25. (1) When any person is sentenced to death, the sentence shall direct that he shall be hanged by the neck until he is dead.

Sentence of death

(2) Sentence of death shall not be pronounced on or recorded against a person convicted of an offence if it appears to the court that, at the time when the offence was committed, he was under the age of eighteen years; but in lieu thereof the court shall sentence him to be detained during the President's pleasure; and when so sentenced he shall be liable to be detained in such place and under such conditions as the President may direct.

(3) When a person has been sentenced to be detained during the President's pleasure under subsection (2), the presiding Judge shall forward to the President a copy of the notes of evidence taken at the trial, with a report in writing signed by him containing such recommendation or observations on the case as he may think fit to make.

(4) Where a woman convicted of an offence punishable with death is found in accordance with the provisions of section *three hundred and six* of the Criminal Procedure Code to be pregnant, the sentence to be passed on her shall be a sentence of imprisonment for life instead of a sentence of death.

(*As amended by No.* 26 *of* 1940 *and No.* 28 *of* 1952)

26. (1) All imprisonment shall be with or without hard labour in the discretion of the court, unless the imposition of imprisonment only without hard labour is expressly prescribed by law.

Imprisonment

(2) A person liable to imprisonment for life or any other period may be sentenced for any shorter term.

(3) A person convicted of a felony, other than manslaughter, may be sentenced to pay a fine in addition to imprisonment:

Provided that, where such person is a corporation, the corporation may be sentenced to a fine instead of imprisonment.

(4) A person convicted of manslaughter or a misdemeanour may be sentenced to pay a fine in addition to or instead of imprisonment.

26A. Where an offender has been sentenced to community service, the offender shall perform community work for the period specified in the order for community service shall be performed in an area where the offender resides.

(*As amended by No.* 26 *of* 1933 *and No.* 76 *of* 1965 *and No 12 of 2000*)

Insertion of new section 26A

Sentence of community service

27. (*No.* 23 *of* 1952 *as amended by No.* 21 *of* 1958, *No.* 18 *of* 1963 *and G.N. No.* 303 *of* 1964 *and Repealed by Act No. 10 of* 2003)

28. Where a fine is imposed under any written law, then, in the absence of express provisions relating to such fine in such written law, the following provisions shall apply:

(*a*) Where no sum is expressed to which the fine may extend, the amount of the fine which may be imposed is unlimited, but shall not be excessive.

Fines

(*b*) In the case of an offence punishable with a fine or a term of imprisonment, the imposition of a fine or a term of imprisonment shall be a matter for the discretion of the court.

(*c*) In the case of an offence punishable with imprisonment as well as a fine in which the offender is sentenced to a fine with or without imprisonment and in every case of an offence punishable with fine only in which the offender is sentenced to a fine, the court passing sentence may, in its discretion-

(i) direct by its sentence that, in default of payment of the fine, the offender shall suffer imprisonment for a certain term, which imprisonment shall be in addition to any other imprisonment to which he may have been sentenced or to which he may be liable under a commutation of sentence; and also

(ii) issue a warrant for the levy of the amount on the immovable and movable property of the offender by distress and sale under warrant:

Provided that if the sentence directs that, in default of payment of the fine, the offender shall be imprisoned, and if such offender has undergone the whole of such imprisonment in default, no court shall issue a distress warrant unless for special reasons to be recorded in writing it considers it necessary to do so.

(*d*) The term of imprisonment ordered by a court in respect of the non-payment of any sum of money adjudged to be paid by a conviction or in respect of the default of a sufficient distress to satisfy any such sum shall be such term as, in the opinion of the court, will satisfy the justice of the case, but shall not exceed in any case the maximum fixed by the following scale:

Maximum CHAPTER *period*

Not exceeding 15 penalty unit . . . . 14 days

Exceeding 15 penalty units but not exceeding 30 penalty units . . . . 1 month

Exceeding 30 penalty units but not exceeding 150 penalty units . . . . 3 months

Exceeding 150 penalty units but not exceeding 600 penalty units . . . . 4 months

Exceeding 600 penalty units but not exceed ing 1500 penalty units. . . . 6 months

Exceeding 1500 penalty units . . . . 9 months

(*e*) The imprisonment which is imposed in default of payment of a fine shall terminate whenever the fine is either paid or levied by process of law.

(*As amended by No.* 26 *of* 1933 *and Act No.* 13 *of* 1994)

29. When any person is convicted of an offence under any of the following sections, namely, sections *ninety four*, *ninety-five*, *ninety-six*, *one hundred and thirty*, *one hundred and fourteen*, *three hundred and eighty-five* and *three hundred and eighty-six*, the count shall, in addition to or in lieu of any penalty which may be imposed, order the forfeiture of any property which has passed in connection with the commission of the offence, or, if

such property cannot be forfeited or cannot be found, of such sum as the court shall assess as the value of the property. Payment of any sum so ordered to be forfeited may be enforced in the same manner and subject to the same provisions as in the case of the payment of a fine.

(*As amended by No.* 26 *of* 1933 *and S.I. No.* 63 *of* 1964 *and Act No.* 29 *of* 1974)

Forfeiture

30. In accordance with the provisions of section *one hundred and seventy-five* of the Criminal Procedure Code, any person who is convicted of an offence may be adjudged to make compensation to any person injured by his offence. Any such compensation may be either in addition to or in substitution for any other punishment;

Provided that where a person is convicted of an offence under section *two hundred and eighty-one A* the court which convicts the person may, in addition to any other penalty imposed under that section, order the person convicted to make compensation to any person who has suffered loss or damage from the convicted person's offence and the order of compensation may include the actual loss suffered and any loss arising from the commission of the offence.

(*As amended by No.* 26 *of* 1933, *No.* 26 *of* 1940 *and No. 20 of* 2000)

Compensation.

31. A person convicted of an offence not punishable with death may, instead of or in addition to any punishment to which he is liable, be ordered to enter into his own recognizance, with or without sureties, in such amount as the court thinks fit, conditioned that he shall keep the peace and be of good behaviour for a time to be fixed by the court, and may be orderd to be imprisoned until such recognizance, with sureties, if so directed, is entered into; but so that the imprisonment for not entering into the recognizance shall not extend for a term longer than one year, and shall not, together with the fixed term of imprisonment, if any, extend for a term longer than the longest term for which he might be sentenced to be imprisoned without fine.

(*No.* 26 *of* 1933 *as amended by No.* 18 *of* 1962)

Security for keeping the peace

32. A court may order any person convicted of an offence to pay the costs of and incidental to the prosecution or any part thereof.

Costs

33. Whenever a court shall sentence to a term of imprisonment any person-

(*a*) who is not a citizen of Zambia; and

(*b*) who has been convicted of an offence under this Code, or under any written law other than an offence relating to the driving of a motor vehicle set out in the Roads and Road Traffic Act or in any regulations for the time being in force made thereunder;

the public prosecutor shall forth with, forward to the Minister responsible for home affairs the particulars of the conviction and sentence and all other particulars specified in the Second Schedule.

(*Act No.* 32 *of* 1972 *and No.* 8 *of* 1974)

Court to send particulars of conviction of non-citizens to Minister responsible for home affairs
Cap. 464

34. (1) Where a person is convicted before the High Court of felony, the High Court may, in addition to or in lieu of any other punishment to which he is liable, recommend to the President that he be deported to such part of Zambia as the President may direct.

Deportation within Zambia- in cases of felony

(2) Where upon any sworn information it appears to the High Court that there is reason to believe that any person is about to commit a breach of the peace or that his conduct is likely to produce or excite to a breach of the peace, the High Court may order him to give security in one or more sureties for peace and good behaviour and in default may order him to be imprisoned until he gives the security ordered, or recommend to the President that he be deported as aforesaid.

In default of security for peace

(3) Where it is shown on oath to the satisfaction of the High Court that any person is conducting himself so as to be dangerous to peace and good order in any part of Zambia, or is endeavouring to excite enmity between any section of the people of Zambia and the President or the Government, or between any section of the people of Zambia and any other section of the same, or is intriguing against constituted power and authority in Zambia, or has been convicted in any court of competent jurisdiction within or without Zambia of any offence which would be likely to excite enmity between any section of the people of Zambia and any other section of the same or by any section of the people against such person, the High Court may recommend to the President that an order be made for his deportation to such part of Zambia as may be specified in such order.

In cases of dangerous conduct

(4) The powers conferred by this section on the High Court shall also be exercisable by subordinate courts:

Powers of subordinate courts

Provided however that any exercise of such powers by subordinate courts shall be liable to revision by and must be reported at once to the High Court.

(5) Where a court recommends under this section that a person be deported, the President may make an order in accordance with such recommendation:

Approval of High Court

Provided however that if such recommendation is made by a subordinate court, the President shall not make an order for deportation without the approval of the High Court.

(6) Any person for whose deportation a recommendation or an order has been made may be detained in the nearest convenient prison pending confirmation or otherwise of the recommendation or the carrying out of the order, as the case may be.

(*As amended by No.* 26 *of* 1933, *No.* 34 *of* 1954, *G.N. No.* 303 *of* 1964 *and S.I. No.* 63 *of* 1964)

Detention pending deportation

35. (1) If a person ordered to be deported to any part of Zambia under the preceding section is sentenced to any term of imprisonment, such sentence of imprisonment shall be served before the order of deportation is carried into effect.

Provisions as to sentences of deportation

(2) An order for deportation may be expressed to be in force for a time to be limited therein or for an unlimited time and may require the deported person to report himself personally at such place, to such person and at such intervals of time, not being less than thirty days, as may be specified in such order.

(3) If a person leaves or attempts to leave the district or place in Zambia to which he has been deported while the order of deportation is still in force without the written consent of the President, which consent may be given subject to any terms as to security for good behaviour or otherwise as to the President may seem good, or wilfully neglects or refuses to report himself as ordered, such person is liable to imprisonment for six months and to be again deported on a fresh warrant under the original order or under a new order.

(4) For the purposes of this section, a person shall be deemed to have served a sentence of imprisonment immediately upon his release after earning remission for good behaviour or on licence issued under any written law relating to prisons.

(*As amended by No.* 1 *of* 1952, *No.* 34 *of* 1954, *No.* 21 *of* 1959, *No.* 18 *of*1962 *and G.N. No.* 303 *of* 1964)

36. With respect to cases where one act constitutes several crimes or where several acts are done in execution of one criminal purpose, the following provisions shall have effect, that is to say:

One act constituting several crimes, etc.

(*a*) Where a person does several acts against or in respect of one person or thing, each of which acts is a crime but the whole of which acts are done in the execution of the same design and in the opinion of the court before which the person is tried form one continuous transaction, the person shall be punished for each act so charged as a separate crime and the court shall upon conviction award a separate punishment for each act. If the court orders imprisonment the order may be for concurrent or consecutive terms of imprisonment:

Against one person or thing

Provided always that-

(i) if the terms of imprisonment ordered are consecutive, the total of the terms so ordered shall not exceed the maximum term of imprisonment allowed by law in respect of that conviction for which the law allows the longest term; and, if the court orders the payment of fines, the fines may or may not be cumulative;

(ii) where the court orders cumulative fines, the total of the fines so ordered shall not exceed the maximum fines allowed by law in respect of that conviction for which the law allows the largest fine.

(*b*) If a person by one act assaults, harms or kills several persons or in any manner causes injury to several persons or things, he shall on conviction be punished in respect of each person so assaulted, harmed or killed or each person or thing injured; in such case the court shall order a separate punishment in respect of each person assaulted, harmed or killed or in respect of each person or thing injured. If the court orders imprisonment, the order may be for concurrent or consecutive terms of imprisonment:

Against several persons or things

Provided always that-

(i) if the terms of imprisonment ordered are consecutive, the total of the terms of imprisonment so ordered shall not exceed the maximum term allowed by law in respect of that conviction for which the law allows the longest term; and, if the court orders the payment of fines, the fines may or may not be cumulative;

(ii) where the court orders cumulative fines, the total of such fines shall not exceed the maximum allowed by law in respect of that conviction for which the law allows the largest fine.

(*As amended by No.* 23 *of* 1952 *and No. 10 of* 2003)

37. Except as otherwise in this Coe or in any other written law provided, a sentence of imprisonment takes effect from and includes the whole of the day on which it was pronounced unless the court shall, at the time of passing sentence, expressly order that it shall take effect from some day prior to that on which it was pronounced;

Date from which sentence takes effect

Provided that such prior day shall not be earlier than the day on which the arrested person was taken into custody for the offence for which sentence is pronounced.

(*As amended by Act No.* 3 *of* 1990)

38. When in this Code no punishment is specially provided for any misdemeanour, it shall be punishable with imprisonment for a term not exceeding two years or with a fine or with both.

General punishment for misdemeanours

39. (1) Where any person is convicted of an offence by a court and at the date of such conviction he has not been sentenced under a prior conviction or his sentence under a prior conviction has not expired, then any sentence imposed by the said court, other than a sentence of death, shall be executed after the expiration of the sentence imposed under the prior conviction, unless the said court otherwise directs.

Sentences cumulative unless otherwise directed

(2) A court may direct that a sentence imposed by it on any person shall be executed concurrently with a sentence or with any part of a sentence imposed on such person under a prior conviction:

Provided that it shall not be lawful for a court to direct that a sentence of imprisonment in default of payment of a fine shall be executed concurrently with a sentence imposed in respect of a prior conviction under sub-paragraph (i) of paragraph (*c*) of section *twenty-eight* or with any part of such sentence.

(*No.* 18 *of* 1962 *as amended by G.N. No.* 268 *of* 1964 *and Act No. 10 of 2003*)

40. (1) When sentence is passed under this Code on an escaped convict, such sentence, if of death or fine, shall, subject to the provisions of this code, take effect immediately, and if of imprisonment, shall take effect according to the following rules, that is to say:

Escaped convicts to serve unexpired sentences when recaptured

(*a*) if the new sentence is severer than the sentence which such convict was undergoing when he escaped, the new sentence shall take effect immediately and he shall serve any period of imprisonment in respect of his former sentence which remained unexpired at the time of his escape after he has completed serving his new sentence;

(*b*) when the new sentence is not severer than the sentence the convict was undergoing when he escaped, the new sentence shall take effect after he has suffered imprisonment for a further period equal to that part of his former sentence which remained unexpired at the time of his escape.

(2) For the purposes of this section, a sentence of imprisonment for whatever period with hard labour shall be deemed severer than a sentence of imprisonment for whatever period without hard labour and, where the conditions as to labour are the same, a longer sentence shall be deemed severer than a shorter sentence.

(*Amended by Act No.* 26 *of* 1940 *and Act No. 10 of* 2003)

41. (1) Where a court by or before which a person is convicted of an offence, not being an offence the sentence for which is fixed by law, is of opinion, having regard to the circumstances including the nature of the offence and the character of the offender, that

it is inexpedient to inflict punishment and that a probation order under the Probation of Offenders Act is not appropriate, the court may make an order discharging him absolutely or subject to the condition that he commits no offence during such period, not exceeding twelve months from the date of the order, as may be specified therein.

Absolute and conditional discharge

(2) An order discharging a person subject to such a condition as aforesaid is in this section and in section *forty-two* referred to as "an order for conditional discharge", and the period specified in any such order as "the period of conditional discharge".

(3) Before making an order for conditional discharge, the court shall explain to the offender in ordinary language that if he commits another offence during the period of conditional discharge he will be liable to be sentenced for the original offence.

(4) A court may, on making an order for conditional discharge, if it thinks it expedient for the purpose of the reformation of the offender, allow any person who consents to do so to execute a bond for the good behaviour of the offender; and the provisions of section *sixty* of the Criminal Procedure Code shall apply in relation to the forfeiture of any such bond.

(5) Subject as hereinafter provided, a conviction for an offence for which an order is made under this section discharging the offender absolutely or conditionally shall not be deemed to be a conviction for any purpose other than the purposes of the proceedings in which the order is made and of any further proceedings which may be taken against the offender under section *forty-two*.

(6) The foregoing provisions of this section shall not affect-

(*a*) any right of any such offender as aforesaid to appeal against his conviction, or to rely thereon in bar of any subsequent proceedings for the same offence;

(*b*) the revesting or restoration of any property in consequence of the conviction of any such offender.

(7) Where, under the provisions of section *forty-two*, a person conditionally discharged under this section is sentenced for the offence in respect of which the order for conditional discharge was made, that order shall cease to have effect.

(*No.* 18 *of* 1962)

42. (1) If it appears to any Judge or magistrate that an offender against whom an order for conditional discharge has been made has been convicted of an offence during the period of conditional discharge, he may issue a summons requiring the offender to appear at the place and time specified therein or may issue a warrant for his arrest:

Commission of further offences by offender against whom an order for conditional discharge has been made

Provided that a magistrate shall not issue such a summons or warrant except on information on oath.

(2) A summons or warrant issued under subsection (1) shall direct the offender to appear or to be brought before the court by which the order for conditional discharge was made.

(3) Where an offender is convicted by a magistrate of an offence committed during the period of conditional discharge, the magistrate may commit the offender to custody or release him on bail, with or without sureties, until he can be brought or appear before the court by which the order of conditional discharge was made.

(4) Where a magistrate commits an offender to custody, or releases him on bail, under the provisions of subsection (3), he shall transmit to the court by which the order for conditional discharge was made-

(*a*) such particulars of the matter as he thinks fit; and

(*b*) a signed certificate of the conviction for the offence committed during the period of conditional discharge;

and for the purposes of the proceedings in the court to which it is transmitted, such certificate, if purporting to be so signed, shall be admitted as evidence of the conviction.

(5) Where it is proved to the satisfaction of the court by which an order for conditional discharge was made that the offender has been convicted of an offence committed during the period of conditional discharge, such court may deal with him in respect of the original offence in any manner in which it could deal with him if he had just then been convicted before the court of such original offence.

(6) Where an offender is convicted before the High Court of an offence committed during the period of conditional discharge, the High Court may deal with him in respect of the original offence in any manner in which the court which made the order for conditional discharge could deal with him if he had just then been convicted before that court of such original offence.

PART II-CRIMES

DIVISION I OFFENCES AGAINST PUBLIC ORDER

CHAPTER VII TREASON AND OTHER OFFENCES

43. (1) A person is guilty of treason and shall be liable to suffer death who-

Treason

(*a*) prepares or endeavours to overthrow by unlawful means the Government as by law established; or

(*b*) prepares or endeavours to procure by force any alteration of the law or the policies of the Government; or

(*c*) prepares or endeavours to procure by force the setting up of an independent state in any part of Zambia or the secession of any part of Zambia from the Republic; or

(*d*) prepares or endeavours to carry out by force any enterprise which usurps the executive power of the State in any matter of both a public and a general nature; or

(*e*) incites or assists any person to invade Zambia with armed force or unlawfully to submit any part of Zambia to attack by land, water or air, to assist in the preparation of any such invasion or attack; or

(*f*) in time of war and with intent to give assistance to the enemy, does any act which is likely to give such assistance.

(2) In paragraphs (*b*), (*c*) and (*d*) of subsection (1), "by force" means either-

(*a*) by force used in such a manner as, whether by reason of the number of persons involved or the means used or both, to imperil or be likely to imperil the safety of the State or to cause or be likely to cause death or grievous harm or serious damage to property; or

(*b*) by a show of force calculated to arouse reasonable apprehension that force will be used in such a manner as is described in paragraph (*a*).

(3) A person who is not a citizen of Zambia shall not be punishable under this section for anything done outside Zambia, but a citizen of Zambia may be tried and punished for an offence under this section as if it had been committed within the jurisdiction of the court.

44. Any person who-

(*a*) becomes an accessory after the fact to treason; or

(*b*) knowing that any person intends to commit treason, does not give information thereof with all reasonable despatch to the President, the Vice-President, a Minister, a Deputy Minister, an Administrative Officer or a police officer, or use other reasonable endeavours to prevent the commission of the offence;

is guilty of the felony termed misprision of treason and is liable to imprisonment for life.

(*As amended by No.* 6 *of* 1965)

Concealment of treason

45. A person is guilty of treason-felony and shall be liable to imprisonment for twenty years who-

Treason-felony

(*a*) prepares or endeavours to procure by unlawful means any alterations of the law or the policies of the Government; or

(*b*) prepares or endeavours to carry out by unlawful means any enterprise which usurps the executive power of the State in any matter of both a public and a general nature.

46. Any person who, without lawful authority, carries on, or makes preparation for carrying on, or aids in or advises the carrying on of, or preparation for, any war or warlike undertaking with, for, by, or against any chief, or with, for, by, or against any tribal group, is guilty of a felony, and is liable to imprisonment for life.

Promoting tribal war

47. Repealed by Act No. 35 of 1973.

48. Any person who advisedly attempts to effect any of the following purposes, that is to say:

Inciting to mutiny

(*a*) to seduce any person serving in the Defence Force or any member of the Zambia Police Force from his duty and allegiance to the President; or

(*b*) to incite any such persons to commit an act of mutiny or any traitorous or mutinous act; or

(*c*) to incite any such persons to make or endeavour to make a mutinous assembly;

is guilty of a felony, and is liable to imprisonment for life.

(*As amended by S.I. No.* 63 *of* 1964)

49. Any person who-

(*a*) aids, abets, or is accessory to, any act of mutiny by; or

(*b*) incites to sedition or to disobedience to any lawful order given by a superior officer;

any non-commissioned officer or private of the Defence Force or any member of the Zambia Police Force, is guilty of a misdemeanour.

Aiding soldiers or police in acts of mutiny

50. Any person who, by any means whatever, directly or indirectly-

(*a*) procures or persuades or attempts to procure or persuade to desert; or

(*b*) aids, abets, or is accessory to the desertion of; or

(*c*) having reason to believe he is a deserter, harbours or aids in concealing;

any non-commissioned officer or private of the Defence Force or any member of the Zambia Police Force, is guilty of a misdemeanour and is liable to imprisonment for six months.

Inducing soldiers or police to desert

51. Any person who-

(*a*) knowingly and advisedly aids an alien enemy of the Republic, being a prisoner of war in Zambia, whether such prisoner is confined in a prison or elsewhere, or is suffered to be at large on his parole, to escape from his prison or place of confinement, or if he is at large on his parole, to escape from Zambia, is guilty of a felony and is liable to imprisonment for life;

(*b*) negligently and unlawfully permits the escape of any such person as is mentioned in paragraph (*a*), is guilty of a misdemeanour.

Aiding prisoners of war to escape

52. In the case of any of the offences defined in this Chapter, when the manifestation by an overt act of an intention to effect any purpose is an element of the offence, every act of conspiring with any person to effect that purpose, and every act done in furtherance of the purpose by any of the persons conspiring, is deemed to be an overt act manifesting the intention.

Definition of overt act

53. (1) If the President is of the opinion that there is in any publication or series of publications published within or without Zambia by any person or association of persons matter which is contrary to the public interest, he may, in his absolute discretion, by order published in the *Gazette* and in such local newspapers as he may consider necessary, declare that that particular publication or series of publications, or all publications or any class of publication specified in the order published by that person or association of persons, shall be a prohibited publication or prohibited publications, as the case may be.

Prohibited publications

(2) If an order made under the provisions of subsection (1) specifies by name a publication which is a periodical publication, such order shall, unless a contrary intention be expressed therein, have effect-

(*a*) with respect to all subsequent issues of such publication; and

(*b*) not only with respect to any publication under that name, but also with respect to any publication published under any other name if the publishing thereof is in any respect a continuation of, or in substitution for, the publishing of the publication named in the order.

(3) If an order made under the provisions of subsection (1) declares that all publications published by a specified person or association of persons shall be prohibited publications, such order shall, unless a contrary intention be expressed therein, have

effect not only with respect to all publications published by that person or association of persons before the date of the order but also with respect to all publications so published on or after such date.

(4) An order made under the provisions of subsection (1) shall, unless a contrary intention is expressed therein, apply to any translation into any language whatsoever of the publication specified in the order.

(5) Where an order has been made under subsection (1) declaring any series of publications or all or any class of publications published by any person or association of persons to be prohibited publications or specifying by name a publication which is a periodical publication, any person who wishes to import into Zambia any particular publication affected by such order may apply to the competent authority for a permit in that behalf and, unless the competent authority is satisfied that the publication contains matter which is contrary to the public interest, he shall grant such a permit and the order shall thereupon cease to have effect with respect to that publication.

(6) Any person whose application to the competent authority under subsection (5) has been refused may appeal in writing against such refusal to the President whose decision thereon shall be final.

(7) For the purpose of this section and of any prosecution in respect of a prohibited publication, any publication which purports to be printed or published outside Zambia by any person or association of persons shall, unless and until the contrary is proved, be deemed to be published outside Zambia by such person or persons.

(*No.* 9 *of* 1954 *as amended by Nos.* 34 *and* 36 *of* 1960, *No.* 18 *of* 1962 *and G.N. No.* 303 *of* 1964)

54. (1) Any person who imports, publishes, sells, offers for sale, distributes, or reproduces any prohibited publication or any extract therefrom, is guilty of an offence and is liable for a first offence to imprisonment for two years or to a fine not exceeding three thousand penalty units or to both, and for a subsequent offence to imprisonment for three years; and such publication or extract therefrom shall be forfeited to the President on behalf of the Government.

Offences in respect of prohibited publications

(2) Any person who, without lawful excuse, has in his possession any prohibited publication or any extract therefrom, is guilty of an offence and is laible for a first offence to imprisonment for one year or to a fine not exceeding one thousand and five hundred penalty units or to both, and for subsequent offence to imprisonment for two years; and such publication or extract therefrom shall be forfeited to the President on behalf of the Government.

(*No.* 48 *of* 1938 *as amended by No.* 9 *of* 1954, *S.I. No.* 63 *of* 1964 *and Act No* 13 *of* 1994)

55. (1) Any person to whom any prohibited publication or any extract therefrom is sent without his knowledge or privity or in response to a request made before the publication was declared to be a prohibited publication, or who has in his possession any prohibited

publication or extract therefrom at the date when the publication is declared to be a prohibited publication, shall forthwith if or as soon as the nature of the contents thereof have become known to him, or in the case of a publication or extract therefrom which is in the possession of such person before an order declaring it to be a prohibited publication has been made, forthwith upon the making of such an order, deliver such publication or extract therefrom at the nearest police station of which an officer of or above the rank of Sub Inspector is in charge or to the nearest Administrative Officer, and in default thereof he is guilty of an offence and is liable on conviction to a fine not exceeding one thousand and five hundred penalty units or to imprisonment for a period not exceeding one year, or to both, and such publication or extract therefrom shall be forfeited.

Delivery of prohibited publication to police station

(2) This section shall not apply to a public officer who receives or is in possession of a prohibited publication or extract therefrom in the course of his duties as such officer.

(3) A person who complies with the provisions of subsection (1) or is convicted of an offence under that subsection shall not be liable to prosecution for an offence under section *fifty-four.*

(*No.* 9 *of* 1954 *as amended by S.I. No.* 63 *of* 1964, *No.* 24 *of* 1977 *and Act No.* 13 *of* 1994)

56. (1) Any of the following officers, that is to say:

Power to examine packages

(*a*) any officer of the General Post Office not below the rank of postmaster;

(*b*) any officer of the Department of Customs and Excise not below the rank of collector;

(*c*) any police officer not below the rank of Sub Inspector;

(*d*) any other officer authorised in that behalf by the President;

may detain, open and examine any package or article which he suspects to contain any prohibited publication or extract therefrom, and during such examination may detain any person importing, distributing, or posting such package or article or in whose possession such package or article is found.

(2) If any such publication or extract therefrom is found in such package or article, the whole package or article may be impounded and retained by the officer, and the person importing, distributing, or posting it, or in whose possession it is found, may forthwith be arrested and proceeded against for the commission of an offence under section *fifty-four* or *fifty-five*, as the case may be.

(*No.* 48 *of* 1938 *as amended by No.* 9 *of* 1954,*G.N. No.* 303 *of* 1964 *and Act No.* 24 *of* 1977)

57. (1) Any person who-

Offences in respect of seditious practices

(*a*) does or attempts to do, or makes any preparation to do, or conspires with any person to do, any act with a seditious intention;

(*b*) utters any seditious words;

(*c*) prints, publishes, sells, offers for sale, distributes or reproduces any seditious publication;

(*d*) imports any seditious publication, unless he has no reason to believe that it is seditious;

is guilty of an offence and is liable for a first offence to imprisonment for seven years or to a fine not exceeding six thousand penalty units or to both; and any seditious publication shall be forfeited.

(2) Any person who, without lawful excuse, has in his possession any seditious publication is guilty of an offence and is liable for a first offence to imprisonment for two years or to a fine not exceeding three thousand penalty units or to both, and for a subsequent offence to imprisonment for five years; and such publication shall be forfeited.

(*No.* 48 *of* 1938 *as amended by No.* 29 *of* 1959,*No.*6 *of* 1965 *and Act No.* 13 *of* 1994)

58. A person shall not be prosecuted for an offence under section *fifty-seven* without the written consent of the Director of Public Prosecutions.

(*No.* 48 *of* 1938 *as amended by No.* 6 *of* 1965)

Legal proceedings

59. No person shall be convicted of an offence under section *fifty-seven*on the uncorroborated testimony of one witness.

Evidence

60. (1) A seditious intention is an intention-

Seditious intention

(*a*) to advocate the desirability of overthrowing by unlawful means the Government as by law established; or

(*b*) to bring into hatred or contempt or to excite disaffection against the Government as by law established; or

(*c*) to excite the people of Zambia to attempt to procure the alteration, otherwise than by lawful means, of any other matter in Zambia as by law established; or

(*d*) to bring into hatred or contempt or to excite disaffection against the administration of justice in Zambia; or (*e*) to raise discontent or disaffection among the people of Zambia; or

(*f*) to promote feelings of ill will or hostility between different communities or different parts of a community; or

(*g*) to promote feelings of ill will or hostility between different classes of the population of Zambia; or

(*h*) to advocate the desirability of any part of Zambia becoming an independent state or otherwise seceding from the Republic; or

(*i*) to incite violence or any offence prejudicial to public order or in disturbance of the public peace; or

(*j*) to incite resistance, either active or passive, or disobedience to any law or the administration thereof:

Provided that an intention, not being an intention manifested in such a manner as to effect or be likely to effect any of the purposes mentioned in the aforegoing provisions of this subsection, shall not be taken to be seditious if it is an intention-

(i) to show that the Government have been misled or mistaken in any of their measures; or

(ii) to point out errors or defects in the Government or Constitution as by law established or in legislation or in the administration of justice, with a view to the reformation of such errors or defects; or

(iii) to persuade the people of Zambia to attempt to procure by lawful means the alteration of any matter in Zambia as by law established; or

(iv) to point out, with a view to their removal, any matters which are producing or have a tendency to produce feelings of ill will or hostility between different classes of the population of Zambia.

(2) In determining whether the intention with which any act was done, any words were spoken, or any document was published, was or was not seditious, every person shall be deemed to intend the consequences which would naturally follow from his conduct at the time and under the circumstances in which he so conducted himself.

(3) For the purposes of paragraph (*f*) of subsection (1), "community" includes any body or group of persons having a common tribal or racial origin.

(*No.* 48 *of* 1938 *as amended by No.* 2 *of* 1955, *No.* 53 *of* 1957, *No.* 34 *of*1960, *No.* 20 *of* 1964, *No.* 6 *of* 1965 *and No.* 36 *of* 1969)

61. (1) In any prosecution for publishing a seditious publication where it is proved that the publication has been published, the following persons shall be deemed to have published such publication:

Persons deemed to have published a seditious publication

(*a*) in the case of a publication of a society, the office-bearers of the society;

(*b*) any person referred to in the publication as being the editor, assistant editor or author of such publication;

(*c*) any person who is proved to be the editor of such publication;

(*d*) any person who is proved to have published such publication.

(2) Notwithstanding the provisions of subsection (1), where any person mentioned in paragraph (*a*), (*b*) or (*c*) of the said subsection is prosecuted for publishing a seditious publication, it shall be a sufficient defence if he proves to the satisfaction of the court that the seditious publication was published without his consent and that the publication of the seditious publication did not arise from want of due care or caution on his part.

(3) A publication shall be treated as being the publication of a society if-

(*a*) it professes by name or otherwise to be a publication of or under the sponsorship of the society;

(*b*) it is published or disseminated by or under the direction or guidance of the society or by any person as an office-bearer of the society.

(4) In any prosecution for publishing a seditious publication, publication by or under the sponsorship of any branch, party or organ of a society shall be deemed to be a publication by the main society and by any headquarters branch of such society.

(5) For the purposes of this section, "office-bearer" and "society" shall have the meaning assigned to them in the Societies Act.

62. For the purposes of sections *fifty-three* to *sixty-one* both inclusive-

Interpretation

"competent authority" means the person appointed as such by the President;

"import" includes-

(*a*) to bring into Zambia; and

(*b*) to bring within the inland waters of Zambia, whether or not the publication is brought ashore, and whether or not there is an intention to bring the same ashore;

"periodical publication" includes every publication issued periodically or in parts or numbers at intervals, whether regular or irregular;

"prohibited publication" means any publication in respect of which an order has been made under the provisions of section *fifty-three*;

"public interest" means the interest of defence, public safety, public order, public morality or public health;

"publication" includes all written or printed matter and everything, whether of a nature similar to written or printed matter or not, containing any visible representation, or by its form, shape, or in any manner capable of suggesting words or ideas, or gramophone record, or other similar means of reproducing speech, and every copy and reproduction of any publication;

"seditious publication" means a publication containing any word, sign or visible presentation expressive of a seditious intention; and

"seditious words" means words having a seditious intention.

(*No.* 48 *of* 1938 *as amended by No.* 9 *of* 1954, *No.* 18 *of* 1962, *G.N. No.* 303 *of* 1964 *and No.* 6 *of* 1965)

63. Any person who-

(*a*) administers, or is present at and consents to the administering of, any oath, or engagement in the nature of an oath, purporting to bind the person who takes it to commit any offence punishable with death; or

(*b*) takes any such oath or engagement, not being compelled to do so;

is guilty of a felony and is liable to imprisonment for life.

Unlawful oaths to commit capital offences

64. Any person who-

(*a*) administers, or is present at and consents to the administering of, any oath, or engagement in the nature of an oath, purporting to bind the person who takes it to act in any of the ways following, that is to say:

Other unlawful oaths to commit offences

(i) to engage in any mutinous or seditious enterprise;

(ii) to commit any offence not punishable with death;

(iii) to disturb the public peace;

(iv) to be of any association, society or confederacy, formed for the purpose of doing any such act as aforesaid;

(v) to obey the orders or commands of any committee or body of men not lawfully constituted, or of any leader or commander or other person not having authority by law for that purpose;

(vi) not to inform or give evidence against any associate, confederate or other person;

(vii) not to reveal or discovery any unlawful association, society or confederacy, or any illegal act done or to be done, or any illegal oath or engagement that may have been administered or tendered to or taken by himself or any other person, or the import of any such oath or engagement; or

(*b*) takes any such oath or engagement, not being compelled to do so;

is guilty of a felony and is liable to imprisonment for seven years.

65. A person who takes any such oath or engagement as is mentioned in the two last preceding sections cannot set up as a defence that he was compelled to do so, unless within fourteen days after taking it, or, if he is prevented by actual force or sickness, within fourteen days after the termination of such prevention, he declares by information on oath before a magistrate, or, if he is on actual service in the Defence Force or in the Zambia Police Force, either by such information or by information to his commanding officer, the whole of what he knows concerning the matter, including the person or persons by whom and in whose presence, and the place where, and the time when, the oath or engagement was administered or taken.

Compulsion: how far a defence

66. (1) Any person who-

Unlawful drilling

(*a*) without the permission of the President, trains or drills any other person to the use of arms or the practice of military exercises, movements, or evolutions; or

(*b*) is present at any meeting or assembly of persons, held without the permission of the President, for the purpose of training or drilling any other persons to the use of arms or the practice of military exercises, movements, or evolutions;

is guilty of a felony and is liable to imprisonment for seven years.

(2) Any person who, at any meeting or assembly held without the permission of the President, is trained or drilled to the use of arms or the practice of military exercises, movements, or evolutions, or who is present at any such meeting or assembly for the purpose of being so trained or drilled, is guilty of a misdemeanour.

(*As amended by G.N. No.* 303 *of* 1964 *and S.I. No.* 63 *of* 1964)

67. (1) Any person who publishes, whether orally or in writing or otherwise, any statement, rumour or report which is likely to cause fear and alarm to the public or to disturb the public peace, knowing or having reason to believe that such statement, rumour or report is false, is guilty of a misdemeanour and is liable to imprisonment for three years.

Publication of false news with intent to cause fear and alarm to the public

(2) It shall be no defence to a charge under subsection (1) that he did not know or did not have reason to believe that the statement, rumour or report was false, unless he proves that, prior to publication, he took reasonable measures to verify the accuracy of such statement, rumour or report.

(*No.* 48 *of* 1938 *as amended by No.* 7 *of* 1958)

68. Any person who does any act or utters any words or publishes any writing, with intent to insult or bring into contempt or ridicule the official national anthem of Zambia, is

guilty of an offence and is liable on conviction to imprisonment for a period not exceeding two years.

Insulting the national anthem

69. Any person who, with intent to bring the President into hatred, ridicule or contempt, publishes any defamatory or insulting matter, whether by writing, print, word of mouth or in any other manner, is guilty of an offence and is liable on conviction to imprisonment for a period not exceeding three years.

Defamation of President

70. (1) Any person who utters any words or publishes any writing expressing or showing hatred, ridicule or contempt for any person or group of persons wholly or mainly because of his or their race, tribe, place of origin or colour is guilty of an offence and is liable on conviction to imprisonment for a period not exceeding two years.

Expressing or showing hatred, ridicule or contempt for persons because of race, tribe, place of origin or colour

(2) A person shall not be prosecuted for an offence under this section without the written consent of the Director of Public Prosecutions.

CHAPTER VIII OFFENCES AFFECTING RELATIONS WITH FOREIGN STATES AND EXTERNAL TRANQUILITY

71. Any person who, without such justification or excuse as would be sufficient in the case of the defamation of a private person, publishes anything intended to be read, or any sign or visible representation, tending to degrade, revile or expose to hatred or contempt any foreign prince, potentate, ambassador or other foreign dignitary with intent to disturb peace and friendship between Zambia and the country to which such prince, potentate, ambassador or dignitary belongs, is guilty of a misdemeanour.

Defamation of foreign princes

72. Any person commits a misdemeanour who does any of the following acts without the authority of the President, that is to say:

(*a*) who prepares or fits out any naval or military expedition to proceed against the dominions of any friendly state, or is engaged in such preparation or fitting-out, or assists therein, or is employed in any capacity in such expedition; or

(*b*) who, being a Zambian subject, accepts or agrees to accept any commission or engagement in the military or naval service of any foreign state at war with any friendly state, or, whether a Zambian subject or not, induces any other person to accept or agree to accept any commission or engagement in the military or naval service of any foreign state as aforesaid; or

(*c*) who, being a Zambian subject, quits or goes on board any vessel with a view of quitting Zambia, with intent to accept any commission or engagement in the military or naval service of any foreign state at war with a friendly state, or, whehter a Zambian subject or not, induces any other person to quit or to go on board any vessel with a view of quitting Zambia with the like intent; or

(*d*) who, being the master or owner of any vessel, knowingly either takes on board, or engages to take on board, or has on board such vessel any illegally enlisted person; or

(*e*) who, with intent or knowledge, or having reasonable cause to believe that the same will be employed in the military or naval service of any foreign state at war with any friendly state builds, agrees to build, causes to be built, equips, despatches, or causes or allows to be despatched, any vessel, or issues or delivers any commission for any vessel:

Foreign enlistment

Provided that a person building, causing to be built or equipping a vessel in any of the cases aforesaid, in pursuance of a contract made before the commencement of such war as aforesaid, is not liable to any of the penalties specified in this section in respect of such building or equipping if-

(i) upon a proclamation of neutrality being issued by the President, he forthwith gives notice to the President or the Minister responsible for foreign affairs that he is so building, causing to be built, or equipping such vessel, and furnishes such particulars of the contract and of any matters relating to, or done, or to be done under the contract as may be required by the President or the Minister responsible for foreign affairs; and

(ii) he gives such security, and takes and permits to be taken such other measures, if any, as the President or the Minister responsible for foreign affairs may prescribe for ensuring that such vessel shall not be despatched, delivered, or removed without the licence of the President until the termination of such war as aforesaid.

73. Any person who is guilty of piracy or any crime connected with or relating or akin to piracy is liable to be tried and punished according to the law of England for the time being in force.

Piracy

CHAPTER IX UNLAWFUL ASSEMBLIES, RIOTS AND OTHER OFFENCES AGAINST PUBLIC TRANQUILITY

74. (1) When three or more persons assemble with intent to commit an offence, or being assembled with intent to carry out some common purpose, conduct themselves in such a manner as to cause persons in the neighbourhood reasonably to fear that the persons so assembled will commit a breach of the peace, or will by such assembly needlessly and without any reasonable occasion provoke other persons to commit a breach of the peace, they are an unlawful assembly. It is immaterial that the original assembling was lawful if, being assembled, they conduct themselves with a common purpose in such a manner as aforesaid.

Definition of unlawful assembly

(2) When an unlawful assembly has begun to execute a common purpose by a breach of the peace and to the terror of the public, the assembly is called a riot, and the persons assembled are said to be riotously assembled.

(As amended by No. 20 of 1964)

Definition of riot

75. Any person who takes part in an unlawful assembly is guilty of a misdemeanour and is liable to imprisonment for five years.

(*As amended by No.* 26 *of* 1961)

Punishment of unlawful assembly

76. Any person who takes part in a riot is guilty of a misdemeanour and is liable to imprisonment for seven years.

(*As amended by No.* 26 *of* 1961)

Punishment of riot

77. Any magistrate, or any police officer of or above the rank of Inspector, or any commissioned officer in the Defence Force, in whose view twelve or more persons are riotously assembled, or who apprehends that a riot is about to be committed by twelve or more persons assembled within his view, may make or cause to be made a proclamation in the President's name, in such form as he thinks fit, commanding the rioters or persons so assembled to disperse peaceably.

(*As amended by No.* 1 *of* 1956 *and S.I. No.* 63 *of* 1964)

Making proclamation for rioters to disperse

78. If upon the expiration of a reasonable time after such proclamation is made, or after the making of such proclamation has been prevented by force, twelve or more persons continue riotously assembled together, any person authorised to make proclamation, or any police officer, or any other person acting in aid of such person or police officer, may do all things necessary for dispersing the persons so continuing assembled, or for apprehending them or any of them, and, if any person makes resistance, may use all such force as is reasonably necessary for overcoming such resistance, and shall not be liable in any criminal or civil proceeding for having, by the use of such force, caused harm or death to any person.

Dispersion of rioters after proclamation made

79. If proclamation is made, commanding the persons engaged in a riot, or assembled with the purpose of committing a riot, to disperse, every person who, at or after the expiration of a reasonable time from the making of such proclamation, takes or continues to take part in the riot or assembly, is guilty of a felony and is liable to imprisonment for ten years.

(*As amended by No.* 26 *of* 1961)

Rioting after proclamation

80. Any person who forcibly prevents or obstructs the making of such proclamation as is in section *seventy-seven* mentioned, is guilty of a felony and is liable to imprisonment for ten years; and if the making of the proclamation is so prevented, every person who, knowing that it has been so prevented, takes or continues to take part in the riot or assembly, is liable to imprisonment for ten years.

(*As amended by No.* 26 *of* 1961)

Preventing or obstructing the making of proclamation

81. Any persons who, being riotously assembled together, unlawfully pull down or destroy, or begin to pull down or destroy any building, railway, machinery or structures are guilty of a felony and each of them is liable to imprisonment for life.

Rioters demolishing buildings, etc.

82. Any persons who, being riotously assembled together, unlawfully damage any of the things in the last preceding section mentioned, are guilty of a felony and each of them is liable to imprisonment for seven years.

Rioters injuring buildings, etc.

83. All persons are guilty of a misdemeanour who, being riotously assembled, unlawfully and with force prevent, hinder or obstruct the loading or unloading of any railway, motor or other vehicle or vessel, or the starting or transit of any railway, motor or other vehicle, or the sailing or navigating of any vessel, or unlawfully and with force board any railway, motor or other vehicle or any vessel with intent so to do.

Riotously interferring with railway, vehicle, etc.

84. Any person who goes armed in public, without lawful occasion, in such a manner as to cause terror to any person is guilty of a misdemeanour and his arms may be forfeited.

Going armed in public

85. (1) Any person who, without lawful authority or excuse, the proof whereof shall lie upon him, has in his possession or in or upon any premises occupied by him any offensive weapon or any offensive material is guilty of an offence and is liable on conviction to imprisonment for a period not exceeding seven years.

Possession of offensive weapons or materials

(2) A police officer may arrest without warrant any person whom he has reasonable cause to believe to be committing an offence under this section.

(3) A person shall not be prosecuted for an offence under this section without the written consent of the Director of Public Prosecutions.

(4) In this section-

"offensive material" means any substance, material or article made or adapted for use for causing or threatening injury to the person or property, or intended by the person in question for such use, and includes-

(*a*) any explosive as defined in the Explosives Act;

(*b*) any ammunition as defined in the Firearms Act;

(*c*) any inflammable liquid or substance, and any acid or gas.

86. (1) Any person who, in order to take possession thereof, enters on any land or tenements in a violent manner, whether such violence consists in actual force applied to any other person or in threats or in breaking open any house or in collecting an unusual number of people, is guilty of the misdemeanour termed "forcible entry".

Forcible entry

(2) It is immaterial whether he is entitled to enter on the land or not, provided that a person who enters upon lands or tenements of his own, but which are in the custody of his servant or bailiff, does not commit the offence of forcible entry.

87. Any person who, being in actual possession of land without colour of right, holds possession of it, in a manner likely to cause a breach of the peace or reasonable apprehension of a breach of the peace, against a person entitled by law to the possession of the land, is guilty of the misdemeanour termed "forcible detainer".

Forcible detainer

8. Any person who takes part in a fight in a public place is guilty of a misdemeanour and is liable to imprisonment for six months or to a fine not exceeding seven hundred and fifty penalty units.

(*As amended by Act No.* 13 *of* 1994)

Affray

89. Any person who challenges another to fight a duel, or attempts to provoke another to fight a duel, or attempts to provoke any person to challenge another to fight a duel, is guilty of a misdemeanour.

Challenge to fight a duel

90. Any person who-

(*a*) threatens another with any injury to his person or property with intent to cause alarm to that person, or to cause that person to do any act which he is not legally bound to do, or to omit to do any act which that person is legally entitled to do, as a means of avoiding the execution of such threat; or

(*b*) discharges loaded firearms or commits any breach of the peace with intent to alarm any person;

is guilty of a misdemeanour and is liable to imprisonment for five years.

(*No.* 28 *of* 1937 *as amended by No.* 26 *of* 1961)

Threatening violence

*91. (1) Any person who, without lawful excuse, to any assembly makes any statement indicating or implying that it would be incumbent or desirable-

*On the expiry of Act No. 70 of 1953, the text of this section set out in Act No. 22 of 1953 will be substituted.

Proposing violence or breaches of the law to assemblies

(*a*) to do any acts calculated to bring death or physical injury to any person or to any class or community of persons; or

(*b*) to do any acts calculated to lead to destruction or damage to any property; or

(*c*) to commit an offence against any law in force in Zambia or in any part thereof;

is guilty of an offence and is liable to imprisonment for seven years:

Provided that a statement which expresses mere disapproval of a law shall, to that extent only, be held not to be a statement which indicates or implies that it would be incumbent or desirable to commit an offence against such law.

(2) A person shall not be prosecuted for an offence under paragraph (*c*) of subsection (1) without the written consent of the Director of Public Prosecutions.

*On the expiry of Act No. 70 of 1953, the text of this section set out in Act No. 22 of 1953 will be substituted.

(3) For the purposes of this section, an assembly means a gathering of three or more persons.

(*No.* 70 *of* 1953 *as amended by No.* 26 *of* 1961 *and S.I. No.* 63 *of* 1964)

92. (1) Whenever the President is satisfied that any boycott is being conducted or is threatened or likely to be conducted in Zambia with the intention or effect of-

Wrongfully inducing a boycott

(*a*) bringing into hatred or contempt, exciting disaffection against or undermining the lawful authority of the Government, or a local authority, or of persuading any such body to alter any law or rule, to appoint or dissolve any commission or committee or to take any action which it is not by law required to take;

(*b*) endangering law and order in the Republic;

(*c*) bringing the economic life of the Republic into jeopardy; or

(*d*) raising discontent or disaffection among the inhabitants of Zambia or engendering feelings of ill will or hostility between different classes or different races of the population of Zambia;

he may, by statutory notice, designate such boycott for the purposes of this section and may, by the same or in a subsequent such notice, specify in relation to a designated boycott any action which he is satisfied is likely to further that boycott, including (but without prejudice to the generality of the foregoing power) any action falling within any of the following classes of action, that is to say:

(i) abstaining from buying goods from or selling goods to any person or class of persons; or

(ii) abstaining from buying or selling any goods or class of goods; or

(iii) abstaining from entering or approaching or dealing at any premises at which any person or class of person carries on trade or business; or

(iv) abstaining from dealing with any person or class of person in the course of his trade or business or abstaining from using or providing any service or class of service; or

(v) abstaining from working for or employing any person or class of person; or

(vi) abstaining from letting, hiring or allowing the use of any land or building to any person or class of person; or

(vii) abstaining from doing any other act which may lawfully be done.

(2) Any person who, with intent to further any designated boycott-

(*a*) by word of mouth; or

(*b*) by making a publication as defined in subsection (6);

advises, induces or persuades or attempts to advise, induce or persuade any person or class of person to take any action which has been specified in relation to such boycott under the provisions of subsection (1), is guilty of an offence and is liable to imprisonment for a period not exceeding six months.

(3) For the purposes of this section, in determining whether any words were spoken or any publication was made with intent to further a designated boycott, every person shall, unless the contrary be proved, be deemed to intend the consequences which would naturally follow from his conduct at the time and the circumstances in which he so conducts himself.

(4) Nothing in this section shall be construed so as to make unlawful any action lawfully taken by a party to a trade dispute as defined in the Industrial and Labour Relations Act, in contemplation or in furtherance of such dispute.

(5) Where any person is charged before any court with an offence under this section, no further proceedings in respect thereof shall be taken against him without the consent of the Director of Public Prosecutions, except such as the court may think necessary by remanding (whether in custody or on bail) or otherwise to secure the due appearance of the person charged, so however, that if such person is remanded in custody, he shall, after the expiration of a period of fourteen days from the date on which he was so remanded, be entitled to be discharged from custody on entering a recognizance without

sureties, unless within such period the Director of Public Prosecutions has consented to such further proceedings as aforesaid.

(6) For the purposes of this section, "publication" has the meaning given to it by section *sixty-two*, and a person is said to make a publication if he prints, publishes, sells, distributes or reproduces such publication.

(7) For the purposes of this section, "boycott" means the withholding by a combination of persons of all relations or any particular relations from any person or class of persons.

(*No.* 29 *of* 1959 *as amended by G.N. No.* 268 *of* 1964, *S.I. No.* 63 *of* 1964 *and No.* 69 *of* 1965)

93. Any persons who assemble together, to the number of two or more, for the purpose of unshipping, carrying, or concealing any goods subject to customs duty and liable to forfeiture under any written law relating to customs, are guilty of a misdemeanour and each of them is liable to imprisonment for six months or to a fine not exceeding three thousand penalty units.

(*As amended by Act No.* 13 *of* 1994)

Assembling for the purpose of smuggling

DIVISION II OFFENCES AGAINST THE ADMINISTRATION OF LAWFUL AUTHORITY

CHAPTER X OFFENCES AGAINST THE ADMINISTRATION OF LAWFUL AUTHORITY

94. Repealed by Act 14 of 1980

95. Repealed by Act 14 of 1980

96. Repealed by Act 14 of 1980

97. Any person who, being employed in the public service, and being charged by virtue of his employment with any judicial or administrative duties respecting property of a special character, or respecting the carrying on of any manufacture, trade or business of a special character, and having acquired or holding, directly or indirectly, a private interest in any such property, manufacture, trade or business, discharges any such duties with respect to the property, manufacture, trade or business in which hc has such intcrest or with respect to the conduct of any person in relation thereto, is guilty of a misdemeanour and is liable to imprisonment for one year.

Officers charged with administration of property of a special character of with special duties

98. Any person who, being employed in the public service in such a capacity as to require him or to enable him to furnish returns or statements touching any sum payable or claimed to be payable to himself or to any other person, or touching any other matter required to be certified for the purpose of any payment of money or delivery of goods to

be made to any person, makes a return or statement touching any such matter which is, to his knowledge, false in any material particular, is guilty of a misdemeanour.

False claims by officials

99. (1) Any person who, being employed in the public service, does or directs to be done, in abuse of the authority of his office, any arbitrary act prejudicial to the rights or interests of the Government or any other person, is guilty of a misdemeanour. If the act is done or directed to be done for purposes of gain, he is guilty of a felony and is liable to imprisonment for three years.

Abuse of authority of office

(2) A prosecution for any offence under this or either of the two last preceding sections shall not be instituted except by or with the sanction of the Director of Public Prosecutions.

(*As amended by S.I. No.* 63 *of* 1964 and Act No 29 of 1976)

100. Any person who, being authorised or required by law to give any certificate touching any matter by virtue whereof the rights of any person may be prejudicially affected, gives a certificate which is, to his knowledge, false in any material particular, is guilty of a misdemeanour.

False certificates by public officers

101. Any person who-

(*a*) not being a judicial officer, assumes to act as a judicial officer; or

(*b*) without authority, assumes to act as a person having authority by law to administer an oath or take a solemn declaration or affirmation or affidavit or to do any other act of a public nature which can only be done by persons authorised by law to do so; or

(*c*) represents himself to be a person authorised by law to sign a document testifying to the contents of any register or record kept by lawful authority, or testifying to any fact or event, and signs such document as being so authorised, when he is not, and knows that he is not, in fact, so authorised;

is guilty of a misdemeanour.

False assumption of authority

102. Any person who-

(*a*) personates any person employed in the public service on an occasion when the latter is required to do any act or attend in any place by virtue of his employment; or

(*b*) falsely represents himself to be a person employed in the public service, and assumes to do any act or to attend in any place for the purpose of doing any act by virtue of such employment;

is guilty of a misdemeanour and is liable to imprisonment for three years.

Personating public officers

103. Whoever holds out any threat of injury to any person employed in the public service, or to any person in whom he believes that person to be interested, for the purpose of inducing that person to do any act, or to forbear or delay to do any act connected with the exercise of the public functions of such person, is guilty of a misdemeanour.

(*No.* 26 *of* 1940)

Threat of injury to persons employed in public service

103A. In this chapter, "public service" means service of the Government or a local authority, or of a statutory board or body including an institution of higher learning, corporation or company in which the Government has majority interest or control.

Definition

CHAPTER XI OFFENCES RELATING TO THE ADMINISTRATION OF JUSTICE

104. (1) Any person who, in any judicial proceeding, or for the purpose of instituting any judicial proceeding, knowingly gives false testimony touching any matter which is material to any question then pending in that proceeding or intended to be raised in that proceeding, is guilty of the misdemeanour termed "perjury".

Perjury

(2) It is immaterial whether the testimony is given on oath or under any other sanction authorised by law.

(3) The forms and ceremonies used in administering the oath or in otherwise binding the person giving the testimony to speak the truth are immaterial, if he assent to the forms and ceremonies actually used.

(4) It is immaterial whether the false testimony is given orally or in writing.

(5) It is immaterial whether the court or tribunal is properly constituted, or is held in the proper place, or not, if it actually acts as a court or tribunal in the proceeding in which the testimony is given.

(6) It is immaterial whether the person who gives the testimony is a competent witness or not, or whether the testimony is admissible in the proceeding or not.

(7) Any person who aids, abets, counsels, procures, or suborns another person to commit perjury is guilty of the misdemeanour termed "subornation of perjury".

Subornation of perjury

104A. (1) Where a witness in any judicial proceeding, other than a person accused of an offence in a criminal proceeding, makes a statement on oath or affirmation on some fact relevant in the proceeding contradicting a material detail in a previous statement made on oath or affirmation by the same witness before any court or tribunal and, the court or tribunal is satisfied that either of the statements whether false or not was made with intent to deceive, shall be guilty of an offence and liable to imprisonment for two years.

Conflicting statements on oath

(2) At the trial of any person for an offence under this section, the record of a court or tribunal containing any statement made on oath or affirmation by the person charged shall be *prima facie* evidence of such statement.

(3) A person shall be liable to be convicted of an offence under this section notwithstanding that any statement made by him before a court or tribunal was made in reply to a question which he was bound by law to answer, any such statement shall be admissible in any proceeding under this section.

(*As amended by Act* 3 *of* 1990)

105. Any person who, having been lawfully sworn as an interpreter in a judicial proceeding, wilfully makes a statement material in that proceeding which he knows to be false, or does not believe to be true, is guilty of the misdemeanour termed "perjury".

(*No.* 26 *of* 1940)

False statements by interpreters

106. Any person who commits perjury or suborns perjury is liable to imprisonment for seven years.

Punishment of perjury and subordination of perjury

107. A person cannot be convicted of committing perjury or of subordination of perjury solely upon the evidence of one witness as to the falsity of any statement alleged to be false.

Evidence on charge of perjury

108. Any person who, with intent to mislead any tribunal in any judicial proceeding-

(*a*) fabricates evidence by any means other than perjury or subordination of perjury; or

(*b*) knowingly makes use of such fabricated evidence;

is guilty of a misdemeanour and is liable to imprisonment for seven years.

Fabricating evidence

109. Any person who swears falsely or makes a false affirmation or declaration before any person authorised to administer an oath or take a declaration upon a matter of public concern under such circumstances that the false swearing or declaration if committed in a judicial proceeding would have amounted to perjury, is guilty of a misdemeanour.

False swearing

110. Any person who practises any fraud or deceit, or knowingly makes or exhibits any false statement, representation, token, or writing, to any person called or to be called as a witness in any judicial proceeding, with intent to affect the testimony of such person as a witness, is guilty of a misdemeanour.

Deceiving witnesses

111. Any person who, knowing that any book, document, or thing of any kind whatsoever, is or may be required in evidence in a judicial proceeding, wilfully removes or destroys it or renders it illegible or undecipherable or incapable of identification, with intent thereby to prevent it from being used in evidence, is guilty of a misdemeanour.

(*As amended by No.* 26 *of* 1940)

Destroying evidence

112. (1) Any person commits a felony who-

Conspiracy to defeat justice and interference with witnesses

(*a*) conspires with any other person to accuse any person falsely of any crime or to do anything to obstruct, prevent, pervert, or defeat the course of justice; or

(*b*) in order to obstruct the due course of justice, dissuades, hinders or prevents any person lawfully bound to appear and give evidence as a witness from so appearing and giving evidence, or endeavours to do so; or

(*c*) obstructs or in any way interferes with or knowingly prevents the execution of any legal process, civil or criminal.

(2) Any person guilty of a felony under sub-section (1) is liable to imprisonment for seven years.

113. Any person who asks, receives, or obtains, or agrees or attempts to receive or obtain, any property or benefit of any kind for himself or any other person upon any agreement or understanding that he will compound or conceal a felony, or will abstain from, discontinue, or delay a prosecution for a felony, or will withhold any evidence thereof, is guilty of a misdemeanour.

Compounding felonies

114. Any person who, having brought, or under pretence of bringing, an action against another person upon a Penal Act or Statute in order to obtain from him a penalty for any offence committed or alleged to have been committed by him, compounds the action without the order or consent of the court in which the action is brought or is to be brought, is guilty of a mis-demeanour.

Compounding penal actions

115. Any person who-

(*a*) publicly offers a reward for the return of any property which has been stolen or lost, and in the offer makes use of any words purporting that no questions will be asked, or that the person producing such property will not be seized or molested; or

(*b*) publicly offers to return to any person who may have bought or advanced money by way of loan upon any stolen or lost property the money so paid or advanced or any other sum of money or reward for the return of such property; or

(*c*) prints or publishes any such offer;

is guilty of a misdemeanour.

Advertisements for stolen property

116. (1) Any person who-

Contempt of court

(*a*) within the premises in which any judicial proceeding is being had or taken, or within the precincts of the same, shows disrespect, in speech or manner, to or with reference to such proceeding, or any person before whom such proceeding is being had or taken; or

(*b*) having been called upon to give evidence in a judicial proceeding, fails to attend or, having attended, refuses to be sworn or to make an affirmation, or having been sworn or affirmed, refuses without lawful excuse to answer a question or to produce a document, or remains in the room in which such proceeding is being had or taken, after the witnesses have been ordered to leave such room; or

(*c*) causes an obstruction or disturbance in the course of a judicial proceeding; or

(*d*) while a judicial proceeding is pending, makes use of any speech or writing, misrepresenting such proceeding, or capable of prejudicing any person in favour of or against any parties to such proceeding, or calculated to lower the authority of any person before whom such proceeding is being had or taken; or

(*e*) publishes a report of the evidence taken in any judicial proceeding which has been directed to be held in private; or

(*f*) attempts wrongfully to interfere with or influence a witness in a judicial proceeding either before or after he has given evidence, in connection with such evidence; or

(*g*) dismisses a servant because he has given evidence on behalf of a certain party to a judicial proceeding; or

(*h*) retakes possession of land from any person who has recently obtained possession by a writ of court; or

(*i*) commits any other act of intentional disrespect to any judicial proceeding, or to any person before whom such proceeding is being had or taken;

is guilty of a misdemeanour and is liable to imprisonment for six months or to a fine not exceeding seven hundred and fifty penalty units.

(2) When any offence against paragraph (*a*), (*b*), (*c*), (*d*) or (*i*) of subsection (1) is committed in view of the court, the court may cause the offender to be detained in custody, and at any time before the rising of the court on the same day may take cognizance of the offence and sentence the offender to a fine not exceeding six hundred penalty units or, in default of payment, to imprisonment without hard labour for one month.

(3) The provisions of this section shall be deemed to be in addition to and not in derogation from the power of a court to punish for contempt of court.

(*As amended by No.* 26 *of* 1940 *and Act No.* 13 *of* 1994)

117. (1) No person shall-

Prohibition on taking photographs, etc., in court

(*a*) take or attempt to take in any court any photograph, or, with a view to publication, make or attempt to make in any court any portrait or sketch, of any person, being a Judge of the court or a juror or a witness in or a party to any proceedings before the court, whether civil or criminal; or

(*b*) publish any photograph, portrait or sketch taken or made in contravention of the provisions of this subsection or any reproduction thereof;

and if any person acts in contravention of this subsection, he shall be liable to a fine not exceeding one thousand five hundred penalty units in respect of each offence;

Provided that this section shall not apply to photographs being taken on any occasion with the consent of the Chief Justice, or where the occasion is the opening of any session of the High Court, with the consent of the Judge holding that session.

(2) For the purposes of this section-

(*a*) "court" means the High Court, any subordinate court, juvenile court, court of a coroner or a local court as defined in the Local Courts Act;

(*b*) "Judge" includes registrar, magistrate, coroner and officer of such local court;

(*c*) a photograph, portrait or sketch shall be deemed to be a photograph, portrait or sketch taken or made in court if it is taken or made in the court-room or in the building or in the precincts of the building in which the court is held, or if it is a photograph, portrait or sketch taken or made of the person while he is entering or leaving the court-room or any such building or precincts as aforesaid.

CHAPTER XII RESCUES, ESCAPES AND OBSTRUCTING OFFICERS OF COURT OF LAW

118. (1) Any person who by force rescues or attempts to rescue from lawful custody any other person-

Rescue

(*a*) is, if such last-named person is under sentence of death or imprisonment for life or charged with an offence punishable with death or imprisonment for life, guilty of a felony and is liable to imprisonment for life; and

(*b*) is, if such other person is imprisoned on a charge or under sentence for any offence other than those specified above, guilty of a felony and is liable to imprisonment for seven years; and

(*c*) is, in any other case, guilty of a misdemeanour.

(2) If the person rescued is in the custody of a private person, the offender must have notice of the fact that the person rescued is in custody.

119. Any person who, being in lawful custody, escapes from such custody, is guilty of a misdemeanour.

Escape from lawful custody

120. Any person who-

(*a*) aids a prisoner in escaping or attempting to escape from lawful custody; or

(*b*) conveys anything or causes anything to be conveyed into a prison with intent to facilitate the escape of a prisoner;

is guilty of a felony and is liable to imprisonment for seven years.

Aiding prisoners to escape

121. Any person who, when any property has been attached or taken under the process of authority of any court, knowingly, and with intent to hinder or defeat the attachment or process, receives, removes, retains, conceals, or disposes of such property, is guilty of a felony and is liable to imprisonment for three years.

Removal etc., of property under lawful seizure

122. Any person who wilfully obstructs or resists any person lawfully charged with the execution of an order or warrant of any court, is guilty of a misdemeanour and is liable to imprisonment for one year.

Obstructing court officers

CHAPTER XIII MISCELLANEOUS OFFENCES AGAINST PUBLIC AUTHORITY

123. Any person employed in the public service who, in the discharge of the duties of his office, commits any fraud or breach of trust affecting the public, whether such fraud or breach of trust would have been criminal or not if committed against a private person, is guilty of a misdemeanour.

Frauds and breaches of trust by public officers

124. Repealed by Act No. 7 of 1990

125. Whoever gives to any person employed in the public service any information which he knows or believes to be false, intending thereby to cause or knowing it to be likely that he will thereby cause such person-

(*a*) to do or omit anything which such person ought not to do or omit if the true state of facts respecting which such information is given were known to him; or

(*b*) to use the lawful power of such person to the injury or annoyance of any person;

is guilty of a misdemeanour and is liable to imprisonment for six months or to a fine of one thousand and five hundred penalty units or to both.

(*As amended by No.* 26 *of* 1933 *and Act No.* 13 *of* 1994)

False information to public officer

126. Everyone who wilfully disobeys any Statute or Act by doing any act which it forbids, or by omitting to do any act which it requires to be done, and which concerns the public or any part of the public, is guilty of a misdemeanour and is liable, unless it appears from the Statute or Act that it was the intention of Parliament to provide some other penalty for such disobedience, to imprisonment for two years.

Disobedience of statutory duty

127. Everyone who disobeys any order, warrant or command duly made, issued or given by any court, officer or person acting in any public capacity and duly authorised in that behalf, is guilty of a misdemeanour and is liable, unless any other penalty or mode of proceeding is expressly prescribed in respect of such disobedience, to imprisonment for two years.

Disobedience of lawful orders

DIVISION III OFFENCES INJURIOUS TO THE PUBLIC IN GENERAL

CHAPTER XIV OFFENCES RELATING TO RELIGION

128. Any person who destroys, damages or defiles any place of worship or any object which is held sacred by any class of persons with the intention of thereby insulting the religion of any class of persons or with the knowledge that any class of persons is likely to consider such destruction, damage or defilement as an insult to their religion, is guilty of a misdemeanour.

Insult to religion of any class

129. Any person who voluntarily causes disturbance to any assembly lawfully engaged in the performance of religious worship or religious ceremony, is guilty of a misdemeanour.

Disturbing religious assemblies

130. Every person who, with the intention of wounding the feelings of any person or of insulting the religion of any person, or with the knowledge that the feelings of any person are likely to be wounded, or that the religion of any person is likely to be insulted thereby, commits any trespass in any place of worship or in any place of sepulture or in any place set apart for the performance of funeral rites or as a depository for the remains of the dead, or offers any indignity to any human corpse, or causes disturbance to any persons assembled for the purpose of funeral ceremonies, is guilty of a misdemeanour.

Trespassing on burial places

131. Any person who, with the deliberate intention of wounding the religious feelings of any person, utters any word, or makes any sound in the hearing of that person, or makes any gesture in the sight of that person, or places any object in the sight of that person, is guilty of a misdemeanour and is liable to imprisonment for one year.

131A. In this Part "child" means a person below the age of sixteen years.

Uttering words with the intent to wound religious feelings

Definition of child

CHAPTER XV OFFENCES AGAINST MORALITY

132. Any person who has unlawful carnal knowledge of a woman or girl, without her consent, or with her consent, if the consent is obtained by force or by means of threats or intimidation of any kind, or by fear of bodily harm, or by means of false representations as to the nature of the act, or, in the case of a married woman, by personating her husband, is guilty of the felony termed "rape".

Definition of rape

133. Any person who commits the offence of rape is liable to imprisonment for life.

(*As amended by No.* 26 *of* 1933 *and No.* 20 *of* 1964)

Punishment of rape

134. Any person who attempts to commit rape is guilty of a felony and is liable to imprisonment for life.

(*As amended by No.* 26 *of* 1933)

Attempted rape

135. Any person who with intent to marry or carnally know a woman of any age, or to cause her to be married or carnally known by any other person, takes her away, or detains her, against her will, is guilty of a felony and is liable to imprisonment for seven years.

Abduction

136. Any person who unlawfully takes an unmarried girl under the age of sixteen years out of the custody or protection of her father or mother or other person having the lawful care or charge of her, and against the will of such father or mother or other person, is guilty of a misdemeanour.

Abduction of children

137. (1) Any person who unlawfully and indecently assaults any woman or girl is guilty of a felony and is liable to imprisonment for fourteen years.

Indecent assault

(2) It shall be no defence to a charge for an indecent assault on a girl under the age of twelve years to prove that she consented to the act of indecency:

Provided that it shall be a sufficient defence to any charge under this subsection if it shall be made to appear to the court before whom the charge shall be brought that the person so charged had reasonable cause to believe, and did in fact believe, that the girl was of or above the age of twelve years.

(3) Any person who is found in any building or dwelling-house or in any verandah or passage attached thereto or in any yard, garden or other land adjacent to or within the curtilage of such building or dwelling-house not being a public place-

Indecently insulting or annoying females

(*a*) for the purpose of and from motives of indecent curiosity gazing at or observing any woman or girl who may be therein while in a state of undress or semi-undress; or

(*b*) with intent to annoy or indecently to insult any woman or girl who may be therein;

is guilty of a misdemeanour and is liable to imprisonment for one year.

(*As amended by No.* 26 *of* 1933)

138. (1) Any person who unlawfully and carnally knows any child commits a felony and is liable, upon conviction, to a term of imprisonment of not less than fifteen years and may be liable to imprisonment for life.

(2) Any person who attempts to have unlawful carnal knowledge of any child commits a felony and is liable, upon conviction, to imprisonment for a term of not less than fourteen years and not exceeding twenty years.

(3) Any person who prescribes the defilement of a child as cure for an ailment commits a felony and is liable, upon conviction, to imprisonment for a term of not less than fifteen years and may be liable to imprisonment for life.

(4) A child above the age of twelve years who commits an offence under subsection (1) or (2) is liable, to such community service or counseling as the court may determine, in the best interests of both children.

Defilement of Child

(As amended by Act No. 15 of 2005)

139. Any person who, knowing a child or other person to be an imbecile or person with mental illness, has or attempts to have unlawful carnal knowledge of that chills or other person in circumstances not amounting to rape, but which prove that the offender knew at the time of the commission of the offence that the child or other person was an idiot or imbecile commits a felony and is a liable, upon conviction, to imprisonment for a term of not less than fourteen years and may be liable to imprisonment for life.

(*As amended by No.* 26 *of* 1933, repealed and replaced by Act No. 15 of 2005)

Defilement of imbeciles or person with mental illness

140. Any person who-

(a) procures or attempts to procure any child or other person to have unlawful carnal knowledge either in Zambia or elsewhere, with an person or other persons for pornography, bestiality or any other purpose;

(b) procures or attempts to procure any child or other person to become, either in Zambia or elsewhere, a common prostitute;

(c) procures or attempts to procure any child or person to leave Zambia, with the intent that the child or person may become an inmate of or frequent a brothel elsewhere; or

(d) procures or attempts to procure any child or person to leave that child's or other person's usual place of abode in Zambia with intent that the child or other person may, for the purposes of prostitution, become an inmate of or frequent a brothel either in Zambia or elsewhere;

commits a felony and is liable, upon conviction, to imprisonment for a term of not less than twenty years and may be liable to imprisonment for life:

Provided that no person shall be convicted of an offence under this section upon the evidence of one witness only, unless such witness be corroborated in some material particular by evidence implicating the accused.

Procuring child or other person for prostitution, etc.

(*As amended by No.* 26 *of* 1933,*No.* 9 *of* 1954 and repealed and replaced by Act No. 15 of 2005)

141. Any person who-

(a) by threat or intimidation procures or attempts to procure any child or other person to have any unlawful carnal knowledge, either in Zambia or elsewhere;

(b) by false pretence or false representation procures any child or other person to have any unlawful carnal knowledge, either in Zambia or elsewhere; or

(c) applies, administers to, or causes to be taken by any child or other person any drug, matter or thing, with intent to stupefy or overpower so as thereby to enable any third person to have unlawful carnal knowledge with such child or other person;

commits a felony and is liable, upon conviction, to imprisonment for a term of not less than twenty years and may be liable to imprisonment for life:

Provided that no person shall be convicted of an offence under this section upon the evidence of one witness only, unless such witness be corroborated in some material particular by evidence implicating the accused.

Procuring defilement by threat or fraud administering drugs

(*As amended by No.* 9 *of* 1954, repealed and replaced by Act No. 15 of 2005)

142. Any person who, being the owner or occupier of premises or having or acting or assisting in the management of control thereof, induces or knowingly permits any child to resort to or be upon such premises for the purpose of being unlawfully and carnally known by any other person, whether such carnal knowledge is intended to be with any particular person or generally, commits a felony and is liable, upon conviction, to imprisonment for a term of not less than twenty years and may be liable to imprisonment for life.

Householder, etc., permitting defilement of child on premises

(As repealed and replaced by Act No. 15 of 2005)

143. Any person who sells or traffics in a child or other person for any purpose or in any form commits an offence is liable, upon conviction, to imprisonment for a term of not less than twenty years:

Provided that where it is proved during the trial of the accused person that the sale or trafficking in a child or other person was for the purpose of causing that child or person to be unlawfully and carnally known by any other person, whether such carnal knowledge was intended to be with any particular person or generally, the person is liable, upon conviction, to imprisonment for life.

Selling or trafficking in children, etc.

(As repealed and replaced by Act No. 15 of 2005)

144. (1) Any person who detains any child or other person against that child or other person's will-

(a) in or upon any premises with intent that the child or other person may be unlawfully and carnally known by any third person, whether particularly or generally or for rituals or any other purpose; or

(b) in any brothel;

commits a felony and is liable, upon conviction, to imprisonment for a term of not less than twenty years and may be liable to imprisonment for life.

(2) When a child or person is in or upon any premises for the purposes of having any lawful carnal knowledge or in any brothel, another person shall be deemed to detain such a child or person in or upon such premises or in such brothel, if, with intent to compel or induce the child or person to remain in or upon such premises or in such brothel, such other person withholds from the child or person any wearing apparel or other property belonging to the child or person, or where wearing apparel has been lent or otherwise supplied to such child or person or by directions of such person, such other person threatens such person with legal proceedings for taking away the wearing apparel so lent or supplied.

(3) No legal proceedings, whether civil or criminal, shall be taken against any child or person for taking away or being found in possession of any such wearing apparel as was necessary to enable the child or person to leave such premises or brothel.

Detention with intent in premises or brothel

(As repealed and replaced by Act No. 15 of 2005)

145. (1) If it appears to any magistrate, on information made before the magistrate, on oath, by any parent, relative or guardian of any child or other person who, in the opinion of the magistrate, is acting *bona fide* in the interests of any child or person, that there is reasonable cause to suspect that such child or other person is unlawfully detained for immoral purposes by any person in any place within the jurisdiction of such magistrate, such magistrate may issue a warrant authorizing the person named therein to search for, and when found to take to and detain in a place of safety such child or person until the child or person can be brought before a magistrate.

(2) The magistrate before whom the child or person is brought in accordance with subsection (1) may cause the child or person to be delivered up to the child's parents or guardians, or be otherwise dealt with as circumstances may permit and require.

(3) A magistrate issuing a warrant under this section may, by the same or any other warrant, cause any person accused of so unlawfully detaining such child or person to be apprehended and brought before a magistrate and proceedings to be taken for punishing such person according to law.

(4) A child or person shall be deemed to be unlawfully detained for the purpose of being unlawfully and carnally known by any other person, whether any particular third person or generally; and

(a) in the case of the child whether the child consented to the detention or not; or

(b) if the person is of, or above the age of, sixteen years and is so detained against the person's will or against the will of the person's father or mother or of any person having the lawful care or charge of that person.

(5) Any person authorised by warrant under this section to search for any child so detained as aforesaid may enter if need be by force, any house, building or other place mentioned in the warrant, and may remove such child or person from there.

Power of search

(*As amended by S.I. No.* 63 *of* 1964, repealed and replaced by Act No. 15 of 2005)

146. (1) A person who-

(a) knowingly lives wholly or in part on the earnings of prostitution; or

(b) in any public place, persistently solicits or importunes for immoral purposes;

commits a felony and is liable, upon conviction, to imprisonment for a term not exceeding fifteen years;

Provided that a child who commits an offence under subsection is liable to such community service or counseling as the court may determine in the best interests of the child.

(2) Where a person is proved to live with or to be habitually in the company of a prostitute or is proved to have exercised control, direction or influence over the movements of a prostitute in such manner as to show that the person is aiding, abetting or compelling the prostitution with any other person, or generally, that person shall, unless the person shall satisfy the court to the contrary, be deemed to be knowingly living on the earnings of prostitution.

Person living on earnings of prostitution or persistently soliciting

(*As repealed and replaced by Act No. 15 of 2005*)

147. (1) Every person who knowingly lives wholly or in part on the earnings of the prostitution of another or who is proved to have, for the purpose of gain, exercised control, direction or influence over the movements of a prostitute in such manner as to show that such person is aiding, abetting or compelling that person's prostitution with any other person, or generally, commits a felony and is liable, upon conviction, to imprisonment for a term not exceeding fifteen years.

(2) Where a person compels a child to become a prostitute that person commits an offence and is liable, upon conviction, to imprisonment for life.

Person living on aiding, etc., prostitution of another for gain

(*As repealed and replaced by Act No. 15 of 2005*)

148. If it is made to appear to a magistrate, by information on oath, that there is reason to suspect that any house or any part of a house is used by a woman or girl for purposes of prostitution, and that any person residing in or frequenting the house is knowingly living wholly or in part on the earnings of the prostitute, or is exercising control, direction or influence over the movements of the prostitute, the magistrate may issue a warrant authorising any police officer to enter and search the house and to arrest such person.

Power of search

149. Any person who keeps a house, room, set of rooms, or place of any kind whatsoever for purposes of prostitution commits a felony and is liable, upon conviction,

to imprisonment for a term of not less than fifteen years and not exceeding twenty five years.

Brothels

(As repealed and replaced by Act No. 15 of 2005)

150. Any person who conspires with another person to induce any person or child, by means of any false pretence or other fraudulent means, to permit any other person to have unlawful carnal knowledge of such person or child, commits a felony and is liable, upon conviction, to imprisonment for a term of not less than fifteen years and may be liable to imprisonment for life.

(As amended by No. 26 of 1933 and repealed and replaced by Act No. 15 of 2005)

Conspiracy to defile

151. Any person who, with intent to procure the miscarriage of a woman or female child, whether she is or is not with child, unlawfully administers to her or causes her to take any poison or other noxious thing, or uses any force of any kind, or uses any other means whatsoever, commits a felony and is liable, upon conviction, to imprisonment for a term not exceeding seven years.

Attempts to procure abortion

(As repealed and replaced by Act No. 15 of 2005)

152. (1) Every woman being pregnant who, with intent to procure her own miscarriage, unlawfully administers to herself any poison or other noxious thing, or uses force of any kind, or uses any other means whatever, or permits any such thing or means to be administered or used, commits a felony and is liable, upon conviction, to imprisonment for a term of fourteen years.

(2) Any female child being pregnant who, with intent to procure her own miscarriage, unlawfully administers to herself any poison or other noxious thing or uses any force of any kind commits an offence and is liable to such community service or counseling as the court may determine, in the best interests of the child:

Provided that where a female child is raped or defiled and becomes pregnant, the pregnancy may be terminated in accordance with the Termination of Pregnancy Act.

(As repealed and replaced by Act No. 15 of 2005)

Abortion by pregnant woman or female child

153. Any person who unlawfully supplies to or procures for any person any thing whatsoever, knowing that it is intended to be unlawfully used to procure the miscarriage of a woman or female child, whether she is or is not with child, commits a felony and is liable, upon conviction, to imprisonment for a term not exceeding fourteen years.

Supplying drugs or instruments to procure abortion

(As repealed and replaced by Act No. 15 of 2005)

154. Except as otherwise expressly stated, it is immaterial in the case of any of the offences committed with respect to a woman or girl under a specified age, that the accused person did not know that the woman or girl was under that age, or believed that she was not under that age.

Knowledge of age of female immaterial

155. Any person who-

(*a*) has carnal knowledge of any person against the order of nature; or

(*b*) has carnal knowledge of an animal; or

(*c*) permits a male person to have carnal knowledge of him or her against the order of nature;

commits a felony and liable, upon conviction, to imprisonment for a term not less than fifteen years and may be liable to imprisonment for life:

Provided that where a person-

(i) has carnal knowledge of a child against the order of nature;

(ii) causes a child to have carnal knowledge of an animal; or

(iii) permits a male person to have carnal knowledge of a male or female child against the order of nature;

that person commits an offence and is liable, upon conviction, to imprisonment for not less than twenty-five years and may be liable to imprisonment for life.

(As amended by No. 26 of 1933 and repealed and replaced by Act No. 15 of 2005)

Unnatural offences

156.Any person who attempts to commit any of the offences specified in section *one hundred and fifty-five* commits a felony and is liable, upon conviction of not less than seven years but not exceeding fourteen years.

(As amended by No. 26 of 1933 and repealed and replaced by Act No. 15 of 2005)

157.(1) Any person who conducts or causes to be conducted a harmful cultural practice on a child commits a felony and is liable, upon conviction, to imprisonment for a term not less than fifteen years and may be liable to imprisonment for life.

(2) In this section "harmful cultural practice" includes sexual cleansing, female genital mutilation or in initiation ceremony that results in injury, the transmission of an infectious or life threatening disease or loss of life to a child but does not include circumcision on a male child.

(As amended by No. 26 of 1933 and repealed and replaced by Act No. 15 of 2005)

158.(1) Any male who, whether in public or private, commits any act of gross indecency with a male child or person, or procures a male child or person to commit any act of gross indecency with him, or attempts to procure the commission of any such act by any male person with himself or with another male child or person, whether in public or private, commits a felony and is liable, upon conviction, to imprisonment for a term of not less than seven years and not exceeding fourteen years.

(2) Any female who, whether in public or private, commits any act of gross indecency with a female child or person, or procures a female child or person to commit any act of gross indecency with her, or attempts to procure the commission of any such act by any female person with himself or with another female child or person, whether in public or private, commits a felony and is liable, upon conviction, to imprisonment for a term of not less than seven years and not exceeding fourteen years.

(3) A child who, whether in public or private, commits any act of gross indecency with another child of the same sex or attempts to procure the commission of any such act by any person with the child's self or with another child or person of the same sex, whether in public or private, commits an offence and is liable, to such community service or counseling as the court may determine in the best interests of the child.

(As amended by No. 26 of 1933 and repealed and replaced by Act No. 15 of 2005)

159. (1) Any male person who has carnal knowledge of a female person who is to that person's knowledge his grandmother, mother, sister, daughter, grand-daughter, aunt or niece commits a felony and is liable, upon conviction, for a term of not less than twenty years and may be liable to imprisonment for life.

(2) Any female person who has carnal knowledge of a male person who is to that person's knowledge her grand-father, father, brother, son, grand-son, uncle or nephew commits a felony and is liable, upon conviction, for a term of not less than twenty years and may be liable to imprisonment for life.

(3) For the purposes of this section, it is immaterial that carnal knowledge was had with consent of the other person.

(4) Any person who attempts to commit incest commits a felony and is liable to imprisonment for a term of not less than ten years and not exceeding twenty-five years.

(As amended by No. 26 of 1933 and repealed and replaced by Act No. 15 of 2005)

160.On the conviction before any court of any person of an offence under section *one hundred and fifty-nine*, or of an attempt to commit the same, against any child it shall be in the power of the court to divest the offender of all authority over such child, and, if the offender is the guardian of such child, to remove the offender from such guardianship, and in any case to appoint any person or persons to be the guardian or guardians of such child during the child's minority or any less period:

Provided that the High Court may at any time vary or rescind the order by the appointment of any other person as such guardian or in any other respect.

(As amended by No. 26 of 1933 and repealed and replaced by Act No. 15 of 2005)

161. (1) Any female person of or above the age of sixteen years who with consent permits her grandfather, father, brother, uncle, nephew, son or grandson to have carnal knowledge of her knowing him to be her grandfather, father, brother, uncle, nephew, son or grandson, as the case may be, commits a felony and is liable, upon conviction, to imprisonment for a term of not less than twenty years and may be liable to imprisonment for life:

Provided that a female child commits an offence under this subsection is liable to such community service or counseling as the court may determine in the best interests of the child.

(2) Any male person of or above the age of sixteen years who with consent permits his grandmother, mother, sister, auntie, niece, daughter or grand-daughter to have carnal knowledge of him knowing her to be her grandmother, mother, sister, aunt, niece, daughter or grand-daughter, as the case may be, commits a felony and is liable, upon conviction, to imprisonment for a term of not less than twenty years and may be liable to imprisonment for life:

Provided that a male child commits an offence under this subsection is liable to such community service or counseling as the court may determine in the best interests of the child.

(As amended by No. 26 of 1933 and repealed and replaced by Act No. 15 of 2005)

Attempt to commit unnatural offences

Harmful cultural practice

Indecent practices between persons of the same sex Incest

Order for guardianship

Consent to incest

162. In sections *one hundred and fifty-nine* and *one hundred and sixty-one*, "brother" and "sister", respectively, include half-brother and half-sister, and the provisions of the said sections shall apply whether the relationship between the person charged with an offence and the person with whom the offence is alleged to have been committed is or is not traced through lawful wedlock.

Test of relationship

163. (1) If, on the trial of any information for or charge of rape, the court is satisfied that the defendant is guilty of an offence under section *one hundred and fifty-nine*, but is not satisfied that the defendant is guilty of rape, the court may acquit the defendant of rape and find him guilty of an offence under section *one hundred and fifty-nine*, and he shall be liable to be punished accordingly.

Conviction of incest lawful on charge of rape

(2) If, on the trial of any information for or charge of an offence under section *one hundred and fifty-nine*, the court is satisfied that the defendant is guilty of an offence

under section *one hundred and thirty-eight* or *one hundred and thirty-nine*, but is not satisfied that the defendant is guilty of an offence under section *one hundred and fifty-nine*, the court may acquit the defendant of an offence under section *one hundred and fifty-nine* and find him guilty of an offence under section *one hundred and thirty-eight* or *one hundred and thirty-nine*, and he shall be liable to be punished accordingly.

Conviction of unlawful carnal knowledge on charge of incest

164. (1) A person shall not without the consent, in writing, given by or on behalf of a child or person publish or disclose to any person otherwise than in the course of duty, the contents of any documents, communication or information which relates to and which has come to that person's knowledge in the course of duty performed in relation to offences under this Part, including the handling, medical treatment or counseling of victims.

(2) A person who contravenes subsection (1) commits an offence and is liable, upon conviction, to a fine of not less than fifty thousand penalty units or to imprisonment for six months, or to both.

(As repealed and replaced by Act No. 15 of 2005)

Prohibition of disclosure of information

CHAPTER XVI OFFENCES RELATING TO MARRIAGE AND DOMESTIC OBLIGATIONS

165. Any person who wilfully and by fraud causes any woman who is not lawfully married to him to believe that she is lawfully married to him and to cohabit or have sexual intercourse with him in that belief, is guilty of a felony and is liable to imprisonment for ten years.

Fraudulent pretence of marriage

166. Any person who, having a husband or wife living, goes through a ceremony of marriage which is void by reason of its taking place during the life of such husband or wife, is guilty of a felony and is liable to imprisonment for five years:

Bigamy

Provided that this section shall not extend to any person whose marriage with such husband or wife has been declared void by a court of competent jurisdiction, nor to any person who contracts a marriage during the life of a former husband or wife, if such husband or wife, at the time of the subsequent marriage, shall have been continually absent from such person for the space of seven years, and shall not have been heard of by such person as being alive within that time.

167. Any person who dishonestly or with a fraudulent intention goes through the ceremony of marriage, knowing that he is not thereby lawfully married, is guilty of a felony and is liable to imprisonment for five years.

Marriage ceremony fraudulently gone through without lawful marriage

168. Any person who being the parent, guardian or other person having the lawful care or charge of a child being able to maintain such child, willfully and without lawful or reasonable cause deserts the child and leaves it without means of support commits an offence and is liable, upon conviction, for a first offence to imprisonment for a term not exceeding three years, or for a subsequent offence to imprisonment for a term not exceeding seven years.

Desertion of children

169. Any person who being the-

(a) parent;

(b) guardian; or

(c) person in charge;

of a child that is unable to provide for itself, refuses or willfully neglects to provide, being able to do so, sufficient food, clothes, bedding or other necessities for such child, and thereby injures the health of such child, commits an offence and is liable, on conviction, to a fine not exceeding one hundred thousand penalty units or to imprisonment for a term not exceeding three years or to both.

Neglecting to provide food, etc., for children

(As repealed and replaced by Act No. 15 of 2005)

170. Any person who, being legally liable either as master or mistress, to provide for any apprentice or servant necessary food, clothing, or lodging, wilfully and without lawful excuse refuses or neglects to provide the same, or unlawfully and maliciously does or causes to be done any bodily harm to such apprentice or servant so that the life of such apprentice or servant is endangered or that his health has been or is likely to be permanently injured, is guilty of a misdemeanour.

Master not providing for servants or apprentices

171. (1) Any person who, with intent to deprive any parent, guardian or other person who has the lawful care or charge of a child under the age of sixteen years, of the possession of such child-

Child stealing

(*a*) forcibly or fraudulently takes or entices away, or detains the child; or

(*b*) receives or harbours the child, knowing it to have been so taken or enticed away or detained;

is guilty of a felony and is liable to imprisonment for fourteen years.

(2) It is a defence to a charge of any of the offences defined in this section to prove that the accused person claimed in good faith a right to the possession of the child, or, in the case of an illegitimate child, is its mother or claimed to be its father.

(*As amended by No.* 20 *of* 1953 *and Act No.* 14*of* 1981)

CHAPTER XVII NUISANCES AND OFFENCES AGAINST HEALTH AND CONVENIENCE

172. (1) Any person who does an act not authorised by law or omits to discharge a legal duty and thereby causes any common injury, or danger or annoyance, or obstructs or causes inconvenience to the public in the exercise of common rights, commits the misdemeanour termed a "common nuisance" and is liable to imprisonment for one year.

Common nuisance

(2) It is immaterial that the act or omission complained of is convenient to a larger number of the public than it inconveniences, but the fact that it facilitates the lawful exercise of their rights by a part of the public may show that it is not a nuisance to any of the public.

173. (1) Every person who, with a view to compelling any other person to abstain from doing or to do any act which such other person has a legal right to do or abstain from doing, wrongfully and without legal authority-

Watching and besetting

(*a*) uses violence to or intimidates such other person or members of his household, or injures his property; or

(*b*) persistently follows such other person about from place to place; or

(*c*) hides any tools, clothes, or other property owned or used by such other person, or deprives him of or hinders him in the use thereof; or

(*d*) follows such other person in a disorderly manner; is guilty of an offence.

(2) Every person who, wrongfully and without legal authority, watches or besets-

(*a*) any premises or the approaches to such premises with a view to preventing any other person from doing any act which such other person has a legal right to do thereat; or

(*b*) the house or other place where any other person resides or works or carries on business, or happens to be, or the approaches to such house or place with a view to preventing such other person from doing or compelling him to do any act which such other person has a legal right to do or abstain from doing;

is guilty of an offence.

(3) Every person who is guilty of an offence under the provisions of this section is liable to a fine not exceeding three thousand penalty units or to imprisonment for a period not exceeding six months, or to both.

(*No.* 60 *of* 1957 *and Act No.* 13 *of* 1994)

174. (1) Any person being the owner or occupier, or having the use of, any house, room or place, who shall open, keep or use the same for the purpose of unlawful gaming being carried on therein, and any person who, being the owner or occupier of any house, room or place, shall knowingly and wilfully permit the same to be opened, kept or used by any other person for the purpose aforesaid, and any person having the care or management of or in any manner assisting in conducting the business of any house, room or place opened, kept or used for the purpose aforesaid, is said to keep a common gaming house.

Gaming houses

(2) In this section, "unlawful gaming" means any game the chances of which are not alike favourable to all the players, including the banker or other person or persons by whom the game is managed or against whom the other players stake, play or bet.

(3) Any person who keeps a common gaming house is guilty of a misdemeanour.

(4) Any person, other than the persons mentioned in subsection (1), who is found in a common gaming house shall be deemed, unless the contrary is proved, to be there for the purpose of unlawful gaming, and is guilty of a misdemeanour and is liable to a fine of one hundred and fifty penalty units for the first offence, and for each subsequent offence to a fine of six hundred penalty units or imprisonment for three months, or to both.

(*As amended by Act No.* 13 *of* 1994)

175. (1) Any house, room or place which is used for any of the purposes following, that is to say:

Betting houses

(*a*) for the purpose of bets being made therein between persons resorting to the place and-

(i) the owner, occupier, or keeper of the place, or any person using the place; or

(ii) any person procured or employed by or acting for or on behalf of any such owner, occupier or keeper, or person using the place; or

(iii) any person having the care or management, or in any manner conducting the business, of the place; or

(*b*) for the purpose of any money or other property being paid or received therein by or on behalf of any such owner, occupier, or keeper, or person using the place, as, or for the consideration-

(i) for an assurance, undertaking, promise, or agreement, express or implied, to pay or give thereafter any money or other property on any event or contingency of or relating to any horse race, or other race, fight, game, sport, or exercise; or

(ii) for securing the paying or giving by some other person of any money or other property on any such event or contingency;

is called a common betting house.

(2) Any person who, being the owner or occupier of any house, room or place, knowingly and wilfully permits it to be opened, kept, or used as a common betting house by another person, or who has the use or management, or assists in conducting the business, of a common betting house, is guilty of a misdemeanour and is liable to imprisonment for one year:

Provided that-

(i) nothing herein contained shall make illegal the use of a totalisator by a race club, gymkhana club or sports club recognised by the Government, with the approval in each case of the Commissioner of Police. In this proviso, "totalisator" means and includes the instrument, machine or contrivance, commonly known as the totalisator and any other instrument, machine or contrivance of a like nature, or any scheme for enabling any number of persons to make bets with one another on the like principles;

(ii) nothing in this section shall be deemed to prohibit any lottery lawfully promoted and conducted under the provisions of the Lotteries Act.

(*As amended by No.* 15 *of* 1946 *and Nos.* 8 *and* 27 *of* 1957)

176. Any person who appears, acts, or behaves as master or mistress, or as the person having the care or management of any such house, room, set of rooms, or place as is mentioned in sections *one hundred and seventy-four* and *one hundred and seventy-five* is to be taken to be the keeper thereof, whether he is or is not the real keeper.

Keeper of premises defined

177. (1) Any person who-

Obscene matters or things

(*a*) makes, produces or has in his possession any one or more obscene writings, drawings, prints, paintings, printed matter, pictures, posters, emblems, photographs, cinematograph films or any other object tending to corrupt morals; or

(*b*) imports, conveys or exports, or causes to be imported conveyed or exported, any such matters or things, or in any manner whatsoever puts any of them in circulation; or

(*c*) carries on or takes part in any business, whether public or private, concerned with any such matters or things, or deals in any such matters or things in any manner whatsoever, or distributes any of them, or exhibits any of them publicly, or makes a business of lending any of them; or (*d*) advertises or makes known by any means whatsoever with a view to assisting the circulation of, or traffic in, any such matters or things, that a person is engaged in any of the acts referred to in this section, or advertises or makes known how, or from whom, any such matters or things can be procured either directly or indirectly; or

(*e*) publicly exhibits any indecent show or performance or any show or performance tending to corrupt morals;

is guilty of a misdemeanour and is liable to imprisonment for five years or to a fine of not less than fifteen thousand penalty units nor more than seventy-five thousand penalty units.

(2) If, in respect of any of the offences specified in paragraph (*a*), (*b*), (*c*) or (*d*) of subsection (1), any constituent element thereof is committed in Zambia, such commission shall be sufficient to render the person accused of such offence triable therefor in Zambia.

(3) A court, on convicting any person of an offence against this section, may order to be confiscated or destroyed any matter or thing made, possessed or used for the purpose of such offence.

(4) Any court may, on the application of a public prosecutor, order the destruction of any obscene matter or thing to which this section relates, whether any person may or may not have been convicted under the provisions of this section in respect of such obscene matter or thing.

(5) No prosecution for an offence under this section shall be instituted without the written consent of the Director of Public Prosecutions.

177A.(1) Any person who engages a child or other person-

(a) in a pornographic performance;

(b) in the production of a pornographic film or other material; or

(c) in a pornographic activity of any nature;

commits an offence and is liable, upon conviction, to a term of imprisonment of not less than fifteen years and may be liable to imprisonment for life.

(2) Any person who-

(a) sells to a child pornographic material;

(b) compels a child to watch a pornographic film or view pornography on the internet or elsewhere or in any form intended to corrupt a child's morals;

commits an offence and is liable, upon conviction, to a term of imprisonment of not less than fifteen years.

(3) A child who commits an offence under subsection (2) is liable, to such community service or counseling as the court may determine in the best interests of the child.

Child pornography

(As amended by Act No. 15 of 2005)

178. The following persons:

(*a*) every common prostitute behaving in a disorderly or indecent manner in any public place;

(*b*) every person wandering or placing himself in any public place to beg or gather alms, or causing or procuring or encouraging any child or children so to do;

(*c*) every person playing at any game of chance, not being an authorised lottery, for money or money's worth in any public place;

(*d*) every person wandering abroad and endeavouring by the exposure of wounds or deformity to obtain or gather alms;

(*e*) every person who, without lawful excuse, publicly does any indecent act;

(*f*) every person who publicly conducts himself in a manner likely to cause a breach of the peace; and

(*g*) every person who in any public place solicits for immoral purposes;

are deemed idle and disorderly persons, and are liable to imprisonment for one month or to a fine not exceeding sixty penalty units or to both.

(*As amended by No.* 15 *of* 1938, *No.* 26 *of* 1940, *No.* 29 *of* 1948 *and Act No.*13 *of* 1994)

Idle and disorderly persons

179. Every person who uses insulting language or otherwise conducts himself in a manner likely to give such provocation to any person as to cause such person to break the public peace or to commit any offence against the person, is liable to imprisonment for three months or to a fine not exceeding four hundred and fifty penalty units or to both.

(*No.* 15 *of* 1938 *and Act No.* 13 *of* 1994)

Use of insulting language

180. (1) Every person found drunk and incapable in any highway or other public place, or on any premises licensed under the Liquor Licensing Act, may be arrested without warrant and is liable to a penalty not exceeding one hundred and fifty penalty units, and on a second conviction within a period of twelve months is liable to a penalty not exceeding three hundred penalty units, and on a third or subsequent conviction within the said period of twelve months is liable to a penalty not exceeding six hundred penalty units.

Nuisances by drunken persons, etc.

(2) Every person who, in any highway or other public place or on any premises licensed under the Liquor Licensing Act, is guilty while drunk of riotous or disorderly behaviour or

who is drunk while in charge on any highway or railway or other public place of any horse, cattle, steam engine, locomotive, wagon, van, carriage or any other vehicle, other than a motor vehicle, or who is drunk when in possession of any loaded firearms, may be arrested without warrant and is liable to a penalty not exceeding seven hundred and fifty penalty units, or to imprisonment with or without hard labour for a period not exceeding three months.

(*No.* 21 *of* 1958 *and Act No.* 13 *of* 1994)

181. The following persons:

(*a*) every person convicted of an offence under section *one hundred and seventy-eight* after having been previously convicted as an idle and disorderly person:

Rogues and vagabonds

(*b*) every person going about as a gatherer or collector of alms, or endeavouring to procure charitable contributions of any nature or kind, under any false or fraudulent pretence;

(*c*) every suspected person or reputed thief who has no visible means of subsistence and cannot give a good account of himself; and

(*d*) every person found wandering in or upon or near any premises or in any road or highway or any place adjacent thereto or in any public place at such time and under such circumstances as to lead to the conclusion that such person is there for an illegal or disorderly purpose;

shall be deemed to be a rogue and vagabond, and are guilty of a misdemeanour and are liable for the first offence to imprisonment for three months, and for every subsequent offence to imprisonment for one year.

182. (1) In this section, unless the context otherwise requires-

"official uniform" means any uniform prescribed for or used by the Defence Force, the Zambia Police Force or any other force or service in Zambia, or such department of the Government as the President may, by statutory instrument, prescribe;

"uniform" includes any distinctive part of such uniform.

Offences relating to official uniform

(2) Any person who unlawfully wears any official uniform, or any dress bearing any of the distinctive marks of any such official uniform-

Wearing of official uniform with intent to commit offence

(*a*) with intent to commit a felony is guilty of an offence and is liable upon conviction to imprisonment for a term not exceeding seven years; or

(*b*) with intent to commit any offence other than a felony is guilty of an offence and is liable upon conviction to a fine not exceeding seven thousand five hundred penalty units or to imprisonment for a term not exceeding three years, or to both.

(3) Any person who, without authority, wears an official uniform, or any dress having the appearance or distinctive marks of such official uniform, is guilty of an offence and is liable upon conviction to a fine not exceeding seven hundred and fifty penalty units or to imprisonment for a term not exceeding two months, or to both.

Unauthorised wearing of official uniform

Provided that nothing in this section shall prevent any person from wearing any official uniform or dress in the course of a stage play performed in any place in which stage plays may lawfully and publicly be performed, or in the course of a music-hall or circus performance, or in the course of any *bona fide* military representation.

(4) Any person who, not being in the service of the Republic or having previously received the written permission of the President or other appropriate authority so to do, imports, manufacturers or sells or has in his possession for sale any official uniform is guilty of an offence and is liable upon conviction to a fine not exceeding seven thousand five hundred penalty units or to imprisonment for a term not exceeding three years, or to both.

Unauthorised importation, manufacture or sale of official uniform, etc.

(5) Any person who wears or uses without authority any badge or insignia of office, decoration, medal or ribbon supplied to or authorised for use by any member of the Defence Force, the Zambia Police Force or any other force or service in Zambia, or of such department of the Government as is prescribed under subsection (1), is guilty of an offence and is liable upon conviction to a fine not exceeding seven hundred and fifty penalty units, or to imprisonment for a term not exceeding two months, or to both.

Unauthorised wearing of badges, etc.

(6) Any person who unlawfully wears any official uniform, or any dress having the appearance of or bearing any of the distinctive marks of any such official uniform, in such manner or in such circumstances as to be likely to bring contempt on that uniform or dress is guilty of an offence and is liable upon conviction to a fine not exceeding seven hundred and fifty penalty units or to imprisonment for a term not exceeding two months, or to both such fine and imprisonment.

Bringing contempt on official uniform

(7) Any uniform, dress, button, badge or other thing which is the subject of an offence under this section is liable to forfeiture, unless the President otherwise directs.

(*As amended by Federal Act No.* 23 *of* 1955, *G.N. No.* 303 *of* 1964, *S.I. No.*63 *of* 1964, *Act No.* 2 *of* 1987 *and No.* 13 *of* 1994)

Forfeiture of official uniform, etc.

183. Any person who unlawfully or negligently does any act which is, and which he knows or has reason to believe to be, likely to spread the infection of any disease dangerous to life, is guilty of a misdemeanour.

Negligent act likely to spread infection

184. Any person who adulterates any article of food or drink, so as to make such article noxious as food or drink, intending to sell such article as food or drink, or knowing it to be likely that the same will be sold as food or drink, is guilty of a misdemeanour.

Adulteration of food or drink intended for sale

185. Any person who sells, or offers or exposes for sale, as food or drink, any article which has been rendered or has become noxious, or is in a state unfit for food or drink, knowing or having reason to believe that the same is noxious as food or drink, is guilty of a misdemeanour.

Sale of noxious food or drink

186. Any person who adulterates any drug or medical preparation in such a manner as to lessen the efficacy or change the operation of such drug or medical preparation, or to make it noxious, intending that it shall be sold or used for, or knowing it to be likely that it will be sold or used for, any medicinal purpose, as if it had not undergone such adulteration, is guilty of a misdemeanour.

Adulteration of drugs

187. Any person who, knowing any drug or medical preparation to have been adulterated in such a manner as to lessen its efficacy, to change its operation, or to render it noxious, sells the same, or offers or exposes it for sale, or issues it from any dispensary for medicinal purposes as unadulterated, or causes it to be used for medicinal purposes by any person not knowing of the adulteration, is guilty of a misdemeanour.

Sale of adulterated drugs

188. Any person who voluntarily corrupts or fouls the water of any public spring or reservoir, so as to render it less fit for the purpose for which it is ordinarily used, is guilty of a misdemeanour.

Fouling water

189. Any person who voluntarily vitiates the atmosphere in any place so as to make it noxious to the health of persons in general dwelling or carrying on business in the neighbourhood or passing along a public way, is guilty of a misdemeanour.

Fouling air

190. Any person who, for the purposes of trade or otherwise, makes loud noises or offensive or unwholesome smells in such places and circumstances as to annoy any considerable number of persons in the exercise of their common rights, commits and is liable to bc punished as for a common nuisance.

Offensive trades

CHAPTER XVIII DEFAMATION

191. Any person who, by print, writing, painting, effigy, or by any means otherwise than solely by gestures, spoken words, or other sounds, unlawfully publishes any defamatory matter concerning another person, with intent to defame that other person, is guilty of the misdemeanour termed "libel".

Libel

192. Defamatory matter is matter likely to injure the reputation of any person by exposing him to hatred, contempt or ridicule, or likely to damage any person in his profession or trade by an injury to his reputation. It is immaterial whether at the time of the publication of the defamatory matter the person concerning whom such matter is published is living or dead:

Definition of defamatory matter

Provided that no prosecution for the publication of defamatory matter concerning a dead person shall be instituted without the consent of the Director of Public Prosecutions.

(*As amended by S.I. No.* 63 *of* 1964)

193. (1) A person publishes a libel if he causes the print, writing, painting, effigy or other means by which the defamatory matter is conveyed, to be dealt with, either by exhibition, reading, recitation, description, delivery, or otherwise, so that the defamatory meaning thereof becomes known or is likely to become known to either the person defamed or any other person.

Definition of publication

(2) It is not necessary for libel that a defamatory meaning should be directly or completely expressed; and it suffices if such meaning and its application to the person alleged to be defamed can be collected either from the alleged libel itself or from any extrinsic circumstances, or partly by the one and partly by the other means.

194. Any publication of defamatory matter concerning a person is unlawful within the meaning of this Chapter, unless-

(*a*) the matter is true and it was for the public benefit that it should be published; or

(*b*) it is privileged on one of the grounds hereafter mentioned in this Chapter.

Definition of unlawful publication

195. (1) The publication of defamatory matter is absolutely privileged, and no person shall, under any circumstances, be liable to punishment under this Code in respect thereof, in any of the following cases, namely:

Cases in which publication of defamatory matter is absolutely privileged

(*a*) if the matter is published by the President, or by the Cabinet or the National Assembly in any official document or proceeding; or (*b*) if the matter is published in the Cabinet or the National Assembly by a Minister or by any member of the National Assembly; or

(*c*) if the matter is published concerning a person subject to military or naval discipline for the time being, and relates to his conduct as a person subject to such discipline, and is published by some person having authority over him in respect of such conduct, and to some person having authority over him in respect of such conduct; or

(*d*) if the matter is published in the course of any judicial proceedings by a person taking part therein as a Judge or magistrate or commissioner or counsel or solicitor or assessor or witness or party thereto; or

(*e*) if the matter published is in fact a fair report of anything said, done, or published in the Cabinet or the National Assembly; or

(*f*) if the person publishing the matter is legally bound to publish it.

(2) Where a publication is absolutely privileged, it is immaterial for the purposes of this Chapter whether the matter be true or false, and whether it be or be not known or believed to be false, and whether it be or be not published in good faith:

Provided that nothing in this section shall exempt a person from any liability to punishment under any other Chapter of this Code or under any other Act or Statute in force within Zambia.

196. A publication of defamatory matter is privileged, on condition that it was published in good faith, if the relation between the parties by and to whom the publication is made is such that the person publishing the matter is under some legal, moral or social duty to publish it to the person to whom the publication is made or has a legitimate personal interest in so publishing it, provided that the publication does not exceed either in extent or matter what is reasonably sufficient for the occasion, and in any of the following cases, namely:

(*a*) if the matter published is in fact a fair report of anything said, done, or shown in a civil or criminal inquiry or proceedings before any court:

Cases in which publication of defamatory matter is conditionally privileged

Provided that if the court prohibits the publication of anything said or shown before it, on the ground that it is seditious, immoral, or blasphemous, the publication thereof shall not be privileged; or

(*b*) if the matter published is a copy or reproduction, or in fact a fair abstract, of any matter which has been previously published, and the previous publication of which was or would have been privileged under the last preceding section; or

(*c*) if the matter is an expression of opinion, in good faith as to the conduct of a person in a judicial, official, or other public capacity, or as to his personal character so far as it appears in such conduct; or (*d*) if the matter is an expression of opinion in good faith as to the conduct of a person in relation to any public question or matter, or as to his personal character so far as it appears in such conduct; or

(*e*) if the matter is an expression of opinion in good faith as to the conduct of any person as disclosed by evidence given in a public legal proceeding, whether civil or criminal, or as to the conduct of any person as a party, witness, or otherwise in any such proceeding, or as to the character of any person so far as it appears in any such conduct as in this paragraph mentioned; or

(*f*) if the matter is an expression of opinion in good faith as to the merits of any book, writing, painting, speech, or other work, performance, or act published, or publicly done or made, or submitted by a person to the judgment of the public, or as to the character of the person so far as it appears therein; or

(*g*) if the matter is a censure passed by a person in good faith on the conduct of another person in any matter in respect of which he has authority, by contract or otherwise, over the other person, or on the character of the other person, so far as it appears in such conduct; or

(*h*) if the matter is a complaint or accusation made by a person in good faith against another person in respect of his conduct in any matter, or in respect of his character so far as it appears in such conduct, to any person having authority, by contract or otherwise, over that other person in respect of such conduct or matter, or having authority by law to inquire into or receive complaints respecting such conduct or matter; or

(*i*) if the matter is published in good faith for the protection of the rights or interests of the person who publishes it, or of the person to whom it is published, or of some person in whom the person to whom it is published is interested.

197. A publication of defamatory matter shall not be deemed to have been made in good faith by a person, within the meaning of the last preceding section, if it is made to appear either-

(*a*) that the matter was untrue, and that he did not believe it to be true; or

Explanation as to good faith

(*b*) that the matter was untrue, and that he published it without having taken reasonable care to ascertain whether it was true or false; or

(*c*) that, in publishing the matter, he acted with intent to injure the person defamed in a substantially greater degree or substantially otherwise than was reasonably necessary for the interest of the public or for the protection of the private right or interest in respect of which he claims to be privileged.

198. If it is proved, on behalf of the accused person, that the defamatory matter was published under such circumstances that the publication would have been justified if made in good faith, the publication shall be presumed to have been made in good faith until the contrary is made to appear, either from the libel itself, or from the evidence

given on behalf of the accused person, or from evidence given on the part of the prosecution.

Presumption as to good faith

DIVISION IV OFFENCES AGAINST THE PERSON

CHAPTER XIX MURDER AND MANSLAUGHTER

199. Any person who by an unlawful act or omission causes the death of another person is guilty of the felony termed "man-slaughter". An unlawful omission is an omission amounting to culpable negligence to discharge a duty tending to the preservation of life or health, whether such omission is or is not accompanied by an intention to cause death or bodily harm.

Manslaughter

200. Any person who of malice aforethought causes the death of another person by an unlawful act or omission is guilty of murder.

Murder

201. (1) Any person convicted of murder shall be sentenced-

Punishment for murder

(*a*) to death; or

(*b*) where there are extenuating circumstances, to any sentence other than death:

Provided that paragraph (*b*) of this subsection shall not apply to murder commited in the course of aggravated robbery with a firearm under section *two hundred and ninety-four.*

(2) For the purpose of this section-

(*a*) an extenuating circumstance is any fact associated with the offence which would diminish morally the degree of the convicted person's guilt;

(*b*) in deciding whether or not there are extenuating circumstances, the court shall consider the standard of behaviour of an ordinary person of a class of the community to which the convicted person belongs.

(*As amended by Act No.* 3 *of* 1990).

202. Any person who commits the felony of manslaughter is liable to imprisonment for life.

Punishment of manslaughter

203. Where a woman by any wilful act or omission causes the death of her child, being a child under the age of twelve months, but at the time of the act or omission the balance of her mind was disturbed by reason of her not having fully recovered from the effect of

giving birth to the child or by reason of the effect of lactation consequent upon the birth of the child, then, notwithstanding that the circumstances were such that but for this section the offence would have amounted to murder, she shall be guilty of felony, to wit of infanticide, and may for such offence be dealt with and punished as if she had been guilty of the offence of manslaughter of the child.

(*No.* 26 *of* 1940)

Infanticide

204. Malice aforethought shall be deemed to be established by evidence proving any one or more of the following circumstances:

(*a*) an intention to cause the death of or to do grievous harm to any person, whether such person is the person actually killed or not;

(*b*) knowledge that the act or omission causing death will probably cause the death of or grievous harm to some person, whether such person is the person actually killed or not, although such knowledge is accompanied by indifference whether death or grievous bodily harm is caused or not, or by a wish that it may not be caused;

(*c*) an intent to commit a felony;

(*d*) an intention by the act or omission to facilitate the flight or escape from custody of any person who has committed or attempted to commit a felony.

Malice aforethought

205. (1) When a person who unlawfully kills another under circumstances which, but for the provisions of this section, would constitute murder, does the act which causes death in the heat of passion, caused by sudden provocation as hereinafter defined, and before there is time for his passion to cool, he is guilty of manslaughter only.

Killing on provocation

(2) The provisions of this section shall not apply unless the court is satisfied that the act which causes death bears a reasonable relationship to the provocation.

(*As amended by No.* 28 *of* 1952)

206. (1) The term "provocation" means and includes, except as hereinafter stated, any wrongful act or insult of such a nature as to be likely, when done or offered to an ordinary person, or in the presence of an ordinary person to another person who is under his immediate care, or to whom he stands in a conjugal, parental, filial, or fraternal relation, or in the relation of master or servant, to deprive him of the power of self-control and to induce him to assult the person by whom the act or insult is done or offered. For the purposes of this section, "an ordinary person" shall mean an ordinary person of the community to which the accused belongs.

Provocation defined

(2) When such an act or insult is done or offered by one person to another, or in the presence of another to a person who is under the immediate care of that other, or to whom the latter stands in any such relation as aforesaid, the former is said to give the latter provocation for an assault.

(3) A lawful act is not provocation to any person for an assault.

(4) An act which a person does in consequence of incitement given by another person in order to induce him to do the act and thereby to furnish an excuse for committing an assault is not provocation to that other person for an assault.

(5) An arrest which is unlawful is not necessarily provocation for an assault, but it may be evidence of provocation to a person who knows of the illegality.

(*As amended by No.* 26 *of* 1933 *and No.* 26 *of* 1940)

207. A person is deemed to have caused the death of another person although his act is not the immediate or sole cause of death in any of the following cases:

(*a*) If he inflicts bodily injury on another person in consequence of which that other person undergoes surgical or medical treatment which causes death. In this case it is immaterial whether the treatment was proper or mistaken, if it was employed in good faith and with common knowledge and skill; but the person inflicting the injury is not deemed to have caused the death if the treatment which was its immediate cause was not employed in good faith or was so employed without common knowledge or skill;

(*b*) If he inflicts bodily injury on another which would not have caused death if the injured person had submitted to proper surgical or medical treatment or had observed proper precautions as to his mode of living;

(*c*) If by actual or threatened violence he causes that other person to perform an act which causes the death of that person, such act being a means of avoiding such violence which in the circumstances would appear natural to the person whose death is so caused;

(*d*) If by any act or omission he hastens the death of a person suffering under any disease or injury which apart from such act or omission would have caused death;

(*e*) If his act or omission would not have caused death unless it had been accompanied by an act or omission of the person killed or of other persons.

Causing death defined

208. A child becomes a person capable of being killed when it has completely proceeded in a living state from the body of its mother, whether it has breathed or not, and whether it has an independent circulation or not, and whether the navel-string is severed or not.

When child deemed to be a person

209. (1) A person is not deemed to have killed another if the death of that person does not take place within a year and a day of the cause of death.

Limitation as to time of death

(2) Such period is reckoned inclusive of the day on which the last unlawful act contributing to the cause of death was done.

(3) When the cause of death is an omission to observe or perform a duty, the period is reckoned inclusive of the day on which the omission ceased.

(4) When the cause of death is in part an unlawful act, and in part an omission to observe or perform a duty, the period is reckoned inclusive of the day on which the last unlawful act was done or the day on which the omission ceased, whichever is the later.

CHAPTER XX DUTIES RELATING TO THE PRESERVATION OF LIFE AND HEALTH

210. It is the duty of every person having charge of another who is unable by reason of age, sickness, unsoundness of mind, detention or any other cause to withdraw himself from such charge, and who is unable to provide himself with the necessaries of life, whether the charge is undertaken under a contract, or is imposed by law, or arises by reason of any act, whether lawful or unlawful, of the person who has such charge, to provide for that other person the necessaries of life; and he shall be deemed to have caused any consequences which adversely affect the life or health of the other person by reason of any omission to perform that duty.

Responsibility of person who has charge of another

211. It is the duty of every person who, as head of a family, has charge of a child under the age of fourteen years, being a member of his household, to provide the necessaries of life for such child; and he shall be deemed to have caused any consequences which adversely affect the life or health of the child by reason of any omission to perform that duty, whether the child is helpless or not.

Duty of head of family

212. It is the duty of every person who as master or mistress has contracted to provide necessary food, clothing, or lodging for any servant or apprentice under the age of sixteen years to provide the same; and he or she shall be deemed to have caused any consequences which adversely affect the life or health of the servant or apprentice by reason of any omission to perform that duty.

Duty of masters and mistresses

213. It is the duty of every person who, except in a case of necessity, undertakes to administer surgical or medical treatment to any other person, or to do any other lawful act which is or may be dangerous to human life or health, to have reasonable skill and to use reasonable care in doing such act; and he shall be deemed to have caused any consequences which adversely affect the life or health of any person by reason of any omission to observe or perform that duty.

Duty of persons doing dangerous acts

214. It is the duty of every person who has in his charge or under his control anything, whether living or inanimate, and whether moving or stationery, of such a nature that, in the absence of care or precaution in its use or management, the life, safety, or health of any person may be endangered, to use reasonable care and take reasonable precautions to avoid such danger; and he shall be deemed to have caused any consequences which adversely affect the life or health of any person by reason of any omission to perform that duty.

Duty of persons in charge of dangerous things

CHAPTER XXI OFFENCES CONNECTED WITH MURDER

215. Any person who-

(*a*) attempts unlawfully to cause the death of another; or

(*b*) with intent unlawfully to cause the death of another does any act, or omits to do any act which it is his duty to do, such act or omission being of such a nature as to be likely to endanger human life;

is guilty of a felony and is liable to imprisonment for life.

Attempt to murder

216. Any person who, being under sentence of imprisonment for three years or more, attempts to commit murder, is liable to imprisonment for life.

(*As amended by No.* 26 *of* 1933)

Attempt to murder by convict

217. Any person who becomes an accessory after the fact to murder is guilty of a felony and is liable to imprisonment for seven years.

Accessory after the fact to murder

218. Any person who, knowing the contents thereof, directly or indirectly causes any person to receive any writing threatening to kill any person, is guilty of a felony and is liable to imprisonment for seven years.

Written threat to murder

219. Any person who conspires with any other person to kill any person, whether such person is in Zambia or elsewhere, is guilty of a felony and is liable to imprisonment for fourteen years.

Conspiracy to murder

220. Any person who, when a woman is delivered of a child, endeavours, by any secret disposition of the dead body of the child, to conceal the birth, whether the child died before, at, or after its birth, is guilty of a misdemeanour.

Concealing the birth of children

221. (1) Subject as hereinafter in this subsection provided, any person who, with intent to destroy the life of a child capable of being born alive, by any wilful act causes a child to die before it has an existence independent of its mother, is guilty of felony, to wit, of child destruction, and is liable on conviction thereof to imprisonment for life:

Child destruction

Provided that no person shall be found guilty of an offence under this section unless it is proved that the act which caused the death of the child was not done in good faith for the purpose only of preserving the life of the mother.

(2) For the purposes of this section, evidence that a woman had at any material time been pregnant for a period of twenty-eight weeks or more shall be *prima facie* proof that she was at that time pregnant of a child capable of being born alive.

(*No.* 28 *of* 1931)

CHAPTER XXII OFFENCES ENDANGERING LIFE OR HEALTH

222. Any person who, by any means calculated to choke, suffocate or strangle, and with intent to commit or to facilitate the commission of a felony or misdemeanour, or to facilitate the flight of an offender after the commission or attempted commission of a felony or misdemeanour, renders or attempts to render any person incapable of resistance, is guilty of a felony and is liable to imprisonment for life.

(*As amended by No.* 26 *of* 1933)

Disabling with intent to commit felony or misdemeanour

223. Any person who, with intent to commit or to facilitate the commission of a felony or misdemeanour, or to facilitate the flight of an offender after the commission or attempted commission of a felony or misdemeanour, administers or attempts to administer any stupefying or overpowering drug or thing to any person, is guilty of a felony and is liable to imprisonment for life.

Stupefying with intent to commit felony or misdemeanour

224. Any person who, with intent to maim, disfigure or disable any person, or to do some grievous harm to any person, or to resist or prevent the lawful arrest or detention of any person-

(*a*) unlawfully wounds or does any grievous harm to any person by any means whatever; or

(*b*) unlawfully attempts in any manner to strike any person with any kind of projectile or with a spear, sword, knife, or other dangerous or offensive weapon; or (*c*) unlawfully causes any explosive substance to explode; or

(*d*) sends or delivers any explosive substance or other dangerous or noxious thing to any person; or

(*e*) causes any such substance or thing to be taken or received by any person; or

(*f*) puts any corrosive fluid or any destructive or explosive substance in any place; or

(*g*) unlawfully casts or throws any such fluid or substance at or upon any person, or otherwise applies any such fluid or substance to the person of any person;

is guilty of a felony and is liable to imprisonment for life.

Acts intended to cause grievous harm or prevent arrest

225. Any person who unlawfully-

(*a*) prevents or obstructs any person who is on board of, or is escaping from a vessel which is in distress or wrecked, in his endeavours to save his life; or

(*b*) obstructs any person in his endeavours to save the life of any person so situated;

is guilty of a felony and is liable to imprisonment for life.

Preventing escape from wreck

226. (1) Any person who, with intent either to injure or endanger the safety of any person travelling by any railway, whether a particular person or not, or to affect or endanger the free and safe use of any railway or who, with intent to derail or cause to be derailed any railway engine, tender, wagon or carriage-

Acts endangering railways and persons travelling thereon

(*a*) places anything on such railway; or

(*b*) interferes with such railway or with anything whatsoever upon or near such railway; or

(*c*) shoots or throws anything at, into or upon, or causes anything to come into contact with, any person or thing on such railway; or

(*d*) shows any light or signal or in any way deals with any existing light or signal upon or near such railway; or

(*e*) wilfully fails to do any act which it is his duty to do;

is guilty of a felony and is liable to imprisonment for life.

(2) Subject to the provisions of the Juveniles Act, where a person has been convicted of an offence under subsection (1) and his intent was to derail or cause to be derailed any railway engine, tender, wagon or carriage, he shall be sentenced to not less than five years' imprisonment.

227. (1) Any person who, save with the express authority of the Zambia Railways or with some other lawful authority or lawful excuse, enters or remains or is found upon any portion of the railway reserve is guilty of a misdemeanour and is liable to a fine not exceeding three thousand penalty units or to imprisonment for a period not exceeding two years, or to both.

Trespass on railway

(2) Any person guilty of an offence under the provisions of subsection (1) who was, at the time such offence was committed, in possession without lawful excuse of any article or implement capable of being used to destroy, damage or dismantle any railway line or part thereof or any railway engine or rolling stock using such railway line, is guilty of a felony and is liable to imprisonment for a period not exceeding fourteen years.

(3) Without prejudice to any other defence which may be open to him, a person shall be deemed to have lawful authority for the purposes of this section if he proves-

(*a*) that he was on a public way or an authorised path; or

(*b*) that he was on a portion of the railway reserve upon which members of the public are admitted for the purposes of the Zambia Railways.

(4) A Divisional Commander of Police may, in his discretion and after consultation with the Zambia Railways, authorise such paths across the railway reserve as he deems necessary for the passage of persons across such reserve, and any path so authorised-

(*a*) shall be entered in a register kept or caused to be kept by the Divisional Commander of Police concerned; and

(*b*) shall be signposted by the Zambia Railways in such manner as the Minister responsible for power, transport and works may from time to time, by statutory notice, prescribe.

(5) In any proceedings under the provisions of this section-

(*a*) the onus of proving that any person had express or other authority or had lawful excuse shall lie upon such person; and

(*b*) every railway line, other than the Zambesi Sawmills Railway Line, over which goods and passengers are carried for fee or reward shall be presumed to be owned by the Zambia Railways unless the contrary is proved; and

(*c*) any document purporting to be an extract or copy of any entry in a register kept under the provisions of subsection (4) and to be certified under the hand of a police officer of or above the rank of Sub-Inspector shall be received in evidence as to the matters stated therein.

(6) For the purposes of this section-

"authorised path" means a path entered in any register kept under the provisions of subsection (4);

"railway reserve" means the strip of land along any railway line owned by the Zambia Railways extending-

(*a*) where the said line consists of a single track, for a distance of one hundred feet outwards from each rail; and

(*b*) where the said line consists of two or more tracks, for a distance of one hundred feet outwards from the outermost rail on each side of such tracks;

and including all the land between the outermost rails.

(*No.* 34 *of* 1960 *as amended by G.N. No.* 493 *of* 1964 *and No.* 24 *of* 1977)

228. Any person who, with intent either to injure or to endanger the safety of any person travelling in any motor vehicle as defined in the Roads and Road Traffic Act, shoots or throws anything at, into or upon or causes anything to come into contact with any such person or any such vehicle, is guilty of a felony and is liable to imprisonment for life.

(*No.* 26 *of* 1961)

Acts endangering the safety of persons travelling in motor vehicles.
Cap. 464

229. Any person who unlawfully does grievous harm to another is guilty of a felony and is liable to imprisonment for seven years.

Grievous harm

230. Any person who unlawfully, and with intent to do any harm to another, puts any explosive substance in any place whatever, is guilty of a felony and is liable to imprisonment for fourteen years.

Attempting to injure by explosive substances

231. Any person who unlawfully, and with intent to injure or annoy another, causes any poison or noxious thing to be administered to, or taken by, any person, and thereby endangers his life, or does him some grievous harm, is guilty of a felony and is liable to imprisonment for fourteen years.

Maliciously administering poison with intent to harm

232. Any person who-

Unlawful wounding or poisoning

(*a*) unlawfully wounds another; or

(*b*) unlawfully, and with intent to injure or annoy any person, causes any poison or other noxious thing to be administered to, or taken by, any person;

is guilty of a felony and is liable to imprisonment for three years.

233. Any person who, being charged with the duty of providing for another the necessaries of life, without lawful excuse fails to do so, whereby the life of that other person is or is likely to be endangered, or his health is or is likely to be permanently injured, is guilty of a felony and is liable to imprisonment for three years.

Failure to supply necessaries

234. A person is not criminally responsible for performing in good faith and with reasonable care and skill a surgical operation upon any person for his benefit, or upon an unborn child for the preservation of the mother's life, if the performance of the operation is reasonable, having regard to the patient's state at the time, and to all the circumstances of the case.

Responsibility as to surgical operation

235. Any person authorised by law or by the consent of the person injured by him to use force is criminally responsible for any excess, according to the nature and quality of the act which constitutes the excess.

Criminal responsibility

236. Notwithstanding anything contained in section *two hundred and thirty-five*, consent by a person to the causing of his own death or his own maim does not affect the criminal responsibility of any person by whom such death or maim is caused.

Exception

CHAPTER XXIII CRIMINAL RECKLESSNESS AND NEGLIGENCE

237. Any person who in a manner so rash or negligent as to en-danger human life or to be likely to cause harm to any other person-

Reckless and negligent acts

(*a*) drives any vehicle or rides on any public way; or

(*b*) navigates, or takes part in the navigation or working of any vessel; or

(*c*) does any act with fire or any combustible matter, or omits to take precautions against any probable danger from any fire or any combustible matter in his possession; or

(*d*) omits to take precautions against any probable danger from any animal in his possession; or

(*e*) gives medical or surgical treatment to any person whom he has undertaken to treat; or

(*f*) dispenses, supplies, sells, administers, or gives away any medicine or poisonous or dangerous matter; or

(*g*) does any act with respect to, or omits to take proper precautions against any probable danger from any machinery of which he is solely or partly in charge;

is guilty of a misdemeanour.

(*As amended by No.* 45 *of* 1969)

238. Any person who unlawfully does any act, or omits to do any act which it is his duty to do, not being an act or omission specified in the preceding section, by which act or omission harm is caused to any person, is guilty of a misdemeanour and is liable to imprisonment for six months.

Unlawful acts causing harm

239. Whoever does, with any poisonous substance, any act in a manner so rash or negligent as to endanger human life, or to be likely to cause hurt or injury to any other person, or knowingly or negligently omits to take such care with any poisonous substance in his possession as is sufficient to guard against probable danger to human life from such poisonous substance, is guilty of a misdemeanour and is liable to imprisonment for six months or to a fine not exceeding three thousand penalty units.

(*No.* 26 *of* 1940 *and Act No.* 13 *of* 1994)

Dealing with poisonous substances in negligent manner

240. Any person who, by any unlawful act or omission not specified in section *two hundred and twenty-six*, causes the safety of any person travelling by any railway to be endangered, is guilty of a misdemeanour.

Endangering safety of persons travelling by railway

241. Any person who exhibits any false light, mark or buoy, intending or knowing it to be likely that such exhibition will mislead any navigator, is liable to imprisonment for seven years.

Exhibition of false light, mark or buoy

242. Any person who knowingly or negligently conveys, or causes to be conveyed for hire, any person by water in any vessel, when that vessel is in such a state or so loaded as to be unsafe, is guilty of a misdemeanour.

Conveying person by water for hire in unsafe or overloaded vessel

243. (1) Any person who, without lawful cause or reasonable excuse, does any act with intent to obstruct or impede the navigation by any vessel of any waters capable of being used for navigation is guilty of an offence and is liable on conviction to imprisonment for a period not exceeding three years.

Obstruction of waterways

(2) For the purposes of this section, "vessel" includes any canoe, boat, ship or raft.

(*No.* 18 *of* 1962)

244. Any person who, by doing any act, or by omitting to take reasonable care with any property in his possession or under his charge, causes danger, obstruction or injury to any person in any public way or public line of navigation, is liable to a fine.

Danger or obstruction in public way or line of navigation

245. (1) Any person who enters upon an aerodrome is guilty of a misdemeanour unless such person proves-

Trespass on aerodromes

(*a*) that he did not know that the land on which he entered was an aerodrome; or

(*b*) that he had reasonable cause for being on such aerodrome.

(2) Any person who, being in charge of an animal, causes or permits such animal to trespass on an aerodrome is guilty of a misdemeanour.

(3) A misdemeanour under this section is punishable with imprisonment for a period not exceeding one month or with a fine not exceeding seven hundred and fifty penalty units, or both.

(4) For the purposes of this section, "aerodrome" includes an airport, landing ground, or other place normally used by aircraft for landing and taking off.

(*No.* 28 *of* 1949 *and Act No.* 13*of* 1994)

246. (1) Any person who, without lawful cause or reasonable excuse, does any act with intent to obstruct, whether partially or otherwise, any road or runway is guilty of an offence and is liable on conviction to imprisonment for a period not exceeding three years.

Obstruction of roads or runways

(2) For the purposes of this section-

"road" shall have the meaning assigned to it by section *two* of the Roads and Road Traffic Act;

"runway" includes any landing ground or other place ordinarily used by aircraft for landing or taking off.

CHAPTER XXIV ASSAULTS

247. Any person who unlawfully assaults another is guilty of a misdemeanour and, if the assault is not committed in circumstances for which a greater punishment is provided in this Code, is liable to imprisonment for one year.

Common assault

248. Any person who commits an assault occasioning actual bodily harm is guilty of a misdemeanour and is liable to imprisonment for five years.

Assaults occasioning actual bodily harm

248A.Any person who commits an assault or battery on a child occasioning actual bodily harm commits an offence and is liable, upon conviction, to a term of imprisonment of not less than five years and not exceeding ten years.

Assault or battering of child

(As amended by Act No. 15 of 2005)

249. Any person who assaults and strikes or wounds any magistrate, officer, or other person lawfully authorised in or on account of the execution of his duty in or concerning the preservation of any vessel in distress, or of any vessel or goods or effects wrecked, stranded, or cast on shore, or lying under water, is guilty of a felony and is liable to imprisonment for seven years.

Assaults on persons protecting wrecks

250. Any person who-

(*a*) assaults any person with intent to commit a felony or to resist or prevent the lawful apprehensive or detainer of himself or of any other person for any offence; or

(*b*) assaults, resists, or wilfully obstructs any police officer in the due execution of his duty, or any person acting in aid of such officer; or

(*c*) assaults any person in pursuance of any unlawful combination or conspiracy to raise the rate of wages, or respecting any trade, business, or manufacture or respecting any person concerned or employed therein; or

(*d*) assaults, resists, or obstructs any person engaged in lawful execution of process, or in making a lawful distress, with intent to rescue any property lawfully taken under such process or distress; or

(*e*) assaults any person on account of any act done by him in the execution of any duty imposed on him by law;

is guilty of a misdemeanour and is liable to imprisonment for five years.

Assaults punishable with five years' imprisonment

CHAPTER XXV OFFENCES AGAINST LIBERTY

251. Any person who conveys any person beyond the limits of Zambia without the consent of that person, or of some person legally authorised to consent on behalf of that person, is said to kidnap that person from Zambia.

Definition of kidnapping from Zambia

252. Any person who takes or entices any minor under fourteen years of age if a male, or under sixteen years of age if a female, or any person of unsound mind, out of the keeping of the lawful guardian of such minor or person of unsound mind, without the

consent of such guardian, is said to kidnap such minor or person from lawful guardianship.

Definition of kidnapping from lawful guardianship

253. Any person who by force compels, or by any deceitful means induces, any person to go from any place, is said to abduct that person.

Definition of abduction

254. Any person who kidnaps any person from Zambia or from lawful guardianship, is guilty of a felony and is liable to imprisonment for seven years.

Punishment for kidnapping

255. Any person who kidnaps or abducts any person in order that such person may be murdered, or may be so disposed of as to be put in danger of being murdered, is guilty of a felony and is liable to imprisonment for ten years.

Kidnapping or abducting in order to murder

256. Any person who kidnaps or abducts any person with intent to cause that person to be secretly and wrongfully confined, is guilty of a felony and is liable to imprisonment for seven years.

Kidnapping or abducting with intent to confine person

257. Any person who kidnaps or abducts any person in order that such person may be subjected, or may be so disposed of as to be put in danger of being subjected, to grievous harm, or slavery, or to the unnatural lust of any person, or knowing it to be likely that such person will be so subjected or disposed of, is guilty of a felony and is liable to imprisonment for ten years.

Kidnapping or abducting in order to subject person to grievous harm, slavery, etc.

258. Any person who, knowing that any person has been kidnapped or has been abducted, wrongfully conceals or confines such person, is guilty of a felony and shall be punished in the same manner as if he had kidnapped or abducted such person with the same intention or knowledge, or for the same purpose, as that with or for which he conceals or detains such person in confinement.

Wrongfully concealing or keeping in confinement kidnapped or abducted person

259. Any person who kidnaps or abducts any child under the age of fourteen years with the intention of taking dishonestly any movable property from the person of such child, is guilty of a felony and is liable to imprisonment for seven years.

Kidnapping or abducting child under fourteen with intent to steal from its person

260. Whoever wrongfully confines any person is guilty of a misdemeanour and is liable to imprisonment for one year or to a fine not exceeding six thousand penalty units.

(*No.* 26 *of* 1940 *and Act No.* 13 *of* 1994)

Punishment for wrongful confinement

261. Any person who imports, exports, removes, buys, sells or disposes of any person as a slave, or accepts, receives or detains against his will any person as a slave, is guilty of a felony and is liable to imprisonment for seven years.

Buying or disposing of any person as a slave

262. Any person who habitually imports, exports, removes, buys, sells, traffics or deals in slaves is guilty of a felony and is liable to imprisonment for ten years.

Habitual dealing in slaves

263. Any person who unlawfully compels any person to labour against the will of that person is guilty of a misdemeanour.

Unlawful compulsory labour

DIVISION V OFFENCES RELATING TO PROPERTY

CHAPTER XXVI THEFT

264. (1) Every inanimate thing whatever which is the property of any person, and which is movable, is capable of being stolen.

Things capable of being stolen

(2) Every inanimate thing which is the property of any person, and which is capable of being made movable, is capable of being stolen as soon as it becomes movable, although it is made movable in order to steal it.

(3) Every tame animal, whether tame by nature or wild by nature and tamed, which is the property of any person, is capable of being stolen.

(4) Animals wild by nature, of a kind which is not ordinarily found in a condition of natural liberty in Zambia, which are the property of any person, and which are usually kept in a state of confinement, are capable of being stolen, whether they are actually in confinement or have escaped from confinement.

(5) Animals wild by nature, of a kind which is ordinarily found in a condition of natural liberty in Zambia, which are the property of any person, are capable of being stolen while they are in confinement and while they are being actually pursued after escaping from confinement, but not at any other time.

(6) An animal wild by nature is deemed to be in a state of confinement so long as it is in a den, cage, sty, tank, or other small enclosure, or is otherwise so placed that it cannot escape, and that its owner can take possession of it at pleasure.

(7) Wild animals in the enjoyment of their natural liberty are not capable of being stolen, but their dead bodies are capable of being stolen.

(8) Everything produced by or forming part of the body of an animal capable of being stolen is capable of being stolen.

265. (1) A person who fraudulently and without claim of right takes anything capable of being stolen, or fraudulently converts to the use of any person other than the general or special owner thereof anything capable of being stolen, is said to steal that thing.

Definition of theft

(2) A person who takes or converts anything capable of being stolen is deemed to do so fraudulently if he does so with any of the following intents, that is to say:

(*a*) an intent permanently to deprive the general or special owner of the thing of it;

(*b*) an intent to use the thing as a pledge or security;

(*c*) an intent to part with it on a condition as to its return which the person taking or converting it may be unable to perform;

(*d*) an intent to deal with it in such a manner that it cannot be returned in the condition in which it was at the time of the taking or conversion;

(*e*) in the case of money, an intent to use it at the will of the person who takes or converts it, although he may intend afterwards to repay the amount to the owner.

(3) When a thing stolen is converted, it is immaterial whether it is taken for the purpose of conversion, or whether it is at the time of the conversion in the possession of the person who converts it. It is also immaterial that the person who converts the thing in question is the holder of a power of attorney for the disposition of it, or is otherwise authorised to dispose of it.

(4) When a thing converted has been lost by the owner and found by the person who converts it, the conversion is not deemed to be fraudulent if at the time of the conversion the person taking or converting the thing does not know who is the owner, and believes on reasonable grounds that the owner cannot be discovered.

(5) A person shall not be deemed to take a thing unless he moves the thing or causes it to move.

(6) For the purposes of this section, "special owner" includes any person who has any charge or lien upon the thing in question, or any right arising from or dependent upon holding possession of the thing in question.

266. (1) When a factor or agent pledges or gives a lien on any goods or document of title to goods entrusted to him for the purpose of sale or otherwise for any sum of money not greater than the amount due to him from his principal at the time of pledging or giving the lien, together with the amount of any bill of exchange or promissory note accepted or made by him for or on account of his principal, such dealing with the goods or document of title is not deemed to be theft.

Special cases

(2) When a servant, contrary to his mater's orders, takes from his possession any food in order that it may be given to an animal belonging to or in the possession of his master, such taking is not deemed to be theft.

267. When a person receives, either alone or jointly with another person, any money or valuable security or a power of attorney for the sale, mortgage, pledge, or other disposition of any property, whether capable of being stolen or not with a direction in either case that such money or any part thereof, or any other money received in exchange for it, or any part thereof, or the proceeds or any part of the proceeds of such security, or of such mortgage, pledge, or other disposition, shall be applied to any purpose or paid to any person specified in the direction, such money and proceeds are deemed to be the property of the person from whom the money, security, or power of attorney was received until the direction has been complied with.

(*As amended by No.* 9 *of* 1968)

Funds, etc., held under direction

268. When a person receives, either alone or jointly with another person, any property from another on terms authorising or requiring him to sell it or otherwise dispose of it, and requiring him to pay or account for the proceeds of the property, or any part of such proceeds, or to deliver anything received in exchange for the property, to the person from whom it is received, or some other person, then the proceeds of the property, and anything so received in exchange for it, are deemed to be the property of the person from whom the property was so received, until they have been disposed of in accordance with the terms on which the property was received, unless it is a part of those terms that the proceeds, if any, shall form an item in a debtor and creditor account between him and the person to whom he is to pay them or account for them, and that the relation of debtor and creditor only shall exist between them in respect thereof.

Funds, etc., received by agents for sale

269. When a person receives, either alone or jointly with another person, any money on behalf of another, the money is deemed to be the property of the person on whose behalf it is received, unless the money is received on the terms that it shall form an item in a debtor and creditor account, and that the relation of debtor and creditor only shall exist between, the parties in respect of it.

Money received for another

270. When any person takes or converts anything capable of being stolen, under such circumstances as would otherwise amount to theft, it is immaterial that he himself has a special property or interest therein, or that he himself is the owner of the thing taken or converted subject to some special property or interest of some other person therein, or that he is lessee of the thing, or that he himself is one of two or more joint owners of the thing, or that he is a director or officer of a corporation or company or society who are the owners of it.

Theft by persons having an interest in the thing stolen

271. A person who, while a man and his wife are living together, procures either of them to deal with anything which is, to his knowledge, the property of the other in a manner which would be theft if they were not married, is deemed to have stolen the thing, and may be charged with theft.

Husband and wife

272. Any person who steals anything capable of being stolen is guilty of the felony termed "theft", and, unless owing to the circumstances of the theft or the nature of the thing stolen some other punishment is provided, is liable to imprisonment for five years.

(*As amended by Act No.* 29 *of* 1974)

General punishment for theft

273. If the thing stolen is a testamentary instrument, whether the testator is living or dead, the offender is liable to imprisonment for ten years.

(*As amended by No.* 28 *of* 1931)

Stolen wills

274. If the thing stolen is postal matter or any chattel, money, or valuable security contained in any postal matter, the offender is liable to imprisonment for ten years.

Stealing postal matter, etc.

275. (1) If the thing stolen is any of the following, that is to say: a horse, mare, gelding, ass, mule, camel, ostrich, ram, ewe, wether, goat or pig, or the young of any such animal, the offender is liable-

Stock theft

(*a*) in the case of a first offence, to imprisonment not exceeding fifteen years;

(*b*) in the case of a second and subsequent offence to imprisonment for a period of not less than seven years and not exceeding fifteen years.

(2) If the thing stolen is a bull, cow or ox, or the young of any such animal, the offender is liable to imprisonment for a period-

(*a*) in the case of a first offence, of not less than five years and not exceeding fifteen years;

(*b*) in the case of a second or subsequent offence, of not less than seven years and not exceeding fifteen years.

275A. (1) Nothwithstanding subsection (2) of section *twenty-six*, if the thing stolen is copper cathodes, copper bars, cobalt, lead, zinc or vanadium the offender is liable to imprisonment for a period not exceeding fifteen years.

Stealing copper cathodes, copper bars, cobalt, lead, zinc or vanadium

(2) Where a person is convicted of an offence under this Act the court which convicts him shall, in addition to any other penalty imposed under subsection (1), order the forfeiture of all the property which is the subject of that offence or which has been used for the commission of that offence:

Provided that no conveyance which has been used for the commission of the offence shall be forfeited if the offence was committed by a person other than the owner or person in charge of the conveyance and it is proved to the court that the use of the conveyance for the commission of the offence was without the consent and knowledge of the owner or person in charge of the conveyance and was not due to any neglect, default or lack of reasonable care by the owner or the person in charge of the conveyance.

(3) Where it is proved to the satisfaction of the court that an offence has been committed under this Section, the court shall make an order for the forfeiture of all property which is the subject matter of that offence or which has been used for the commission of that offence, notwithstanding that no person may have been convicted of the offence:

Provided that the proviso to subsection (2) shall apply in relation to an order for forfeiture under this subsection.

(*As amended by Act No.* 23 *of* 1993)

276. If a theft is committed under any of the circumstances following, that is to say:

(*a*) if the thing is stolen from the person of another;

(*b*) if the thing is stolen in a dwelling-house and its value exceeds one hundred and fifty fee units or the offender, at or immediately before or after the time of stealing uses or threatens to use violence to any person in the dwelling-house;

(*c*) if the thing is stolen from any kind of vessel or vehicle or place of deposit used for the conveyance or custody of goods in transit from one place to another;

(*d*) if the thing stolen is attached to or forms part of a railway;

(*e*) if the thing is stolen from a vessel which is in distress or wrecked or stranded;

(*f*) if the thing is stolen from a public office in which it is deposited or kept;

(*g*) if the offender, in order to commit the offence, opens any locked room, box, or other receptacle, by means of a key or other instrument;

the offender is liable to imprisonment for seven years.

(*As amended by Act No.* 13 *of* 1994)

Stealing from the person; stealing goods in transit, etc.

277. If the offender is a person employed in the public service and the thing stollen is the property of the Government, a local authority or a corporation, body or board, including an institution of higher learning in which the Government has a majority or con-trolling interest, or came into his possession by virtue of his employment, he is liable to imprisonment for fifteen years.

(*As amended by Act No.* 29 *of* 1974)

Stealing by persons in public service

278. If the offender is a clerk or servant and the thing stolen is the property of his employer, or came into the possession of the offender on account of his employer, he is liable to imprisonment for seven years.

Stealing by clerks and servants

279. If the offender is a director or officer of a corporation or company and the thing stolen is the property of the corporation or company, he is liable to imprisonment for seven years

Stealing by directors or officers of companies

280. If the thing stolen is any of the things following, that is to say:

(*a*) property which has been received by the offender with a power of attorney for the deposition thereof;

(*b*) property which has been entrusted to the offender either alone or jointly with any other person for him to retain in safe custody or to apply, pay, or deliver for any purpose or to any person the same or any part thereof or any proceeds thereof;

(*c* property which has been received by the offender either alone or jointly with any other person for or on account of any other person;

Stealing by agents etc.

(*d*) the whole or part of the proceeds of any valuable security which has been received by the offender with a direction that the proceeds thereof should be applied to any purpose or paid to any person specified in the direction;

(*e*) the whole or part of the proceeds arising from any disposition of any property which has been received by the offender by virtue of a power of attorney for such disposition, such power of attorney having been received by the offender with a direction that such proceeds should be applied to any purpose or paid to any person specified in the direction;

the offender is liable to imprisonment for seven years.

281. If the thing stolen is a fixture or chattel let to the offender to be used by him with a house or lodging and its value exceeds one hundred and fifty fee units, he is liable to imprisonment for seven years.

Stealing by tenants or lodgers

(*As amended by Act No.* 13 *of* 1994)

281A. (1) If the thing stolen is a motor vehicle, the offender is liable to imprisonment for a period-

Stealing of motor vehicle

(*a*) in the case of a first offence, of not less than five years and not exceeding fifteen years;

(*b*) in the case of a second or subsequent offence, of not less than seven years and not exceeding fifteen years.

(2) In this section, "motor vehicle" means a motor vehicle or trailer-

(*a*) which is registered or registrable under the provisions of section *sixty-six* of the Roads and Road Traffic Act; or

(*b*) which is exempted from the need for registration under any of the provisions of the Roads and Road Traffic Act or any regulation made thereunder.

(3) Where a person is convicted of an offence under subsection (1) the court which convicts the person shall, in addition to any other penalty imposed under that sunsection, order the forfeiture of all the property which has been used for or derived from the commission of that offence:

Provided that no property which has been used for the commission of the offence shall be forfeited if the offence was committed by a person other than the owner or person in charge of the property and it is proved to the court that the use of the property for the commission of the offence was without the consent and knowledge of the owner or person in charge of the property.

(4) Where a person is charged with an offence under subsection (1) the trial court may, notwithstanding that the person was not originally charged with that offence, convict the person of a lesser offence and the person shall, upon such conviction, be liable to a fine of not less than fifty-eight thousand penalty units or to imprisonment for a term of not less than five years, or to both.

281B. (1) A policy officer may, without a warrant, stop, search and arrest any person found driving, or in possession, charge or control of a motor vehicle, where the officer believes, on reasonable grounds, that the vehicle is stolen.

(2) Where an arrest is made under subsection (1) the police officer may seize the vehicle and any documents relating to the vehicle.

(3) A police officer who arrests any person or seizes a motor vehicle under this section shall as soon as practicable take the person, the vehicle and any documents relating to the nearest police station.

(4) A person arrested and any motor vehicle seized under this section shall, within forty-eight hours of arrest and seizure, be brought before a court.

(5) Any motor vehicle-

(a) returned, by the court, to the police at the conclusion of the case; or

(b) found abandoned on any road or inn any public place or premises;

and of which the owner is not known or cannot be found, may be removed to a police station, and if not previously claimed by its owner, shall be dealt with in accordance with the provisions of subsection (6).

(6) The Officer-In-Charge of the police station to which a motor vehicle is removed in terms of subsection (5) shall cause to be published, once in the *Gazzette,* and once in a newspaper of general circulation in Zambia, a notice containing-

(a) particulars of the vehicle concerned; or

(b) where no particulars are available, fair description of the vehicle; and

(c) a warning that if the vehicle remians unclaimed within six minths from

the date of publication of the notice, it shall be forfeited to the State

and dealt with as the Minister may, by notice in the *Gazzette,* direct,

which may include sale by public auction.

(*As amended by Act No.* 9 *of* 1974 *and No. 20 of* 2000)

Search, seizure and arrest of person in relation to theft of motor vehicle

282. Repealed by Act No. 29 of 1974

CHAPTER XXVII OFFENCES ALLIED TO STEALING

283. Any person who, with intent to defraud, conceals or takes from its place of deposit any register which is authorised or required by law to be kept for authenticating or recording the title to any property, or for recording births, baptisms, marriages, deaths or burials, or a copy of any part of any such register which is required by law to be sent to any public office, is guilty of a felony and is liable to imprisonment for ten years.

Concealing registers

284. Any person who, with intent to defraud, conceals any testamentary instrument, whether the testator is living or dead, is guilty of a felony and is liable to imprisonment for ten years.

Concealing wills

85. Any person who, with intent to defraud, conceals the whole or part of any document which is evidence of title to any land or estate in land, is guilty of a felony and is liable to imprisonment for three years.

Concealing deeds

286. Any person who kills any animal capable of being stolen with intent to steal the skin or carcass, or any part of the skin or carcass, is guilty of an offence and is liable to the same punishment as if he had stolen the animal.

Killing animals with intent to steal

287. Any person who makes anything movable with intent to steal it is guilty of an offence and is liable to the same punishment as if he had stolen the thing after it had become movable.

Severing with intent to steal

288. (1) Any person who, being the mortgagor of mortgaged goods, removes or disposes of the goods without the consent of the mortgagee, and with intent to defraud, is guilty of a misdemeanour.

Fraudulent disposition of mortgaged goods

(2) In this section, "mortgaged goods" includes any goods and chattels of any kind, and any animals, and any progeny of any animals, and any crops or produce of the soil, whether growing or severed, which are subject for the time being, by virtue of the provisions of any Act or of any written instrument, to a valid charge or lien by way of security for any debt or obligation.

289. Notwithstanding subsection (2) of section *twenty-six*, any person who takes, conceals, or otherwise disposes of any ore or any metal or mineral with intent to defraud any person, is guilty of a felony and is liable to imprisonment for a period not exceeding fifteen years.

289B. (1) Any person who-

(a) takes, conceals, sells, or otherwise disposes of a motor

vehicle or any part of it with intent to defraud any person; or

(b) knowing or believing that a motor vehicle is stolen,

dishonestly receives such motor vehicle or undertakes or

assists in its retention, removal disposal or realisation by or

for the benefit of another person or arranges to do so;

commits an offence and is liable, upon conviction, to a fine of not less than twenty-eight thousand penalty units but not exceeding fifty-six thousand penalty units or imprisonment for a term of five years or to both.

(2) Where a person is convicted of an offence under this section the court which convicts the person shall, in addition to any penalty imposed under subsection (1), order the forfeiture of all property which is used for or derived from the commission of the offence.

(3) Any sentence imposed under subsection (1) shall be consecutive to, and not concurrent with, any sentence imposed on the convicted person and no part of such sentence shall be suspended.

(*As amended by Act No.* 23 *of* 1993*and No. 20 of* 2000)

Fraudulently dealing with metals or minerals

Fraidulently dealing with motor vehicles

290. Any person who fraudulently abstracts or diverts to his own use or to the use of any other person any mechanical, illuminating, or electrical power derived from any machine, apparatus, or substance, the property of another person, is guilty of a felony and is liable to imprisonment for five years.

Fraudulent appropriation of power

291. Any person who unlawfully and without colour of right, but not so as to be guilty of theft, takes or converts to his use or to the use of any other person any draught or riding animal or any vehicle or cycle however propelled, or any vessel, is guilty of a misdemeanour and is liable to imprisonment for six months or to a fine not exceeding one thousand five hundred penalty units, or to both.

(*As amended by Act No.* 13 *of* 1994)

Conversion not amounting to theft

CHAPTER XXVIII ROBBERY AND EXTORTION

292. Any person who steals anything, and, at or immediately before or immediately after the time of stealing it, uses or threatens to use actual violence to any person or property to obtain or retain the thing stolen or to prevent or overcome resistance to its being stolen or retained, is guilty of the felony of robbery and is liable on conviction to imprisonment for fourteen years.

(*No.* 18 *of* 1963)

Robbery

293. Any person who assaults any person with intent to steal anything is guilty of a felony and is liable on conviction to imprisonment for seven years.

(*No.* 18 *of* 1963)

Assault with intent to steal

294. (1) Any person who, being armed with any offensive weapon or instrument, or being together with one person or more, steals anything, and, at or immediately before or immediately after the time of stealing it, uses or threatens to use actual violence to any person or property to obtain or retain the thing stolen or to prevent or overcome

resistance to its being stolen or retained, is guilty of the felony of aggravated robbery and is liable on conviction to im-prisonment for life, and, notwithstanding subsection (2) of section *twenty-six*, shall be sentenced to imprisonment for a period of not less than fifteen years.

Aggravated robbery

(2) Notwithstanding the provisions of subsection (1), the penalty for the felony of aggravated robbery under subsection (1) shall be death-

(*a*) where the offensive weapon or instrument is a firearm, unless the court is satisfied by the evidence in the case that the accused person was not armed with a firearm and-

(i) that he was not aware that any of the other persons involved in committing the offence was so armed; or

(ii) that he dissociated himself from the offence immediately on becoming so aware; or

(*b*) where the offensive weapon or instrument is not a firearm and grievous harm is done to any person in the course of the offence, unless the court is satisfied by the evidence in the case that the accused person neither contemplated nor could reasonably have contemplated that grievous harm might be inflicted in the course of the offence.

(3) In this section "firearm" has the meaning assigned to it in section *two* of the Firearms Act.

(*No.* 18 *of* 1963 *as amended by No.* 40 *of* 1969 *and*
Act No. 29 *of* 1974)

295. Any person who, being armed with any offensive weapon or instrument, or being together with one person or more, assaults any person with intent to steal anything, is guilty of a felony and is liable on conviction to imprisonment for a period (notwithstanding subsection (2) of section *twenty-six*) of not less than ten years and not exceeding twenty years.

(*No.* 18 *of* 1963 *as amended by No.* 40 *of* 1969)

Aggravated assault with intent to steal

296. Any person who, with intent to extort or gain anything from any person, and knowing the contents of the writing, causes any person to receive any writing demanding anything from any person without reasonable or probable cause, and containing threats of any injury or detriment of any kind to be caused to any person, either by the offender or any other person, if the demand is not complied with, is guilty of a felony and is liable to imprisonment for fourteen years.

Demanding property by written threats

297. (1) Any person who, with intent to extort or gain anything from any person-

Attempts at extortion by threats

(*a*) accuses or threatens to accuse any person of committing any felony or misdemeanour, or of offering or making any solicitation or threat to any person as an inducement to commit or permit the commission of any felony or misdemeanour; or

(*b*) threatens that any person shall be accused by any other person of any felony or misdemeanour, or of any such act; or

(*c*) knowing the contents of the writing, causes any person to receive any writing containing any such accusation or threat as aforesaid;

is guilty of a felony, and if the accusation or threat of accusation is of-

(i) an offence for which the punishment of death or imprisonment for life may be inflicted; or

(ii) any of the offences defined in Chapter XV, or an attempt to commit any of such offences; or

(iii) an assault with intent to have carnal knowledge of any person against the order of nature, or an unlawful and indecent assault upon a male person; or

(iv) a solicitation or threat offered or made to any person as an inducement to commit or permit the commission of any of the offences aforesaid;

the offender is liable to imprisonment for fourteen years. In any other case the offender is liable to imprisonment for three years.

(2) It is immaterial whether the person accused or threatened to be accused has or has not committed the offence or act of which he is accused or threatened to be accused.

298. Any person who, with intent to defraud, and by means of any unlawful violence to, or restraint of, the person of another, or by means of any threat of violence or restraint to be used to the person of another, or by means of accusing or threatening to accuse any person of committing any felony or misdemeanour, or by offering or making any solicitation or threat to any person as an inducement to commit or permit the commission of any offence, compels or induces any person-

Procuring execution of deeds, etc., by threats

(*a*) to execute, make, accept, endorse, alter, or destroy the whole or any part of any valuable security; or

(*b*) to write any name or impress or affix any seal upon or to any paper or parchment, in order that it may be afterwards made or converted into or used or dealt with as a valuable security;

is guilty of a felony and is liable to imprisonment for fourteen years.

299. Any person who, with intent to steal any valuable thing, demands it from any person with menaces or force, is guilty of a felony and is liable to imprisonment for five years.

Demanding property with menaces with intent to steal

CHAPTER XXIX BURGLARY, HOUSEBREAKING AND SIMILAR OFFENCES

300. (1) A person who breaks any part, whether external or internal, of a building, or opens by unlocking, pulling, pushing, lifting, or any other means whatever, any door, window, shutter, cellar flap, or other thing, intended to close or cover an opening in a building, or an opening giving passage from one part of a building to another, is deemed to break the building.

Definition of breaking and entering

(2) A person is deemed to enter a building as soon as any part of his body or any part of any instrument used by him is within the building.

(3) A person who obtains entrance into a building by means of any threat or artifice used for that purpose, or by collusion with any person in the building, or who enters any chimney or other aperture of the building permanently left open for any necessary purpose, but not intended to be ordinarily used as a means of entrance, is deemed to have broken and entered the building.

301. Any person who-

(*a*) breaks and enters any dwelling house with intent to commit a felony therein; or

(*b*) having entered any dwelling house with intent to commit a felony therein, or having committed a felony in any such dwelling house, breaks out thereof;

is guilty of the felony termed "housebreaking" and is liable to imprisonment for seven years. If the offence is committed in the night, it is termed "burglary" and the offender is liable to imprisonment for ten years.

(*As amended by Act No.* 3 *of* 1990)

House-breaking and burglary

302. (1) Any person who enters or is in any dwelling house with intent to commit a felony in it is guilty of a felony and liable upon conviction to imprisonment for a period not exceeding five years or if the offence is committed at night to imprisonment for a period not exceeding seven years.

Entering dwelling house or other building with intent to commit felony

(2) Any person who enters or is in any building other than a dwelling house, with intent to commit a felony in it is guilty of a felony and liable upon conviction to imprisonment for a period not exceeding five years or if the offence is committed at night to imprisonment for a period not exceeding seven years.

303. Any person who-

(*a*) breaks and enters into any building other than a dwelling house and commits a felony in it; or

(*b*) having committed a felony in any building other than a dwelling house, breaks out of it, is guilty of a felony and is liable to imprisonment for seven years;

is guilty of a felony and is liable to imprisonment for seven years.

(*As amended by Act No.* 3 *of* 1990)

Breaking into building and committing felony

304. Any person who breaks and enters a schoolhouse, shop, warehouse, store, office, or counting-house, or a building which is adjacent to a dwelling-house and occupied with it but is not part of it, or any building used as a place of worship with intent to commit a felony therein, is guilty of a felony and is liable to imprisonment for five years.

Breaking into building with intent to commit felony

305. Any person who is found under any of the circumstances following, that is to say:

(*a*) being armed with any dangerous or offensive weapon or instrument, and being so armed with intent to break or enter a dwelling-house, and to commit a felony therein;

(*b*) being armed as aforesaid by night, and being so armed with intent to break or enter any building whatever, and to commit a felony therein;

(*c*) having in his possession by night without lawful excuse, the proof of which lies on him, any instrument of housebreaking, explosive or petroleum;

(*d*) having in his possession by day any such instrument, explosive or petroleum with intent to commit a felony;

(*e*) having his face masked or blackened or being otherwise disguised with intent to commit a felony;

(*f*) being in any building whatever by night with intent to commit a felony therein;

(*g*) being in any building whatever by day with intent to commit a felony therein, and having taken precautions to conceal his presence;

is guilty of a felony and is liable to imprisonment for three years. If the offender has been previously convicted of a felony relating to property, he is liable to imprisonment for seven years.

(*As amended by No.* 7 *of* 1960)

Persons found armed, etc., with intent to commit felony

306. Any person who-

(*a*) unlawfully enters into or upon any property in the possession of another with intent to commit an offence or to intimidate, insult or annoy any person in possession of such property;

(*b*) having lawfully entered into or upon such property unlawfully remains there with intent thereby to intimidate, insult or annoy any such person or with intent to commit any offence;

is guilty of the misdemeanour termed "criminal trespass" and is liable to imprisonment for three months. If the property upon which the offence is committed is any building, tent or vessel used as a human dwelling or any building used as a place of worship or as a place for the custody of property, the offender is liable to imprisonment for one year.

Criminal trespass

307. When any person is convicted of an offence under this Chapter, the court shall order that any dangerous or offensive weapon or instrument of housebreaking carried or used in connection with any such offence shall be forfeited.

(*As amended by S.I. No.* 63 *of* 1964 *and No.* 5 *of* 1972)

Forfeiture

CHAPTER XXX FALSE PRETENCES

308. Any representation made by words, writing or conduct, of a matter of fact or of law, either past or present, including a representation as to the present intentions of the person making the representation or of any other person, which representation is false in fact, and which the person making it knows to be false or does not believe to be true, is a false pretence.

(*As amended by No.* 5 *of* 1972)

Definition of false pretence

309. Any person who, by any false pretence and with intent to defraud, obtains from any other person anything capable of being stolen, or induces any other person to deliver to any person anything capable of being stolen, is guilty of a misdemeanour and is liable to imprisonment for three years.

Obtaining goods by false pretences

309A. (1) Any person who, by any false pretence, dishonestly obtains for himself or another any pecuniary advantage, is guilty of a misdemeanour and is liable to imprisonment for five years.

Obtaining pecuniary advantage by false pretences

(2) The cases in which a pecuniary advantage within the meaning of this section is to be regarded as obtained for a person are cases where-

(*a*) any debt or charge for which he makes himself liable or is or may become liable (including one not legally enforceable) is reduced or in whole or in part evaded or deferred; or

(*b*) he is allowed to borrow by way of overdraft, or to take out any policy of insurance or annuity contract, or obtains an improvement of the terms on which he is allowed to do so; or

(*c*) he is given the opportunity to earn remuneration or greater remuneration in an office or employment, or to win money by betting.

310. Any person who, by any false pretence and with intent to defraud, induces any person to execute, make, accept, endorse, alter, or destroy the whole or any part of any valuable security, or to write any name or impress or affix any seal upon or to any paper or parchment in order that it may be afterwards made or converted into or used or dealt with as a valuable security, is guilty of a misdemeanour and is liable to imprisonment for three years.

Obtaining execution of a security by false pretences

310A. An intent to deceive exists where one person induces another person-

(*a*) to believe that a thing is true which is false, and which the person practising the deceipt knows or believes to be false; or

(*b*) to believe a thing to be false which is true, and which the person practising the deceipt knows or believes to be true;

and in consequence of having been so induced does or omits to do an act whether or not any injury or loss is thereby suffered by any person.

(*As amended by Act No.* 5 *of* 1972)

Intent to deceive

311. Any person who, by means of any fraudulent trick or device, obtains from any other person anything capable of being stolen or induces any other person to deliver to any person anything capable of being stolen or to pay or deliver to any person any money or goods or any greater sum of money or greater quantity of goods than he would have paid or delivered but for such trick or device, is guilty of a misdemeanour and is liable to imprisonment for three years.

Cheating

312. Any person who-

(*a*) in incurring any debt or liability, obtains credit by any false pretence or by means of any other fraud; or

(*b*) with intent to defraud his creditors or any of them, makes or causes to be made any gift, delivery, or transfer of or any charge on his property; or (*c*) with intent to defraud his creditors or any of them, conceals, sells or removes any part of his property after or within three months before the date of any unsatisfied judgment or order for payment of money obtained against him;

is guilty of a misdemeanour and is liable to imprisonment for one year.

Obtaining credit, etc., by false pretences

313. Any person who conspires with another by deceit or any fraudulent means to affect the market price of anything publicly sold, or to defraud the public, or any person, whether a particular person or not, or to extort any property from any person, is guilty of a misdemeanour and is liable to imprisonment for three years.

Conspiracy to defraud

314. Any person who, being a seller or mortgagor of any property, or being the solicitor or agent of any such seller or mortgagor, with intent to induce the purchaser or mortgagee to accept the title offered or produced to him, and with intent to defraud-

(*a*) conceals from the purchaser or mortgagee any instrument material to the title, or any incumbrance; or

(*b*) falsifies any pedigree on which the title depends or may depend; or

(*c*) makes any false statement as to the title offered or conceals any fact material thereto;

is guilty of a misdemeanour.

Frauds on sale or mortgage of property

315. Any person who for gain or reward undertakes to tell fortunes, or pretends from his skill or knowledge in any occult science to discover where or in what manner anything supposed to have been stolen or lost may be found, is guilty of a misdemeanour.

Pretending to tell fortunes

316. Any person who wilfully procures or attempts to procure for himself or any other person any registration, licence or certificate under any Act by any false pretence, is guilty of a misdemeanour and is liable to imprisonment for one year.

Obtaining registration, etc., by false pretences

317. Any person who makes a statement which is to his know-ledge untrue for the purpose of procuring a passport, whether for himself or for any other person, is guilty of a misdemeanour.

False declaration for passport

CHAPTER XXXI RECEIVING PROPERTY STOLEN OR UNLAWFULLY OBTAINED AND LIKE OFFENCES

318. (1) Any person who receives or retains any chattel, money, valuable security or other property whatsoever, knowing or having reason to believe the same to have been feloniously stolen, taken, extorted, obtained or disposed of, is guilty of a felony and is liable to imprisonment for seven years.

Receiving stolen property, etc.

(2) Any person who received or retains any chattel, money, valuable security or other property whatsoever, knowing or having reason to believe the same to have been unlawfully taken, obtained, converted or disposed of in a manner which constitutes a misdemeanour, is guilty of a misdemeanour and is liable to the same punishment as the offender by whom the property was unlawfully obtained, converted or disposed of.

Receiving property unlawfully obtained

319. Any person who shall be brought before a court charged with-

(*a*) having in his possession anything which may be reasonably suspected of having been stolen or unlawfully obtained; or

(*b*) conveying in any manner anything which may be reasonably suspected of having been stolen or unlawfully obtained;

and who shall not give an account to the satisfaction of such court of how he came by the same, is guilty of a misdemeanour.

(*No.* 22 *of* 1969)

Person suspected of having or conveying stolen property

320. Every person who, without lawful excuse, knowing or having reason to believe the same to have been stolen or obtained in any way whatsoever under such circumstances that if the act had been committed in Zambia the person committing it would have been guilty of felony or misdemeanour, receives or has in his possession any property so stolen or obtained outside Zambia, is guilty of an offence of the like degree (whether felony or misdemeanour) and is liable to imprisonment for seven years.

Receiving goods stolen outside Zambia

CHAPTER XXXII ILLEGAL POSSESSION OF DIAMONDS AND EMERALDS

321. (1) Any person who, without the written permission of the Chief Mining Engineer, has in his possession or disposes of any diamond or emerald shall be guilty of a misdemeanour.

Illegal possession of diamonds or emeralds

(2) For the purposes of this section-

"Chief Mining Engineer" means the person appointed as such in pursuance of section *six* of the Mines and Minerals Act, 1969;

"diamond" means any rough or uncut diamond and includes any diamond which has been partially cut, shaped or polished out of the rough;

"emerald" means any rough or uncut emerald and includes any emerald which has been partially cut, shaped or polished out of the rough.

(3) Any police officer of or above the rank of Sub Inspector may arrest without warrant any person reasonably suspected by him of having committed or of attempting to commit an offence under this section.

322. (1) When a person has been found guilty by a court of an offence under section *three hundred and twenty one* in addition to any other punishment imposed on the accused person, the diamonds or emeralds in respect of which the offence has been committed shall be forfeited to the state upon such finding by the court.

Forfeiture on conviction

(2) Any diamonds or emeralds which have been forfeited under subsection (1) shall be released to the Minister of Finance or such other person as may be authorised by him in writing.

(*As amended by Act No.* 5 *of* 1972)

CHAPTER XXXIII FRAUDS BY TRUSTEES AND PERSONS IN A POSITION OF TRUST, AND FALSE ACCOUNTING

323. (1) Any person who, being a trustee of any property, destroys the property with intent to defraud, or, with intent to defraud, converts the property to any use not authorised by the trust, is guilty of a felony and is liable to imprisonment for seven years.

Trustees fraudulently disposing of trust property

(2) For the purposes of this section, "trustee" includes the following persons and no others, that is to say:

(*a*) trustees upon express trusts created by a deed, will, or instrument in writing, whether for a public or private or charitable purpose;

(*b*) trustees appointed by or under the authority of an Act or Statute for any such purpose;

(*c*) persons upon whom the duties of any such trust as aforesaid devolve;

(*d*) executors and administrators.

324. Any person who-

(*a*) being a director or officer of a corporation or company, receives or possesses himself as such of any of the property of the corporation or company otherwise than in payment of a just debt or demand, and, with intent to defraud, omits either to make a full and true entry thereof in the books and accounts of the corporation or company, or to cause or direct such an entry to be made therein; or

(*b*) being a director, officer, or member of a corporation or company, does any of the following acts with intent to defraud, that is to say:

Directors and officers of corporations or companies fraudulently appropriating property or keeping fraudulent accounts or falsifying books or accounts

(i) destroys, alters, mutilates or falsifies any book, document, valuable security or account, which belongs to the corporation or company, or any entry in any such book, document, or account, or is privy to any such act; or

(ii) makes, or is privy to making, any false entry in any such book, document, or account; or

(iii) omits, or is privy to omitting, any material particular from any such book, document or account;

is guilty of a felony and is liable to imprisonment for seven years.

325. Any person who, being a promoter, director, officer or auditor of a corporation or company, either existing or intended to be formed, makes, circulates or publishes, or concurs in making, circulating, or publishing, any written statement or account which, in any material particular, is to his knowledge false, with intent thereby to effect any of the purposes following, that is to say:

(*a*) to deceive or to defraud any member, shareholder, or creditor of the corporation or company, whether a particular person or not;

(*b*) to induce any person, whether a particular person or not, to become a member of, or to entrust or advance any property to, the corporation or company, or to enter into any security for the benefit thereof;

is guilty of a felony and is liable to imprisonment for seven years.

False statements by officials of companies

326. Any person who, being a clerk or servant, or being employed or acting in the capacity of a clerk or servant, does any of the acts following with intent to defraud, that is to say:

(*a*) destroys, alters, mutilates or falsifies any book, document, valuable security or account, which belongs to or is in the possession of his employer, or has been received by him on account of his employer, or any entry in any such book, document or account, or is privy to any such act; or

(*b*) makes, or is privy to making, any false entry in any such book, document, or account; or

(*c*) omits, or is privy to omitting, any material particular from any such book, document or account;

is guilty of a felony and is liable to imprisonment for seven years.

Fraudulent false accounting

327. Any person who, being an officer charged with the receipt, custody or management of any part of the public revenue or property, knowingly furnishes any false statement or return of any money or property received by him or entrusted to his care, or of any balance of money or property in his possession or under his control, is guilty of a misdemeanour.

DIVISION VI

MALICIOUS INJURIES TO PROPERTY

False accounting by public officer

CHAPTER XXXIV OFFENCES CAUSING INJURY TO PROPERTY

328. Any person who wilfully and unlawfully sets fire to-

(*a*) any building or structure whatever, whether completed or not; or

(*b*) any vessel or any motor vehicle as defined in the Roads and Road Traffic Act, whether completed or not; or

(*c*) any stack of cultivated vegetable produce, or of mineral or vegetable fuel; or

(*d*) a mine, or the workings, fittings, or appliances of a mine;

is guilty of a felony and is liable to imprisonment for life.

(*As amended by No.* 26 *of* 1961)

Arson

329. Any person who-

(*a*) attempts unlawfully to set fire to any such thing as is mentioned in the last preceding section; or

(*b*) wilfully and unlawfully sets fire to anything which is so situated that any such thing as is mentioned in the last preceding section is likely to catch fire from it;

is guilty of a felony and is liable to imprisonment for fourteen years.

Attempts to commit arson

330. Any person who wilfully and unlawfully sets fire to-

(*a*) a crop of cultivated produce, whether standing, picked or cut; or (*b*) a crop of hay or grass under cultivation, whether the natural or indigenous product of the soil or not, and whether standing or cut; or

(*c*) any standing trees, saplings, or shrubs, whether indigenous or not, under cultivation;

is guilty of a felony and is liable to imprisonment for fourteen years.

(*As amended by No.* 26 *of* 1940)

Setting fire to crops and growing plants

331. Any person who-

(*a*) attempts unlawfully to set fire to any such thing as is mentioned in the last preceding section; or

(*b*) wilfully and unlawfully sets fire to anything which is so situated that any such thing as is mentioned in the last preceding section is likely to catch fire from it;

is guilty of a felony and is liable to imprisonment for seven years.

Attempts to set fire to crops, etc.

332. Any person who-

(*a*) wilfully and unlawfully casts away or destroys any vessel, whether completed or not; or

(*b*) wilfully and unlawfully does any act which tends to the immediate loss or destruction of a vessel in distress; or

(*c*) with intent to bring a vessel into danger, interferes with any light, beacon, buoy, mark, or signal used for purposes of navigation, or exhibits any false light or signal;

is guilty of a felony and is liable to imprisonment for life.

(*As amended by No.* 26 *of* 1933)

Casting away vessels

333. Any person who attempts unlawfully to cast away or destroy a vessel, whether completed or not, or attempts unlawfully to do any act tending to the immediate loss or destruction of a vessel in distress, is guilty of a felony and is liable to imprisonment for fourteen years.

(*As amended by No.* 26 *of* 1933)

Attempts to cast away vessels

334. (1) Any person who wilfully and unlawfully kills, maims or wounds any animal capable of being stolen is guilty of an offence.

Injuring animals

(2) If the animal in question is a horse, mare, gelding, ass, mule, camel, bull, cow, ox, goat, pig, ram, ewe, wether, or ostrich, or the young of any such animal, the offender is guilty of a felony and is liable to imprisonment for seven years. In any other case the offender is guilty of a misdemeanour.

335. (1) Any person who wilfully and unlawfully destroys or damages any property is guilty of an offence, which, unless otherwise stated, is a misdemeanour and he is liable, if no other punishment is provided, to imprisonment for two years.

Punishment for malicious injuries in general

(2) If the property in question is a dwelling-house or a vessel, and the injury is caused by the explosion of any explosive substance, and if-

In special cases- destroying or damaging an inhabited house or a vessels with explosives

(*a*) any person is in the dwelling-house or vessel; or

(*b*) the destruction or damage actually endangers the life of any person;

the offender is guilty of a felony and is liable to imprisonment for life.

(3) If the property in question-

River bank or wall, or navigation works, or bridges

(*a*) is a bank or wall of a river, canal, aqueduct, reservoir, or inland water, or work which appertains to a dock, reservoir, or inland water, and the injury causes actual danger of inundation or damage to any land or building; or

(*b*) is a railway or is a bridge, viaduct, or aqueduct which is constructed over a highway, railway, or canal, or over which a railway, highway, or canal passes, and the property is destroyed; or

(*c*) being a railway or being any such bridge, viaduct, or aqueduct, is damaged, and the damage is done with intent to render the railway, bridge, viaduct, or aqueduct, or the highway, or canal passing over or under the same or any part thereof, dangerous or impassable, and the same or any part thereof is thereby rendered dangerous or impassable;

the offender is guilty of a felony and is liable to imprisonment for life.

(4) If the property in question is a testamentary instrument, whether the testator is living or dead, or a register which is authorised or required by law to be kept for authenticating or recording the title to any property or for recording births, baptisms, marriages, deaths, or burials, or a copy of any part of any such register which is required by law to be sent to any public officer, the offender is guilty of a felony and is liable to imprisonment for fourteen years.

Wills and registers

(5) If the property in question is a vessel in distress or wrecked, or stranded, or anything which belongs to such vessel, the offender is guilty of a felony and is liable to imprisonment for seven years.

Wrecks

(6) If the property in question is any part of a railway, or any work connected with a railway, the offender is guilty of a felony and is liable to imprisonment for fourteen years.

Railways

(7) If the property in question-

Other things of special value

(*a*) being a vessel, whether completed or not, is destroyed; or

(*b*) being a vessel, whether completed or not, is damaged, and the damage is done with intent to destroy it or render it useless; or

(*c*) is a light, beacon, buoy, mark, or signal, used for the purposes of navigation, or for the guidance of persons engaged in navigation; or

(*d*) is a bank or wall of a river, canal, aqueduct, reservoir, or inland water, or a work which appertains to a dock, canal, aqueduct, reservoir, or inland water, or which is used for the purposes of lading or unlading goods; or

(*e*) being a railway, or being a bridge, viaduct, or aqueduct which is constructed over a highway, railway, or canal, or over which a highway, railway, or canal passes, is damaged, and the damage is done with intent to render the railway, bridge, viaduct, or aqueduct, or the highway, railway, or canal passing over or under the same, or any part thereof, dangerous or impassable; or

(*f*) being anything in process of manufacture, or an agricultural or manufacturing machine, or a manufacturing implement, or a machine or appliance used or intended to be used for performing any process connected with the preparation of any agricultural or pastoral produce, is destroyed; or

(*g*) being any such thing, machine, implement, or appliance, as last aforesaid, is damaged, and the damage is done with intent to destroy the thing in question or to render it useless; or

(*h*) is a shaft or a passage of a mine, and the injury is done with intent to damage the mine or to obstruct its working; or

(*i*) is a machine, appliance, apparatus, building, erection, bridge, or road, appertaining to or used with a mine, whether the thing in question is completed or not; or

(*j*) being a rope, chain, or tackle, of whatever material, which is used in a mine, or upon any way or work appertaining to or used with a mine, is destroyed; or

(*k*) being any such rope, chain, or tackle, as last aforesaid, is damaged, and the damage is done with intent to destroy the thing in question or to render it useless; or (*l*) is a well, or bore for water, or the dam, bank, wall, or floodgate of a millpond or pool;

the offender is guilty of a felony and is liable to imprisonment for seven years.

(8) If the property in question is a document which is deposited or kept in a public office, or which is evidence of title to any land or estate in land, the offender is guilty of a felony and is liable to imprisonment for seven years.

(*As amended by No.* 26 *of* 1933)

Deeds and records

336. Any person who, unlawfully and with intent to destroy or damage any property, puts any explosive substance in any place whatever, is guilty of a felony and is liable to imprisonment for fourteen years.

Attempts to destroy property by explosives

337. Any person who wilfully and unlawfully causes, or is concerned in causing, or attempts to cause, any infectious disease to be communicated to or among any animal or animals capable of being stolen, is guilty of a felony and is liable to imprisonment for seven years.

Communi-cating infectious diseases to animals

338. Any person who wilfully and unlawfully, and with intent to defraud, removes or defaces any object or mark which has been lawfully erected or made as an indication of the boundary of any land, is guilty of a felony and is liable to imprisonment for three years.

Removing boundary marks with intent to defraud

339. Any person who-

(*a*) wilfully removes, defaces or injuries any survey mark or boundary mark which shall have been made or erected by or under the direction of any Government department or in the course of or for the purposes of a Government survey; or

(*b*) being under an obligation to maintain in repair any boundary mark made or erected as aforesaid, neglects or refuses to repair the same; or

(*c*) wilfully removes, defaces or injures any mark erected by an intending applicant for any lease, licence or right under an Act relating to mines or minerals;

is guilty of a misdemeanour and is liable to imprisonment for three months or to a fine of six hundred penalty units, and may further be ordered by the court to pay the cost of repairing or replacing the survey mark or boundary mark and of making any survey rendered necessary by the offender's act or neglect.

(*As amended by No.* 13 *of* 1994)

Wilful damage, etc., to survey and boundary marks

340. Any person who-

(*a*) wilfully damages, injuries, or obstructs any work, way, road, building, turnstile, gate, toll bar, fence, weighing machine, engine, tender, carriage, wagon, truck, material or plant, acquired for or belonging to any railway works; or

(*b*) pulls up, removes, defaces, or destroys, or in any way interferes with, any poles, stakes, flags, pegs, lines, marks, or anything driven or placed in or upon the ground, trees, stones, or buildings, or any other material, belonging to any railway works; or

(*c*) commits any nuisance or trespass in or upon any land, buildings, or premises, acquired for or belonging to any railway works; or

(*d*) wilfully molests, hinders, or obstructs the officer in charge of any railway or his assistants or workmen in the execution of any work done or to be done in reference to the construction or maintenance of any such railway;

is guilty of a misdemeanour and is liable to imprisonment for three months or to a fine of six hundred penalty units.

(*As amended by No.* 13 *of* 1994)

Penalties for damage, etc., to railway works

341. Any person who, knowing the contents thereof, sends, delivers, utters or directly or indirectly causes to be received any letter or writing threatening to burn or destroy any house, barn, or other building, or any rick or stack of grain, hay, or straw, or other agricultural produce, whether in or under any building or not, or any vessel, or to kill, maim, or wound any cattle, is guilty of a felony and is liable to imprisonment for ten years.

Threats to burn or destroy

DIVISION VII FORGERY, COINING, COUNTERFEITING AND SIMILAR OFFENCES

CHAPTER XXXV DEFINITIONS

342. Forgery is the making of a false document with intent to defraud or to deceive.

(*As amended by No.* 26 *of* 1940)

Definition of forgery

343. In this Division, "document" does not include a trade mark or any other sign used in connection with articles of commerce though they may be written or printed.

Definition of document

344. Any person makes a false document who-

(*a*) makes a document purporting to be what in fact it is not;

(*b*) alters a document without authority in such a manner that if the alteration had been authorised it would have altered the effect of the document;

(*c*) introduces into a document without authority whilst it is being drawn up matter which if it had been authorised would have altered the effect of the document;

(*d*) signs a document-

Making a false document

(i) in the name of any person without his authority whether such name is or is not the same as that of the person signing;

(ii) in the name of any fictitious person alleged to exist, whether the fictitious person is or is not alleged to be of the same name as the person signing;

(iii) in the name represented as being the name of a different person from that of the person signing it and intended to be mistaken for the name of that person;

(iv) in the name of a person personated by the person signing the document, provided that the effect of the instrument depends upon the identity between the person signing the document and the person whom he professes to be.

344A. An intent to deceive exists where one person induces another person-

(*a*) to believe that a thing is true which is false, and which the person practising the deceit knows or believes to be false; or

(*b*) to believe a thing to be false which is true, and which the person practising the deceit knows or believes to be true;

and in consequence of having been so induced does or omits to do an act whether or not any injury or loss is thereby suffered by any person.

Intent to deceive

345. An intent to defraud is presumed to exist if it appears that, at the time when the false document was made, there was in existence a specific person ascertained or unascertained capable of being defrauded thereby, and this presumption is not rebutted by proof that the offender took or intended to take measures to prevent such person from being defrauded in fact, nor by the fact that he had or thought he had a right to the thing to be obtained by the false document.

Intent to defraud

CHAPTER XXXVI PUNISHMENTS FOR FORGERY

346. In this Chapter, "currency notes" includes any notes (by whatever name called) which are legal tender in the country in which they are issued.

Definition of currency notes

347. Any person who forges any document is guilty of an offence which, unless otherwise stated, is a felony and he is liable, unless owing to the circumstances of the forgery or the nature of the thing forged some other punishment is provided, to imprisonment for three years.

General punishment for forgery

348. Any person who forges any will, document of title to land, judicial record, power of attorney, bank note, currency note, bill of exchange, promissory note or other negotiable instrument, policy of insurance, cheque or other authority for the payment of money by a person carrying on business as a banker, is liable to imprisonment for life and the court may in addition order that any such document as aforesaid shall be forfeited.

(*As amended by S.I. No.*63 *of* 1964)

Forgeries punishable by imprisonment for life

349. Any person who forges any judicial or official document is liable to imprisonment for seven years.

Forgery of judicial or official document

350. Any person who-

(*a*) forges any stamp, whether impressed or adhesive, used for the purpose of revenue or accounting by any Government department; or

(*b*) without lawful excuse, the proof whereof shall lie upon him, makes or has knowingly in his possession any die or instrument capable of making the impression of any such stamp; or

(*c*) fraudulently cuts, tears in any way, or removes from any material any stamp used for purposes of revenue or accounting by the Government, with intent that another use shall be made of such stamp or any part thereof; or

(*d*) fraudulently mutilates any such stamp as last aforesaid, with intent that another use shall be made of such stamp; or

(*e*) fraudulently fixes or places upon any material or upon any such stamp as last aforesaid any stamp or part of a stamp which, whether fraudulently or not, has been cut, torn, or in any way removed from any other material or out of or from any other stamp; or

(*f*) fraudulently erases or otherwise either really or apparently removes from any stamped material any name, sum, date, or other matter or thing whatsoever written thereon with the intent that another use shall be made of the stamp upon such material; or (*g*) knowingly and without lawful excuse, the proof whereof shall lie upon him, has in his possession any stamp or part of a stamp which has been fraudulently cut, torn, or otherwise removed from any material, or any stamp which has been fradulently mutilated, or any stamped material out of which any name, sum, date, or other matter or thing has been fradulently erased or otherwise really or apparently removed;

is liable to imprisonment for seven years.

Forgeries punishable by imprisonment for seven years

351. Any person who, without lawful authority or excuse, the proof whereof lies upon him-

(*a*) makes, uses, or knowingly has in his custody or possession any paper intended to resemble and pass as special paper such as is provided and used for making any currency note or bank note;

(*b*) makes, uses, or knowingly has in his custody or possession, any frame, mould or instrument for making such paper, or for producing in or on such paper any words, figures, letters, marks, lines or devices peculiar to and used in or on any such paper;

(*c*) engraves or in any wise makes upon any plate, wood, stone, or other material, any words, figures, letters, marks, lines or devices, the print whereof resembles in whole or in part any words, figures, letters, marks, lines or devices peculiar to and used in or on any bank note, or in or on any document entitling or evidencing the title of any person to any share or interest in any public stock, annuity, fund, or debt of the Republic or of any foreign state, or in any stock, annuity, fund or debt of any body corporate, company or society, whether within or without the Republic;

(*d*) uses or knowingly has in his custody or possession any plate, wood, stone, or other material, upon which any such words, figures, letters, marks, lines, or devices have been engraved or in any wise made as aforesaid; or

(*e*) uses or knowingly has in his custody or possession, any paper upon which any such words, figures, letters, marks, lines or devices have been printed or in any wise made as aforesaid;

is guilty of a felony and is liable to imprisonment for seven years.

(*No.* 48 *of* 1938 *as amended by S.I. No.* 63 *of* 1964)

Making or having in possession paper or implements for forgery

352. Any person who knowingly and fraudulently utters a false document is guilty of an offence of the same kind, and is liable to the same punishment, as if he had forged the thing in question.

Uttering false documents

353. Any person who knowingly utters as and for a subsisting and effectual document, any document which has by any lawful authority been ordered to be revoked, cancelled, or suspended, or the operation of which has ceased by effluxion of time, or by death, or

by the happening of any other event, is guilty of an offence of the same kind, and is liable to the same punishment, as if he had forged the document.

Uttering cancelled or exhausted documents

354. Any person who, by means of any false and fraudulent representations as to the nature, contents or operation of a document, procures another to sign or execute the document, is guilty of an offence of the same kind, and is liable to the same punishment, as if he had forged the document.

Procuring execution of documents by false pretences

355. Any person who, with intent to defraud-

(*a*) obliterates, adds to, or alters the crossing on a cheque; or

(*b*) knowingly utters a crossed cheque, the crossing on which has been obliterated, added to, or altered;

is guilty of a felony and is liable to imprisonment for seven years.

Obliterating crossings on cheques

356. Any person who, with intent to defraud or to deceive-

(*a*) without lawful authority or excuse, makes, signs, or executes, for or in the name or on account of another person, whether by procuration or otherwise, any document or writing; or

(*b*) knowingly utters any document or writing so made, signed, or executed by another person;

is guilty of a felony and is liable to imprisonment for seven years.

(*As amended by No.* 26 *of* 1940)

Making documents without authority

357. Any person who procures the delivery or payment to himself or any other person of any property or money by virtue of any probate or letters of administration granted upon a forged testamentary instrument, knowing the testamentary instrument to have been forged, or upon or by virtue of any probate or letters of administration obtained by false evidence, knowing the grant to have been so obtained, is guilty of an offence of the same kind, and is liable to the same punishment, as if he had forged the document or thing by virtue whereof he procures the delivery or payment.

Demanding property upon forged testamentary instrument

358. Any person who, without lawful authority or excuse, the proof of which lies on him, purchases or receives from any person, or has in his possession a forged bank note or currency note, whether filled up or in blank, knowing it to be forged, is guilty of a felony and is liable to imprisonment for seven years.

Purchasing forged notes

359. Any person who, being employed in the public service, knowingly and with intent to defraud makes out or delivers to any person a warrant for the payment of any money payable by public authority, for a greater or less amount than that to which the person on whose behalf the warrant is made out is entitled, is guilty of a felony and is liable to imprisonment for seven years.

Falsifying warrants for money payable under public authority

360. Any person who, having the actual custody of any register or record kept by lawful authority, knowingly permits any entry which in any material particular is to his knowledge false, to be made in the register or record, is guilty of a felony and is liable to imprisonment for seven years.

Falsification of register

361. Any person who signs or transmits to a person authorised by law to register marriages, a certificate of marriage, or any document purporting to be a certificate of marriage, which in any material particular is to his knowledge false, is guilty of a felony and is liable to imprisonment for seven years.

Sending false certificate of marriage to registrar

362. Any person who, knowingly and with intent to procure the same to be inserted in a register of births, deaths, or marriages, mato any false statement touching any matter required by law to be registered in any such register, is guilty of a felony and is liable to imprisonment for three years.

False statements for registers of births, deaths and marriages

CHAPTER XXXVII OFFENCES RELATING TO COIN

363. In this Chapter-

Definitions of counterfeit coin and current coin

"counterfeit coin" means coin not genuine but resembling or apparently intended to resemble or pass for genuine current coin; and includes genuine current coin prepared or altered so as to pass for current coin of a higher denomination;

"current", applied to any coin, includes any coin coined in Zambia or lawfully current in Zambia or any coin lawfully current in any foreign country.

(*No.* 48 *of* 1938 *as amended by S.I. No.* 63 *of* 1964)

364. Any person who makes or begins to make any counterfeit coin is guilty of a felony and is liable to imprisonment for life.

(*As amended by No.* 48 *of* 1938)

Counterfeiting coin

365. Any person who-

(*a*) gilds or silvers any piece of metal of a fit size or figure to be coined, with intent that it shall be coined into counterfeit coin; or

(*b*) makes any piece of metal into a fit size or figure to facilitate the coining from it of any counterfeit coin, with intent that such counterfeit coin shall be made from it; or

(*c*) without lawful authority or excuse, the proof of which lies on him-

Preparations for coining

(i) buys, sells, receives, pays, or disposes of any counterfeit coin at a lower rate than it imports or is apparently intended to import, or offers to do any such thing; or

(ii) brings or receives into Zambia any counterfeit coin, knowing it to be counterfeit; or

(iii) makes or mends, or begins or prepares to make or mend, or has in his possession, or disposes of any stamp or mould which is adapted to make the resemblance of both or either of the sides of any coin, or any part of either side thereof, knowing the same to be a stamp or mould or to be so adapted; or

(iv) makes or mends, or begins or prepares to make or mend, or has in his possession, or disposes of any tool, instrument or machine which is adapted and intended to be used for marking coin round the edges with marks or figures apparently resembling those on the edges of any coin, knowing the same to be so adapted and intended; or

(v) makes or mends, or begins or prepares to make or mend, or has in his possession, or disposes of any press for coinage, or any tool, instrument, or machine which is adapted for cutting round blanks out of gold, silver, or other metal, knowing such press, tool, instrument, or machine to have been used or to be intended to be used for making any counterfeit coin;

is guilty of a felony and is liable to imprisonment for life.

(*As amended by No.* 48 *of* 1938)

366. Any person who deals with any current coin in such a manner as to diminish its weight, with intent that when so dealt with it may pass as current coin is guilty of a felony and is liable to imprisonment for seven years.

(*As amended by No.* 48 *of* 1938)

Clipping

367. Any person who melts down, breaks up, defaces by stamping thereon any name, word or mark, or uses otherwise than as currency, any silver coin current for the time being in Zambia, is guilty of a misdemeanour and is liable to imprisonment for six months or to a fine not exceeding three thousand penalty units, or to both.

(*As amended by Act No.* 26 *of* 1940 *and No.* 13 *of* 1994)

Melting down of currency

368. Any person who unlawfully has in his possession, or disposes of any filings, or clippings of gold or silver, or any gold or silver in bullion, dust, solution, or any other state, obtained by dealing with current gold or silver coin in such a manner as to diminish its weight, knowing the same to have been so obtained, is guilty of a felony and is liable to imprisonment for seven years.

Possession of clippings

369. Any person who utters any counterfeit coin, knowing it to be counterfeit, is guilty of a misdemeanour.

(*As amended by No.* 48 *of* 1938)

Uttering counterfeit coin

370. Any person who-

(*a*) utters any counterfeit coin, knowing it to be counterfeit, and at the time of such uttering has in his possession any other counterfeit coin; or

(*b*) utters any counterfeit coin, knowing it to be counterfeit, and either on the same day or on any of the ten days next ensuing, utters any other counterfeit coin, knowing it to be counterfeit; or

(*c*) has in his possession three or more pieces of counterfeit coin, knowing them to be counterfeit, and with intent to utter any of them;

is guilty of a felony and is liable to imprisonment for three years.

(*As amended by No.* 48 *of* 1938)

Repeated uttering

371. Any person who, with intent to defraud, utters as and for current coin-

(*a*) any coin which is not such current coin; or

(*b*) any medal or piece of metal, whether a coin or not, which is of less value than the current coin as and for which it is uttered;

is guilty of a misdemeanour and is liable to imprisonment for one year.

(*As amended by No.* 48 *of* 1938)

Uttering foreign coin or metal as current coin

372. Any person who, without lawful authority or excuse, the proof of which lies on him, exports or puts on board of a vessel or vehicle of any kind for the purpose of being exported from Zambia, any counterfeit coin whatever, knowing it to be counterfeit, is guilty of a felony and is liable to imprisonment for fourteen years.

(*As amended by No.* 48 *of* 1938)

Exporting counterfeit coin

373. When any person is convicted of an offence under this Chapter, or Chapter XXXVI, the court shall order the forfeiture of any forged bank note or currency note or of any counterfeit coin, or any stamp, mould, tool, instrument, machine, press, or any coin, bullion or metal used or employed in the commission of any such offence.

(*As amended by No.* 48 *of* 1938 *and S.I. No.* 63 *of* 1964)

Forfeiture

XXXVIII COUNTERFEIT STAMPS

374. Any person who, without lawful authority or excuse, the proof of which lies on him-

(*a*) makes or mends, or begins or prepares to make or mend, or uses, or knowingly has in his possession, or disposes of any die, plate, or instrument capable of making an impression resembling that made by any die, plate or instrument used for the purpose of making any stamp, whether impressed or adhesive, which is used for the purposes of the public revenue or of the postal administration in Zambia, or in any foreign country, or capable of producing in or on paper any words, figures, letters, marks or lines resembling any words, figures, letters, marks, or lines used in or on any paper specially provided by the proper authority for any such purpose; or

(*b*) knowingly has in his possession or disposes of any paper or other material which has on it the impression of any such die, plate, or instrument, or any paper which has on it or in it any such words, figures, letters, marks or lines as aforesaid; or

(*c*) fraudulently, and with intent that use may be made of any such stamp as aforesaid, or of any part of it, removes the stamp from any material in any way whatever; or

(*d*) fraudulently, and with intent that use may be made of any part of such stamp, mutilates the stamp; or

(*e*) fraudulently fixes or places upon any material or upon any such stamp, any stamp or part of a stamp which has been in any way removed from any other material, or out of or from any other stamp; or

(*f*) fraudulently, and with intent that use may be made of any such stamp which has been already impressed upon or attached to any material, erases or otherwise removes, either really or apparently, from such material anything whatever written on it; or

(*g*) knowingly has in his possession or disposes of anything ob-tained or prepared by any such unlawful act as aforesaid; or

(*h*) fraudulently or with intent to cause loss to the public revenue, uses for any purpose a stamp issued by Government for the purposes of revenue which he knows to have been previously used;

is guilty of a felony and is liable to imprisonment for seven years, and any die, plate, instrument, paper or other thing as aforesaid which is found in his possession shall be forfeited.

(*As amended by No.* 26 *of* 1940, *G.N. No.* 303 *of* 1964
and S.I. No. 63 *of* 1964)

Possession of die used for purpose of making stamps

375. (1) Any person who, without lawful authority or excuse, the proof of which lies on him-

Paper and dies for postage stamps

(*a*) makes, or begins or prepares to make, or uses for any postal purpose, or has in his possession, or disposes of any imitation or representation on paper or any other material, of any stamp used for denoting any rate of postage of the Republic, or of any foreign country; or

(*b*) makes or mends, or begins or prepares to make or mend, or uses, or has in his possession or disposes of any die, plate, instrument, or material for making any such imitation or representation;

is guilty of a misdemeanour, and is liable to imprisonment for one year, or to a fine of one thousand and five hundred penalty units, and any stamps and any other such things as aforesaid, which are found in his possession, shall be forfeited.

(2) For the purposes of this section, a stamp purporting to denote a rate of postage of any country is to be taken to be a stamp used for postal purposes in that country until the contrary is shown.

(*As amended by S.I. No.* 63 *of* 1964 *and Act No.* 13 *of* 1994)

CHAPTER XXXIX COUNTERFEITING TRADE MARKS

376. A trade mark is-

(*a*) a mark lawfully used by any person to denote any chattel to be an article or thing of the manufacture, workmanship, production, or merchandise of such person or to be an article or thing of any peculiar or particular description made or sold by such person;

(*b*) any mark or sign which in pursuance of any written law in force for the time being relating to registered designs is to be put or placed upon or attached to any chattel or article during the existence or continuance of any copyright or other sole right acquired under the provision of such law.

Definition of trade mark

377. (1) Any person who does any of the following things with intent to defraud or to enable another to defraud any person, that is to say:

Counterfeiting trade marks a misdemeanour

(*a*) forges or counterfeits any trade mark;

(*b*) applies any trade mark or any forged or counterfeited trade mark to any chattel or article not being the merchandise of any person whose trade mark is so forged or counterfeited;

(*c*) applies any trade mark or any forged or counterfeited trade mark to any chattel or article not being the particular or peculiar description of merchandise denoted or intended to be denoted by such trade mark or by such forged or counterfeited trade mark;

(*d*) applies any trade mark or any forged or counterfeited trade mark to any thing intended for any purpose of trade or manufacture, or in, on, or with which any chattel or article is intended to be sold, or is sold or offered or exposed for sale;

(*e*) encloses or places any chattel or article in, upon, under, or with anything to which any trade mark has been falsely applied, or to which any forged or counterfeit trade mark has been applied;

(*f*) applies or attaches any chattel or article to any case, cover, reel, ticket, label, or other thing to which any trade mark has been falsely applied, or to which any false or counterfeit trade mark has been applied;

(*g*) encloses, places, or attaches any chattel or article in, upon, under, with, or to any thing having thereon any trade mark of any other person;

is guilty of a misdemeanour.

(2) Every person committing any such misdemeanour as mentioned in subsection (1) shall forfeit-

(*a*) all chattels and articles to which any such trade mark or counterfeit trade mark is applied or caused or procured to be applied;

(*b*) every instrument for applying any such trade mark or counterfeit trade mark in his possession or power;

(*c*) the chattels and articles and the things mentioned in paragraphs (*d*), (*e*) and (*g*) of subsection (1), and all similar things made to be used in like manner in his possession or power.

(*As amended by S.I. No.* 63 *of* 1964)

CHAPTER XL PERSONATION

378. (1) Any person who, with intent to defraud any person, falsely represents himself to be some other person, living or dead, is guilty of a misdemeanour.

Personation in general

(2) If the representation is that the offender is a person entitled by will or operation of law to any specific property and he commits the offence to obtain such property or possession thereof, he is liable to imprisonment for seven years.

379. Any person who, without lawful authority or excuse, the proof of which lies on him, makes in the name of any other person, before any court or person lawfully authorised to take such an acknowledgment, an acknowledgment of liability of any kind, or an acknowledgment of a deed or other instrument, is guilty of a misdemeanour.

Falsely acknowledging deeds, recognizances, etc.

380. Any person who utters any document which has been issued by lawful authority to another person, and whereby that other person is certified to be a person possessed of any qualification recognised by law for any purpose, or to be the holder of any office, or to be entitled to exercise any profession, trade or business, or to be entitled to any right or privilege, or to enjoy any rank or status, and falsely represents himself to be the person named in the document, is guilty of an offence of the same kind and is liable to the same punishment as if he had forged the document.

Personation of person named in certificate

381. Any person who, being a person to whom any document has been issued by lawful authority whereby he is certified to be a person possessed of any qualification recognised by law for any purpose, or to be the holder of any office, or to be entitled to exercise any profession, trade or business, or to be entitled to any right or privilege, or to enjoy any rank or status, sells, gives, or lends the document to another person with intent that that other may represent himself to be the person named therein, is guilty of a misdemeanour.

Lending, etc., certificate for personation

382. Any person who, for the purpose of obtaining any employment, utters any document of the nature of a testimonial of character given to another person, is guilty of a misdemeanour and is liable to imprisonment for one year.

Personation of person named in testimonial of character

383. Any person who, being a person to whom any such document as is mentioned in the last preceding section has been given, gives, sells, or lends such document to another person with the intent that that other person may utter such document for the purpose of obtaining any employment, is guilty of a misdemeanour.

DIVISION VIII

Lending, etc., testimonial for personation

CHAPTER XLI 384. Repealed by Act 14 of 1980.

385. Repealed by Act 14 of 1980.

386. Repealed by Act 14 of 1980.

387. Repealed by Act 14 of 1980.

388. Repealed by Act 14 of 1980.

DIVISION IX ATTEMPTS AND CONSPIRACIES TO COMMIT CRIMES, AND ACCESSORIES AFTER THE FACT

CHAPTER XLII ATTEMPTS

389. (1) When a person, intending to commit an offence, begins to put his intention into execution by means adapted to its fulfilment, and manifests his intention by some overt act, but does not fulfil his intention to such an extent as to commit the offence, he is deemed to attempt to commit the offence.

Definition of attempt

(2) It is immaterial, except so far as regards punishment, whether the offender does all that is necessary on his part for completing the commission of the offence, or whether the complete fulfilment of his intention is prevented by circumstances independent of his will, or whether he desists of his own motion from the further prosecution of his intention.

(3) It is immaterial that by reason of circumstances not known to the offender it is impossible in fact to commit the offence.

390. Any person who attempts to commit a felony or misdemeanour is guilty of an offence which, unless otherwise stated, is a misdemeanour.

Attempts to commit offences

391. Any person who attempts to commit a felony of such a kind that a person convicted of it is liable to the punishment of death or imprisonment for a term of fourteen years or upwards, with or without other punishment, is guilty of a felony and is liable, if no other punishment is provided, to imprisonment for seven years.

Punishment of attempts to commit certain felonies

392. (1) Any person who attempts to procure another to do an act or make an omission of such a nature that if he himself were to do the act or make the omission he would be guilty of an offence, is himself to be deemed guilty of attempting to commit such offence and to be punishable accordingly.

Attempts to procure commission of criminal acts

(2) Any person who, while in Zambia, attempts to procure another to do an act or make an omission at a place not in Zambia of such a nature-

(*a*) that if he were himself to do the act or make the omission in Zambia he would be guilty of an offence; and

(*b*) that if he were himself to do the act or make the omission at the place where the act or omission is proposed to be done or made he would himself be guilty of an offence under the laws in force at that place;

is guilty of an offence of the same kind and is liable to the same punishment as if he were himself to attempt to do the same act or make the same omission in Zambia.

(*No.* 28 *of* 1931)

393. Every person who, knowing that a person designs to commit or is committing a felony, fails to use all reasonable means to prevent the commission or completion thereof, is guilty of a misdemeanour.

Neglect to prevent commission of a felony

CHAPTER XLIII CONSPIRACIES

394. Any person who conspires with another to commit any felony, or to do any act in any part of the world which if done in Zambia would be a felony, and which is an offence under the laws in force in the place where it is proposed to be done, is guilty of a felony and is liable, if no other punishment is provided, to imprisonment for seven years, or, if the greatest punishment to which a person convicted of the felony in question is liable is less than imprisonment for seven years, then to such lesser punishment.

Conspiracy to commit felony

395. Any person who conspires with another to commit a misdemeanour, or to do any act in any part of the world which if done in Zambia would be a misdemeanour, and which is an offence under the laws in force in the place where it is proposed to be done, is guilty of a misdemeanour.

Conspiracy to commit misdemeanour

396. Any person who conspires with another to effect any of the purposes following, that is to say:

(*a*) to prevent or defeat the execution or enforcement of any Act, Statute, or Order; or

(*b*) to cause any injury to the person or reputation of any person, or to depreciate the value of any property of any person; or

(*c*) to prevent or obstruct the free and lawful disposition of any property by the owner thereof for its fair value; or

(*d*) to injure any person in his trade or profession; or

(*c*) to prevent or obstruct, by means of any act or acts which if done by an individual person would constitute an offence on his part, the free and lawful exercise by any person of his trade, profession, or occupation; or

(*f*) to effect any unlawful purpose; or

(*g*) to effect any lawful purpose by any unlawful means;

is guilty of a misdemeanour:

Other conspiracies

Provided that an agreement or combination by two or more persons to do or procure to be done any act in contemplation or furtherance of a trade dispute, as defined in the Industrial and Labour Relations Act, shall not be punishable under the provisions of this section if such act committed by one person would not be punishable as a crime.

(*As amended by No.* 1 *of* 1952 *and No.* 7 *of* 1958)

CHAPTER XLIV ACCESSORIES AFTER THE FACT

397. (1) Any person who receives or assists another who is, to his knowledge, guilty of an offence, in order to enable him to escape punishment, is said to become an accessory after the fact to the offence.

Definition of accessories after the fact

(2) A wife does not become an accessory after the fact to an offence of which her husband is guilty by receiving or assisting him in order to enable him to escape punishment; or by receiving or assisting, in her husband's presence and by his authority, another person who is guilty of an offence in the commission of which her husband has taken part, in order to enable that other person to escape punishment; nor does a husband become accessory after the fact to an offence of which his wife is guilty by receiving or assisting her in order to enable her to escape punishment.

398. Any person who becomes an accessory after the fact to a felony is guilty of a felony, and is liable, if no other punishment is provided, to imprisonment for three years.

Punishment of accessories after the fact to felonies

399. Any person who becomes an accessory after the fact to a misdemeanour is guilty of a misdemeanour.

Punishment of accessories after the fact to misdemeanours

BUSINESS TRAVEL

US STATE DEPARTMENT SUGGESTIONS

COUNTRY DESCRIPTION: Zambia is a developing southern African country. Tourist facilities outside of well-known game parks are not fully developed. The capital is Lusaka.

ENTRY/EXIT REQUIREMENTS: A passport and visa are required. A visa should be obtained in advance. American citizens arriving for tourism or business at Lusaka International Airport or major land borders, can obtain a one-entry visa for 25 dollars (US) or a multiple entry visa for 80 dollars (US). Long-term visitors or persons coming for employment may also obtain a visa at the border. All Americans who are not residents of Zambia must pay an airport departure tax of 20 dollars (US).

In an effort to prevent international child abduction, many governments have initiated procedures at entry/exit points. These often include requiring documentary evidence of relationship and permission for the child's travel from the parent(s) or legal guardian not present. Having such documentation on hand, even if not required, may facilitate entry/departure.

SAFETY AND SECURITY: U.S. citizens are advised to avoid all travel in Zambia's Northern Luapula Province, including the entire Lake Mweru lakefront, and in directly adjacent areas in the northern province near the border with the Democratic Republic of Congo (DRC) due to instability in the area. In December 2000, military action near the DRC town of Pweto caused armed combatants and refugees to flood into northeastern Zambia. Armed gunman occasionally attack vehicles near the DRC-Zambian border.

U.S. Government personnel are restricted from traveling to the northeast Zambian border region, and from using the Pedicle Road, which traverses the southeast portion of DRC between Mufulira in Copperbelt Province and Mansa in Luapula Province unless they have received prior permission to travel to those areas.

Large numbers of travelers visit tourist destinations, including South Luangwa National Park and Victoria Falls, without incident. However, in 1998, armed gunmen attacked cars traveling on the Lusaka-Mongu Road in the immediate vicinity of the Kafue National Park. American citizens are advised defer any unnecessary travel to the region along the western border with Angola, where conditions remain unsettled as a result of periodic cross-border military activity. Armed gunman occasionally attack traffic near the western border with Angola, and, in the past, bombs have fallen into Zambian territory.

Land mines in the Gwembe Valley near Sinazongwe (along the southwest end of Lake Kariba on the Livingstone to Siavonga Road) make travel to that area potentially hazardous. U.S. citizens are advised not to travel on this road and not to drive off established roads in this area.

U.S. citizens should avoid political rallies and street demonstrations and maintain security awareness at all times.

CRIME: Crime in Zambia is widespread. Armed carjackings, muggings and petty theft are commonplace in Lusaka and other major cities, especially in downtown commercial districts and housing compounds. Carjackers target four-wheel drive vehicles, but anyone who does not practice sound security procedures may be targeted. Thieves steal possessions from automobiles and public transport vehicles stopped in traffic. Lock car doors and roll up windows at all times. Travel at night is particularly risky, both in Lusaka and on roads outside of the city.

The loss or theft abroad of a U.S. passport should be reported immediately to local police and to the nearest U.S. Embassy or Consulate. The pamphlets *A Safe Trip Abroad* and *Tips for Travelers to Sub-Saharan Africa* provide useful information on protecting personal security while traveling abroad and on travel in the region in general. Both are available from the Superintendent of Documents, U.S. Government Printing Office, Washington, D.C. 20402, via the Internet at http://www.access.gpo.gov/su_docs, or via the Bureau of Consular Affairs home page at http://travel.state.gov/.

MEDICAL FACILITIES: Government hospitals and clinics are often understaffed and lack supplies. Private medical clinics in major cities can provide reasonable care in many cases, but major medical emergencies usually require medical evacuation to South Africa or the U.S. Basic medical care outside of major cities is extremely limited. Doctors and hospitals often expect immediate cash payment for health services.

MEDICAL INSURANCE: The Department of State strongly urges Americans to consult with their medical insurance company prior to traveling abroad to confirm whether their policy applies overseas and whether it will cover emergency expenses such as medical evacuation. U.S. medical insurance plans seldom cover health costs incurred outside the United States unless supplemental coverage is purchased. Further, U.S. Medicare and Medicaid programs do not provide payment for medical services outside the United States. However, many travel agents and private companies offer insurance plans that will cover health care expenses incurred overseas including emergency services such as medical evacuations.

When making a decision regarding health insurance, Americans should consider that many foreign doctors and hospitals require payment in cash prior to providing service and that a medical evacuation to the U.S. may cost well in excess of 50,000 dollars (US). Uninsured travelers who require medical care overseas often face extreme difficulties, whereas travelers who have purchased overseas medical insurance have, when a medical emergency occurs, found it life-saving. When consulting with your insurer prior to your trip, ascertain whether payment will be made to the overseas healthcare provider or whether you will be reimbursed later for expenses you incur. Some insurance policies also include coverage for psychiatric treatment and for disposition of remains in the event of death.

Useful information on medical emergencies abroad, including overseas insurance programs, is provided in the Department of State's Bureau of Consular Affairs brochure *Medical Information for Americans Traveling Abroad*, available via the Bureau of Consular Affairs home page or autofax: (202) 647-3000.

OTHER HEALTH INFORMATION: Information on vaccinations and other health precautions may be obtained from the Centers for Disease Control and Prevention's hotline for international travelers at 1-877-FYI-TRIP (1-877-394-8747); fax 1-888-CDC-FAXX (1-888-232-3299), or via the CDC's Internet site at http://www.cdc.gov/.

TRAFFIC SAFETY AND ROAD CONDITIONS: While in a foreign country, U.S. citizens may encounter road conditions that differ significantly from those in the United States. The information below concerning Zambia is provided for general reference only, and may not be totally accurate in a particular location or circumstance.

Safety of Public Transportation: Poor
Urban Road Conditions/Maintenance: Fair
Rural Road Conditions/Maintenance: Poor
Availability of Roadside Assistance: Poor

Driving on Zambian roads can be hazardous. Since most roads do not have shoulders or sidewalks, pedestrians and livestock use the roadways both day and night. While the main roads in Lusaka are maintained, many secondary roads are in poor repair. Driving at night can be hazardous and is discouraged. Mini-buses and cars break down often. When breakdowns occur, local drivers place a few branches behind the car to indicate trouble, but this is hardly visible at night. Many drivers use their high beams at night to detect stopped vehicles and pedestrians.

There are no emergency services for stranded drivers. It is advisable to have a cell phone when undertaking a trip outside of town, although many parts of the country do not yet have cell phone service. During the rainy season (end of October to mid-March), travelers who do not have a four-wheel drive vehicle will encounter problems driving on rural roads. The stretch between Lusaka and Livingstone is more difficult during that time of year, as well as the Great East Road and roads in the eastern and northern parts of the country. The road from Lusaka to the Copperbelt cities of Ndola and Kitwe is generally in good shape year-round. It is not unusual to see elephants and antelopes on or near the road while driving to Victoria Falls or in the vicinity of the Kafue National Park.

Mini-buses serve as the primary means of inter-city travel in Zambia. They are often overcrowded and seldom punctual. City traffic is comprised mostly of cars and mini-buses; motorcycles are rare. Over 1,000 car accidents, many alcohol-related, were reported in 2000. No American citizens have been involved in serious car accidents. Carjackings occur in Lusaka during the daytime. For security reasons, the Embassy discourages travelers from driving on rural roads, especially near the borders with DRC and Angola. American citizens who must drive there are encouraged to drive in convoy and to carry cellular phones and two-way radios.

Seat belts are mandatory, as are helmets for motorcyclists. A child's seat is not mandatory. Traffic circulates on the left side of the road. There is no is no left turn on red, however, many motorists do turn. The speed limit is 50 km/30 mph in Lusaka and 100 km/60 mph outside of city limits. However, speed limits are rarely respected and most cars drive 80 km/50 mph in the city and 120 km/75 mph outside town. It is not unusual to see four-wheel drive vehicles, trucks and buses driving at even higher speeds on the stretch between Lusaka and Livingstone. Drivers under the influence of alcohol who are involved in accidents are tested at Lusaka's University Teaching Hospital (UTH) and then taken to court. The penalty for drivers involved in an accident resulting in injury is 6,000 Kwacha (approximately 2 US dollars).

For additional general information about road safety, including links to foreign government sites, see the Department of State, Bureau of Consular Affairs home page at http://travel.state.gov/road_safety.html. For specific information concerning Zambian driving permits, vehicle inspection, road tax and mandatory insurance, contact the Zambia National Tourist Board at www.zntb@zamnet.zm. The Road Safety Commission is responsible for road safety in Zambia, telephone 260-1-25-24-38 or 25-19-77.

AVIATION SAFETY OVERSIGHT: As there is no direct commercial air service by local carriers at present, or economic authority to operate such service, between the U.S. and Zambia, the U.S. Federal Aviation Administration (FAA) has not assessed Zambia's Civil Aviation Authority for compliance with international aviation safety standards.

For further information, travelers may contact the Department of Transportation within the U.S. at 1-800-322-7873, or visit the FAA Internet home page at http://www.faa.gov/avr/iasa/. The U.S. Department of Defense (DOD) separately assesses some foreign air carriers for suitability as official providers of air services. For information regarding the DOD policy on specific carriers, travelers may contact DOD at (618) 229-4801.

CRIMINAL PENALTIES: While in a foreign country, a U.S. citizen is subject to that country's laws and regulations, which sometimes differ significantly from those in the United States and may not afford the protections available to the individual under U.S. law. Penalties for breaking the law can be more severe than in the United States for similar offenses. Persons violating Zambian laws, even unknowingly, may be expelled, arrested or imprisoned. Penalties for possession, use, or trafficking in illegal drugs in Zambia are strict and convicted offenders can expect jail sentences and heavy fines.

U.S. citizens importing prescription drugs into Zambia without a physician's prescription may be arrested and incarcerated. Travelers should carry their prescription drugs and medications in original labeled containers, as well as the written prescription from their physician. Persons overstaying their visa or attempting to work while on a tourist visa risk imprisonment and deportation.

Zambian police do not always provide the U.S. Embassy with timely notification of the arrest of American citizens. If you are detained, insist on your right to contact a U.S. Consular Officer.

CURRENCY ISSUES: American Express and Visa cards are accepted in major supermarkets, restaurants, stores and hotels in Lusaka and Victoria Falls. American travelers cannot withdraw money from ATMs unless they have an account with a bank in Zambia. U.S. travelers checks are easy to cash provided travelers have identification. There are no currency restrictions in Zambia.

PHOTOGRAPHY RESTRICTIONS: Travel to military areas and photographing military facilities are prohibited. Authorities may also challenge photography of areas other than tourist attractions.

DANGERS POSED BY WILD ANIMALS: Travelers are advised that, even in the most serene settings, the animals are wild and can pose a threat to life and safety. Travelers are cautioned to observe all local or park regulations and heed all instructions given by tour guides.

CHILDREN'S ISSUES: For information on international adoption of children and international parental child abduction please refer to our Internet site at http://travel.state.gov/children's_issues.html or telephone (202) 736-7000.

REGISTRATION/EMBASSY LOCATION: U.S. citizens living in or visiting Zambia are encouraged to register with the Consular Section of the U.S. Embassy in Lusaka at the corner of Independence and United Nations Avenues, and to obtain updated information on travel and security in Zambia. U.S. citizens may contact the American Embassy during regular work hours, Monday through Thursday from 8:00 a.m. to 5:00 p.m., and on Friday from 8:00 a.m. to 12:30 p.m. The telephone number is (260-1) 250-955. After hours, the Embassy duty officer can be reached at (260-1) 252-234. The mailing address is P.O. Box 31617, Lusaka, Zambia. The telephone number is (260-1) 250-955 or 250-230; the fax number is (260-1) 252-225.

IMPORTANT INFORMATION

BUSINESS CUSTOMS

Zambia inherited the British legal system at independence in 1964. Business law is based mostly on British law, and business customs are similar to those in the U.S. and Europe.

TRAVEL ADVISORY AND VISAS:

Visas are required for U.S. passport holders, and it is highly recommended that travelers obtain visas in advance of arrival. Multiple entry visas may be obtained from the Embassy of the Republic of Zambia, 2419 Massachusetts Avenue, NW, Washington DC 20008, telephone (202) 265-9717. A multiple entry visa costs forty U.S. dollars, and a single entry visa costs twenty-five dollars. Zambian Embassy officials generally require a letter of invitation from the individual or entity in Zambia with whom one intends to do business. Tourist visas may be obtained at the border pr at the airport upon arrival. These visas are usually single entry visas valid for 3 months and cost twenty dollars.

Crime is a problem in Zambia. Mugging is relatively rare, but car thefts and house and car break-ins are not uncommon. The Copperbelt towns along the border with the Democratic Republic of Congo (Zaire) have seen periodic surges in crime due to problems across the border. There are no internal travel restrictions in Zambia, although areas around military bases may have restricted access. Police/traffic checkpoints do occur, fining vehicles deemed not to meet safety regulations. Many observers see this as corruption problem.

Medical facilities are generally limited. Doctors and hospitals often require immediate cash payment for health care services. Medical insurance covering air ambulance evacuation is highly advisable. For the most recent travel information on Zambia, call (202) 647-5225. For fax information, call (202) 647-3000, or check "travel.state.gov" on the Internet.

HOLIDAYS:

Date	Weekday	Holiday name	Holiday type
Jan 1	Friday	New Year	Public Holiday
Mar 8	Tuesday	International Women's Day	Public Holiday
Mar 12	Saturday	Youth Day	Public Holiday
Mar 20	Sunday	March equinox	Season
Mar 25	Friday	Good Friday	Public Holiday
Mar 27	Sunday	Easter Day	Public Holiday
Mar 28	Monday	Easter Monday	Public Holiday
May 1	Sunday	May Day	Public Holiday
May 8	Sunday	Mother's Day	Observance
May 25	Wednesday	Africa Freedom Day	Public Holiday
Jun 19	Sunday	Father's Day	Observance
Jun 20	Monday	June Solstice	Season
Jul 6	Wednesday	Heroes Day	Public Holiday
Jul 7	Thursday	Unity Day	Public Holiday
Aug 3	Wednesday	Farmers Day	Public Holiday
Sep 22	Thursday	September equinox	Season
Oct 24	Monday	Independence Day	Public Holiday
Dec 21	Wednesday	December Solstice	Season
Dec 25	Sunday	Christmas Day	Public Holiday

BUSINESS INFRASTRUCTURE

English is the official language and the language of government and business in Zambia.

There are weekly or more frequent airline connections to Lusaka from London, Dar es Salaam, Harare, Johannesburg, Lilongwe, Nairobi and among other cities. Domestic flights are available between Lusaka, Ndola or Kitwe (Copperbelt Province), Mfuwe and Chipata (Eastern Province), Livingstone (Southern Province), and Kasama (Northern Province). There are also five flights per week from Johannesburg to Ndola and four per week from Johannesburg to Livingstone.

The railway system is rundown and undergoing restructuring. Passenger train travel is unreliable and can be uncomfortable. There are numerous private city bus lines, but they are overcrowded and often unsafe. There are well-maintained and affordable luxury coach services on inter-city runs, including Lusaka-Harare, Lusaka-Johannesburg, and Livingstone -Lusaka- Copperbelt routes.

Road transportation is the preferred means of transport for many goods. The road network is uneven: quite good on some stretches and abysmal on others.

Zambia is landlocked and goods come in and out via air freight, or four ports: Dar es Salaam, Tanzania; Beira, Mozambique; Durban, South Africa; and Walvis Bay, Namibia.

Telecommunications are generally adequate but can be unreliable, especially during the rainy season. Cellular service is currently offered in Lusaka, Copperbelt towns, and some towns along the line of rail. International telephone calls are expensive, about 8 U.S. dollars per 3 minute call to the U.S., including tax. AT&T's USA Direct service is available, as well as similar services to Britain, Sweden and some other European countries. A number of callback service companies are operating, although their legality and blocks their operations are disputed by the parastatal telephone company, ZAMTEL. Fax machines are widely used in Zambia. The Internet is also becoming a popular communications tool.

Good quality housing is available but generally in short supply, particularly for rental housing.

Malaria is endemic in Zambia; cases occur in Lusaka, as well. Prophylaxis is strongly recommended if traveling outside the city. HIV prevalence is very high in Zambia, with estimated rates of 30-40% of the adult population in urban areas. The water in major city hotels is safe. When traveling outside the major cities, water should be filtered and boiled if possible.

Fresh meat, dairy products, fruits and vegetables are readily available and of high quality. Most processed food is imported from South Africa and is available in urban supermarkets, although it may be expensive. Lusaka has a number of good restaurants.

Guide For Business Representatives: This guide is available for sale by the Superintendent of Documents, U.S. Government Printing Office, Washington DC 20402, Tel: (202) 512-1800; Fax: (202) 512-2250. Business travelers to Zambia are encouraged to seek appointments with U.S. Embassy Lusaka officials. Such visitors should contact the Commercial Section in advance. The Commercial Section can be reached at Tel: (260-1) 250-955 or Fax: (260-1) 252-225.

MAJOR CITIES

LUCAKA

Lusaka is a city whose bustling chaos has a certain charm that is just Zambia.

The tourist passing through the capital may not see any reason to stay, but Lusaka is the product of a country battling to find its way in a new world, caught between colonial beginnings, years of socialist independence and now democracy. It typifies the problems many African countries face as they find their "independent" footing in world that's surging ahead.

The fascinating thing about Lusaka is its energy. Not perhaps of the same ilk as the Big Apple, but an African energy, propelled by that need to survive.

Lusaka is as much a part of "the real Africa" as the rich national parks and stunning scenery. Well over 60% of its 2 million inhabitants are unemployed, but there are surprisingly few beggars. Although petty theft occurs, most people try to make an honest living, selling their wares or services and smiling to boot.

The markets are a hive of activity, the thousands of stalls are filled and cleared every day. A myriad of motor spares dealers, restaurants, hairdressers, fishmongers, fruitsellers and rows and rows of "salaula" - discarded clothing from the West sold to Africa by the bale.

Venture out to a nightclub or roadside shebeen and "get in the groove", so to speak, of the local people. Dance the night away to the sounds of rhumba, kwela, techno or good old rock 'n roll.

But Lusaka is also a city undergoing a facelift. A walk around the city will reveal new shops-including a new market and a multi-million dollar shopping mall under construction; smart fast food outlets; freshly mended roads old buildings being refurbished and the transformation of the city's parks.

For many, this is the perfect example of what economic liberalisation has done for the country. And viewed from the villages, Lusaka is the glittering capital which still persuades rural Zambians to take the bus there in search of jobs and dreams.

The capital covers an area of over 70km sqare and is one of the fastest-growing cities in central Africa. It's population almost trebled in the immediate post-independence era and continues to grow daily. There has been no influx control and the city is bursting at the seams. Grossly inadequate municipal facilities are hard-pressed to cope with the ever-increasing demand.

It is a sprawling, unplanned metropolis with many multi-storey buildings, high-walled suburbs and busy shanty towns. Fast-growing industrial development has brought together people of many nationalities, making it a bustling centre for economic, political and cultural activities.

The city lies at the junction of the main highways to the north, east, south and west at an altitude of 1 300m above sea level. There are air links to most of the major tourist destinations in Zambia from Lusaka International Airport.

The shops are mainly grouped along the broad double carriageway of Cairo Rd, but the government buildings are about 6km away along Independence Ave.

For maps of the city, try the **Zambian National Tourist Board**, the craft shop at the Pamodzi Hotel or the Map Centre, Mulungushi House, opposite the US embassy.

There is a local magazine called the **Lusaka Lowdown** which is a mine of information on what's happening in town and full of useful adverts for local services and products. Check out the online version.

CLIMATE

The most appealing factor to many who have made Lusaka their home is the superb climate. Warm sunny summers, interspersed with cooling thunderstorms and mild winters with loads of sunshine.

It can get very hot between October and March if there's no rain. The average rainfall, between November and April, is about 950mm. Summer temperatures range from 20 degrees to 32 degrees C. Winter temperatures from 10 degrees to about 26 degrees. Humidity is usually below 40%.

GETTING THERE

Lusaka is close to the centre of Zambia between the eastern and western bulges. **All major routes to the east, west, north and south flow through the city**.

The Great North Road comes down from Tanzania via Kapiri Mposhi, and is about 1 100km from the Tanzanian border.

The Great East Rd from Chipata to Lusaka is 570km.

The road from Livingstone in the south meets up with the "Kafue Road" and is 470km long. From the Chirundu border with Zimbabwe, the route is well paved and 136km long.

The Mongu road coming in from the west via the **Kafue National Park** is 591km long.

The domestic railway goes to Livingstone, Kapiri Mposhi and the Copperbelt. The Tanzania Zambia Railway - Tazara - comes down as far as Kapiri Mposhi, where the Zambia Railways train links it to Lusaka. Buses arrive from Harare, Lilongwe, Johannesburg, Livingstone and the Copperbelt.

Lusaka International Airport, which is 14km from the city centre, receives most international flights.

Zambian Airways will flies to and from Johannesburg and currently has scheduled flights to Mfuwe, Chipata, the Copperbelt and Livingstone.

Zambia Skyways has scheduled domestic flights to Lusaka from: Ndola, Kasama, Kasaba Bay, Mongu, Livingstone, Mfuwe and Chipata.

InterAir Flies into Ndola from Johannesburg and Entebbe from where a connecting flight to Lusaka can be taken.

Getting around -

No scheduled bus services - taxis range from 12 seater minibuses to dilapidated cars to good dial up cabs to chauffeur driven vehicles.

WHERE TO STAY

Accommodation in Lusaka is plentiful and there are choices to suit all tastes and budgets. From Five star hotels, Well known hotel chains, Game lodges on private game reserves, to motels and quiet guesthouses in the suburbs.

A few kilometres from the CBD are the three top hotels, the **Holiday Inn,** the **Inter-Continental Hotel** and the **Pamodzi.**

For cheaper accommodation try the **Fairview Hotel, Chrismar, Hillview, Kafue Rd Garden, Garden House** or **Ndeke Hotels.** The oldest hotel in the City is the **Lusaka Hotel** just off Cairo Rd.

Comfortable Guesthouses in the suburbs include the **Wayside Bed & Breakfast** just 4km South of the City Centre, and **Juls Guesthouse** just off the Great East Rd. Lusaka's newest Lodge **Villa Lodge Gardens** and another one with very convenient shopping access **Chita Lodge.**

There are various motels in and around town which offer basic but reasonably priced accommodation.

RESTAURANTS AND NIGHTLIFE

See Supplement

SHOPPING

Most of the banks and many bureaux de change can be found along Cairo Road.

For groceries and general **supplies**, the newly opened Manda Hill shopping centre is where it's all at. This is Lusaka's first shopping mall and it's becoming a big hit with an excellent range of shops and boutiques. There's also a big supermarket in Cairo Rd. There are several suburban shopping centres, not of the mall type, but with a variety of shops that usually supply anything you need, mostly imported from Zimbabwe or South Africa and a little pricey. These are called Kabulonga, Northmead and Woodlands.

If not for shopping, but just for the experience of how the local masses shop, a visit to one of Lusaka's **markets** is a must. It's an interesting experience and well worth a visit, if just for the colourful and lively atmosphere. The Soweto Market is two roads west of Cairo Road, and the other opposite the Tazara building in Independence Ave. A new, smarter, roofed market has just been built along Freedom Way.

Curios and crafts can be found at Zambili in Luanshya Rd. The Book House shop, in the Manda Hills Shopping Center. Zintu Handicrafts are at the Holiday Inn. Moore Pottery on Kabalenga Road has an excellent range of ceramics, and Zintu Za Nyimba at the bottom end of Panganani Road sells a wide range of locally made wooden furniture, batiks, candle holders, lamps shades, hand-dyed cloths and carvings. Definitely worth a visit. Hope House in Luanshya Road is a charitable organisation providing support to Aids victims and sell a range of home-made crafts.

For **Gemstones** and fine **jewellery**, try **Jagoda** at the Holiday Inn or the Intercontinental Hotel.

You can buy **film** and get photographs processed at Phoenix Photographics halfway down Cairo Road. Books can be found at Tower Books at the Castle in Makeni, the Book House SHop at Manda Hills and Mary's Bookshop on the Leopards Hill Rd.

A word of warning - Lusaka is famous for car thieves, pick-pockets and bag snatchers, but if you have someone who can mind your vehicle and keep a good grip on your bags, it's quite safe.

SIGHTSEEING

A good place for locally hand-crafted curios is the **Kabwata Cultural Village**, which is in the suburb of Kabwata along Burma Road. The residents are carving all day and a wide variety of items are for sale at reasonable prices. Test your bargaining skills.

Lusaka National Museum on Independence Avenue is undoubtedly one of the most attractive public buildings in the city.This cultural history museum tells the story of Zambia in four main sections; ethnography, witchcraft, history and contemporary art. The ground floor presents the works of artists from Zambia's independence (1964) to date: contemporary paintings, sculpture and ceramics. With no national art gallery, this provides the visitors with a rare opportunity to sample Zambian Art. The upper floor houses historical and cultural artifacts. Particularly fascinating is the witchcraft exhibit which will give the visitor the opportunity to learn about a part of Zambian life that is rarely discussed, but is deeply imbedded in every sphere of daily life. Facilities: The museum has a small library, a small conference room and a snack shop. Opening hours: 9am-4. 30pm daily; closed public holidays. Admission: US$2 adults, US$1 children. Guided tours possible. Parking available.

Bente Lorens Ceramic Studio in Longacres has a fine collection of bowls, plates and ornaments which are also for sale. **The Henry Tayali Visual Arts Centre** at the showgrounds has a fine selection of works by Zambian artists. Single-exhibitor and group shows are held every month. Open daily from 10h00. (See listings for Galleries)

Kalimba Reptile Park has an impressive collection of snakes, all found in the surrounding area, crocodiles, tortoises and some of the most unusual chameleons found in Africa. The park is set in a lush garden with a kids playground, putt putt course and a verandah where refreshments are served. Head out of town on the Great East Road towards the airport and turn left at the last Caltex garage before the airport turnoff. Follow the signs for about 11km. The park, which is part of a fish farm, also sells fresh frozen fish and crocodile tails, as well as a range of crocodile bags, purses, belts, etc. Mundawanga Park has been renovated and is back operating.

The Aylermer May Cemetery in Lagos Rd, Rhodes Park. This was Lusaka's first Cemetery and is currently undergoing extensive renovations.

There are several car-hire companies in Lusaka to help you get around: see **car hire** listings for contact numbers.

DAY TRIPS

Lilayi Game Ranch, 20 minutes outside of town, is set on a 700 hectare farm, a part of which has been uncultivated and left in its pristine bush state. There are 19 different antelope species but no predators,so they're a lot less skitttish than in the national parks. Over 200 birds species have been recorded here, which can be spotted on walking trails, game drives or horseback trails. Bookings are essential .

Chaminuka Private Game Reserve just 45 minutes north of Lusaka offers a superb wildlife Safari and lunch in beautiful surroundings. One can also take a horseback trail through the Reserve, go fishing, enjoy a swim, play tennis and relax in their outdoor jacuzzi and sauna. The Reserve has more species of animals than any other game park in Zambia, including, lion cheetah, giraffe, elephant, ostrich and even the elusive sitatunga. It does offer day package special which can be found at the rates section of their web site.

Another reason to visit Chaminuka is their extensive **Art Gallery** . Historically the Sardanis family have been serious promoters of Zambian Art. Chaminuka, has a collection of more than 1000 pieces of art, ranging from traditional artefacts collected in over 35 countries in Africa, to contemporary sculpture and painting collections.

Zambili Crafts and Cafe D'Afrique near the centre of town is a great place to stop over for lunch. Traditional foods and cultural performances, situated in Kalundu.

JLazyJ Farm is a 1 500 hectare bird sanctuary also 20 minutes from town. The owner will take you horseback riding through the pristine miombo woodland or one can simply do walks and birdwatching on one's own.

Trotover Equestrian Centre offers horseback hacks through indigenous forest with natural obstacles, or birdwatching walks. This is a great spot for a family picnic - with a pool and a few streams.

Foxdale Ostrich Farm

Lechwe Game and Fish Farm is within an hour of Lusaka on the banks of the Kafue River. The river's proximity attracts many waterbirds. Sixteen different antelope species can be seen in the woodlands and floodplains of the area. On offer are horse trails and boat rides down the river. Booking essential.

At the **Kafue Marina**, also within an hour's drive from town, one can hire a boat or canoe and there are picnic facilities with barbecues and rondavels. Take the Kafue Road out of town and turn left just before the Kafue Bridge, followed by another left and a right. (See listings for Daytrips)

LIVINGSTON

Named after the famous Victorian missionary explorer, Dr. David Livingstone, the Town was established in 1905. As a major European settlement, the town was made the capital of Northern Rhodesia in 1911. As the capital, it enjoyed excellent facilities far superior to anything in the country, as can be seen from the surviving Edwardian colonial buildings that line the city's main road, and even had the distinction of having the country's first newspaper.

The capital was moved to Lusaka in 1935 and the bustling city has become a quiet town, a little neglected but still retaining a special charm. The proximity to the Zambezi River and the spectacular Victoria Falls has led it to become a base for travelers from all over the world wanting to explore this Seventh wonder of the World.
Stop in at the Adventure Centre for a wide range of adventure activities, services and shops. There are several Adventure Companies offering Riverboarding, White water rafting, Canoeing, Horse riding trails, Abseiling, local tours to the Victoria Falls and around Livingstone. There are Safari operators, a Restaurant, an Internet Cafe, a Backpackers Lodge and an excellent Arts and Crafts Gallery. You'll find them in Mosi-o-Tunya road heading towards the Falls (corner of Nakatindi rd out to Kazungula) Don't miss it! You can also book all these adventures from the Pocket Guide Office at the Victoria falls Border post on the Zambian side. Two great new books on Dr. Livingstone just released - order here

GETTING THERE

- **Zambian Airways** has scheduled planes to Livingstone from Lusaka and will soon be flying from Livingstone to Johannesburg.

- **Zambia Skyways** has scheduled flights to Livingstone from Lusaka.

By Road, Livingstone can be approached from three directions. If you're coming **from Zimbabwe,** cross the border at the town of Victoria Falls over the famous Victoria Falls Bridge, carry straight on this road for about 11 kilometres. **From Botswana**, cross the border at Kazungula by ferry, and continue east for about 60kms. **From Lusaka**, Livingstone is 470 kms. Take the southbound Kafue Road out of Lusaka and just after the Kafue River Bridge, turn right towards Mazabuka. This road leads straight to Livingstone.

WHERE TO STAY

In Livingstone Town itself there are 3 hotels, and several backpackers establishments

- **Wasawange Lodge** in Libala Drive which is also the road to the airport, has very comfortable ethnically decorated chalets with all the conveniences of a modern hotel.

- The **New Fairmount** Hotel in Mosi o Tunya Rd and the Northwestern Hotel have standard air-conditioned rooms and a Casino and night club.

- **Ngolide Lodge** in Mosi-o-Tunya Rd, Livingstone offers comfortable, affordable accommodation in a convenient location, just 8 kms from the falls.

- **Fawlty Towers** is right in the middle of Livingstone on the Mosi-o-Tunya Road in the Adventure Centre and has great inexpensive accommodation with a pool.

There are several hotels and lodges in the Victoria Falls area and along the Zambezi, providing a wide range of accommodation.

- **Stanley Safari Lodge** is the newest lodge in the area opening June 2002. It has a direct view over the spray of the Victoria Falls and the National Park. They are offering excellent opening specials at the moment.

- **Tongabezi** is a very stylish lodge built from stone and set into the surrounding cliffs. It has comfortable safari tented accommodation on the rivers edge as well as three stone, wood and thatch chalets on the cliff edge overlooking the river. They also have island camps in the Zambezi River.

- **Taita Falcon Lodge** is perched on the edge of the cliffs and has superb views of the spectacular Batoka gorge.

- **Zambezi Royal Chundu Fishing and Safari Lodge** is further upstream of the Zambezi.

- **Mukolo Island Tented Camp** run by the stylish Chilongozi Safari Company who also conduct canoeing safaris on the upper Zambezi.

- **Chundukwa Tree Lodge** Camp has wood and thatch chalets on stilts over the River and offers horse trails and canoeing.

- **Thorntree** is another bush camp up river with spacious tented accommodation on the rivers edge.

- The newest additions are the **River Club** on the banks of the Zambezi and the **Waterfront**. Sun International is planning a luxurious complex to open in 2001.

- **Kubu Cabins** is a quaint bush lodge about 25kms up river with an excellent riverside site, renowned for superb food and a quiet homely atmosphere. This lodge is currently being refurbished.

- **Mawala Lodge** is 30 kms upstream of Victoria Falls with an upstairs bar and dining area offering great views of the Zambezi and wildlife coming down to the rivers edge to drink.

- A new **Sun International Resort** just opened very close to the Falls. There are two hotels, **The Zambezi Sun** (3 star hotel) as well as **The Royal Livingstone** (5 star hotel). Each of the hotels has its own design, specific character and identity. The needs of the widest possible range of clients are provided for, including families and corporate and conference groups, as well as top end individual travellers.

RESTAURANTS

Several new restaurants have opened in Livingstone recently:
Utsav is the first Indian Restaurant to appear in Livingstone - found in the main Mosi-o-

tunya rd. They also have a take-away section called Exciting Biting !
The Laughing Dragon is a new Chinese establishment just off the main rd near the **Hungry Lion.**
Hippo's pub behind Fawlty Towers serves great meals and has a pool table and darts.
ZigZag also doubles as a booking office for various adventures as well as a small shop but serves lunches and cakes on the pavement.
The **Pigs Head**, Kabompo Road is one of the local pubs, also serving food.
Eatrite Fast Foods, in the main road
For excellent light lunches with good wholesome food try **Pilgrims** just on the outskirts of Town on the way to the Falls. They also have a curio shop there.
Chanters is a good new restaurant in Lukulu Rd with accommodation as well.
Flying Pizza on the main rd near the Adventure Centre serves great pizzas, shwarmas, burrittos, soft drinks.
The **Waterfront** always has meals available on their great terrace on the river's edge
Both **Sun International Hotels** have several good restaurants although they're quite pricey.

CURIO SHOPS

African Visions is a great new addition to Livingstone with a wide selection of Zambian and other African works of art and craftwork. Find them at the **Adventure Centre** in Mosi-o-Tunya Rd.
Kubu Crafts sells fine wood crafted furniture among other curios and souvenirs.

GETTING AROUND

Imperial Car Hire offers a full range of vehicles to tour around Livngstone, and the Falls.
AJ Car Hire and Tours offers chauffeur driven cars or self drive hire and takes tours around the area as well as airport transfers.
Makoro Quest, Bundu Adventures and **Bushtracks Africa** also do day trips and transfers

SUPPLEMENTS

CRIME STTISTICS

NATIONAL CRIME STATISTICS ON MAJOR OFFENCES AS FROM 2011 TO 2015

Murder cases reported from 2011 to 2015

Year	Reported
2011	863
2012	885
2013	867
2014	825
2015	853

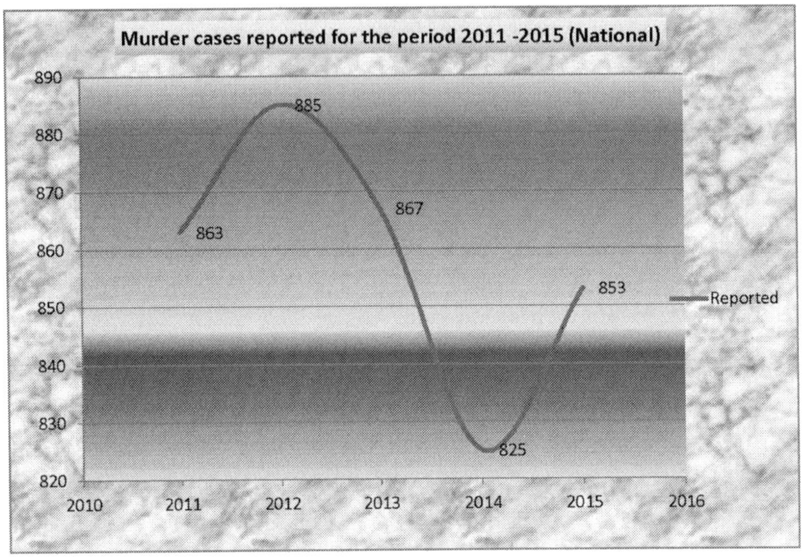

Aggravated cases reported from 2011 to 2015

Year	Reported
2011	2114
2012	1415
2013	1167
2014	898
2015	835

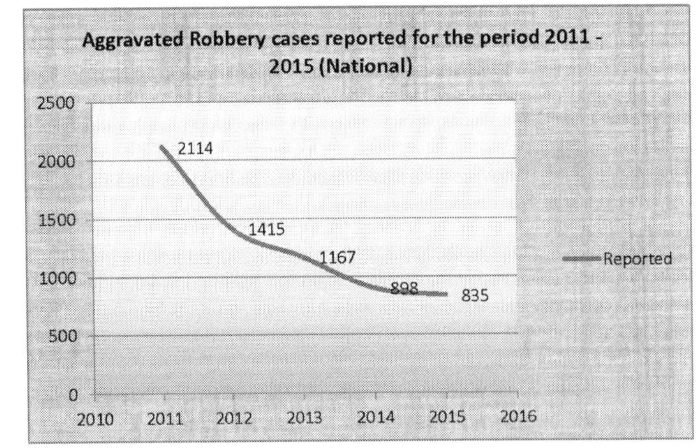

Year	Reported
2011	250
2012	323
2013	294
2014	339
2015	324

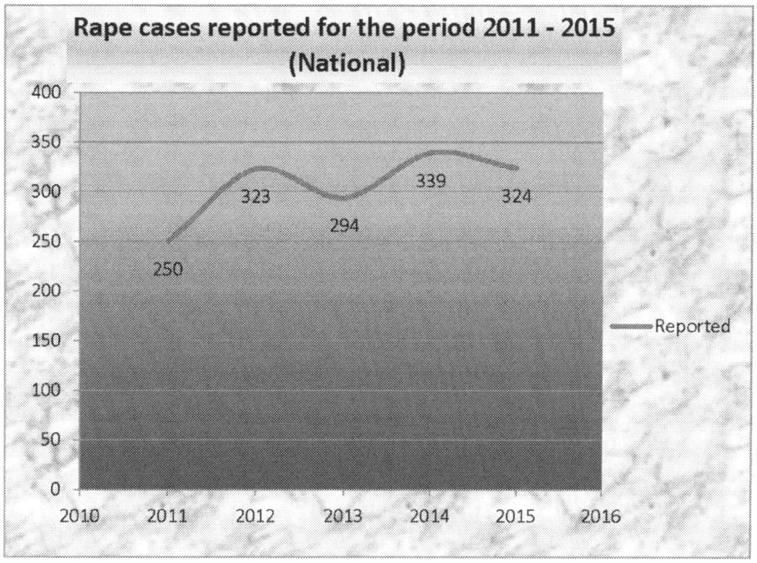

Defilement

Year	Reported
2011	1354
2012	3392
2013	1159
2014	1246
2015	1181

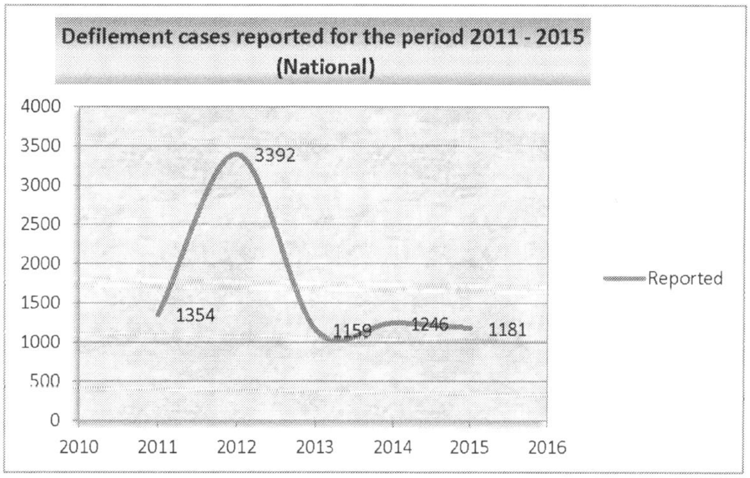

Stock Theft cases reported from 2011 to 2015

Year	Reported
2011	1829
2012	2042
2013	1650
2014	1691
2015	1681

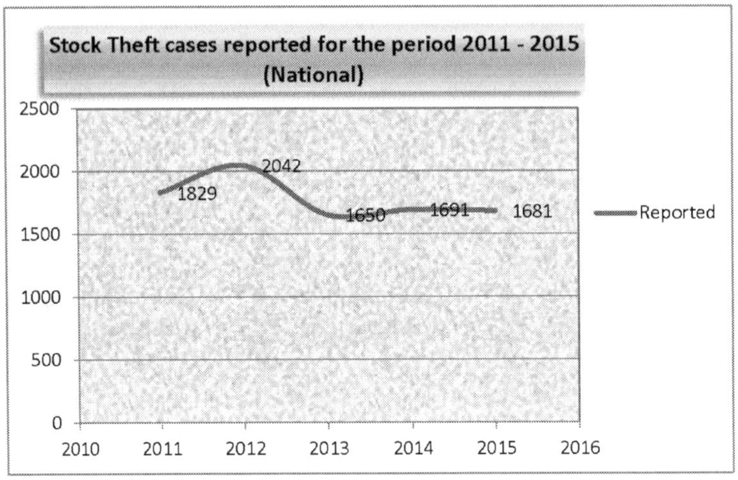

Arson cases reported from 2011 to 2015

Year	Reported
2011	795
2012	812
2013	696
2014	594
2015	585

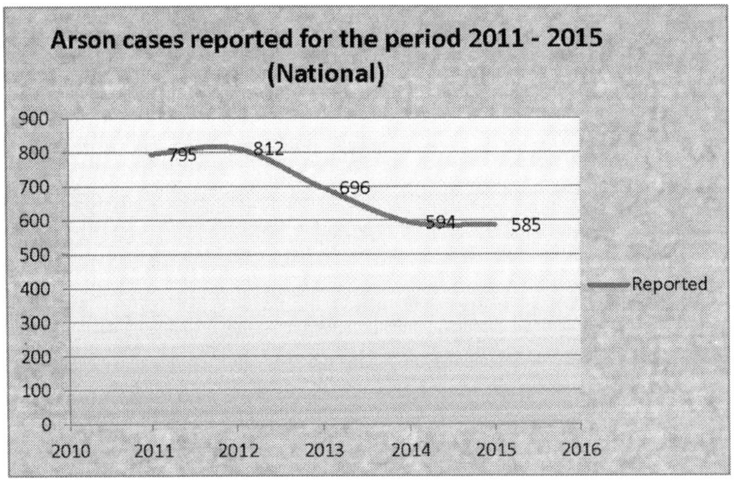

Theft cases reported from 2011 to 2015

Year	Reported
2011	15750
2012	16682
2013	15786
2014	13582
2015	12674

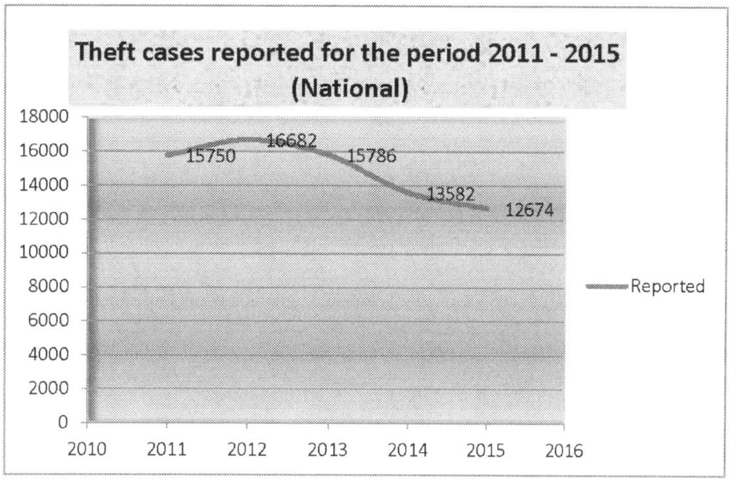

IMPORTANT CONTACTS

Ministry of Home Affairs www.homeaffairs.gov.zm
Drug Enforcement Commission www.deczambia.gov.zm
Immigration www.zambiaimmigration.gov.zm
Prisons Service www.zambiaprison.gov.zm
Lost and Found: Property & Persons
www.lf.zambiapolice.org.zm

POLICE CONTACTS

TELEPHONE NUMBERS FOR PROVINCES

LUSAKA
-0979-810007, -0950-180007, -0969-180008

COPPERBELT	
MUFULIRA	-0212-410037
LUANSHYA	-0212-510600
CHINGOLA	-0212-313111
KITWE	-0212-231888
NDOLA	
CHILILABOMBWE	
SOUTHERN	
CHOMA	-221464
MAZABUKA	-230600
LIVINGSTONE	-323575
MONZE	-250109
NAMWALA	-220055
MAAMBA	-278182
GWEMBE	-240026
NORTHERN	-04-222016
LUAPULA	-02-821644
EASTERN (CHIPATA)	
PETAUKE	-371011
LUNDAZI	-480112
KATETE	-252211
CHADIZA	-251142
NYIMBA	-374283
SINDA	-256187
MFUWE	-24009/245046
CENTRAL	-0215-222271
N/WESTERN	-08-821031/ 0975-916100

	-0962-420208
	-0953-467884
WESTERN	-0955-897643
MUCHINGA	-0955-373939
AIRPORT	-0211-271363

LAWYERS IN ZAMBIA[2]

KABWE

Kabesha & Company

Specializes in family law, adoptions, child custody, parental child abduction, child protection, insurance, banking/financial, commercial/business law, civil law, criminal law, damages, narcotics, collections, commercial law, contracts, estates, labor relations, immigration and auto/accidents

Mulilo Kabesha: 3rd Floor Mukuni Hse Independence Way, Kabwe, Zambia, PH: +260-215-222596, Mobile: 260-97-7-780511, Email:mdkabesha@gmail.com.

Speaks: French and most Zambian languages

KITWE

Jacques & Partners

Specializes in family law, marriage/divorce, insurance, commercial/business law, civil law, damages, collections, commercial law, contracts, estates, labor relations and auto/accidents

Kafunya Mbindo: Jaques and Partners, Plot 6669 Kabengele Ave, Kafunya House Kitwe, Zambia Ph:+260 -212 229171 Fax: :+260 -212- 229177 Mobile:+260-97-8-280407 jaqueslegal@zamnet.zm. In Practice for over 30 years.

Speaks: Most Local languages

Nyirongo & CO

The firm specializes in family law, adoption, child custody, parental child abduction, child protection, commercial/business law, civil law, criminal law, damages, narcotics, collections, commercial law, contracts, corporations, labor relations, immigration and auto/accidents.

Gavu Nyirongo: Nyirongo & CO, Hse NO. 21 kalunwishi Ave Nkana East Kitwe, Zambia. Mobile: +260-97-3-193668, Email: nyirongoandco@yahoo.com. In practice for over 22 years.

Speaks: Tumbuka and Bemba

[2] All lawyers listed speak English (English is the first language) and most can provide transcription and notary services.

Partner: Kondwani Musukwa

Pasi Advocates

The firm specializes in family law, adoptions, child custody, parental child abductions, child protection, marriage/divorce, insurance, banking/financial, commercial/business law. Foreign investments, marketing agreements, intellectual property law, civil law, commercial law, conflicts, transportation law, corporations, estates, and labor relations.

Hastings Siakoola Pasi: Pasi Advocates, Suite 215, 1st floor Mukuba Pension Hse, President Ave, Kitwe. Mobile: 260-96-2-555010, Mobile: 260-97-7-318076, Email: hpasi@pasiadvocates.com.

Speaks: Local Languages

Suba Tafeni and Associates

Specializes in all disciplines of Law

Inutu Etambuyu Suba: Solidarity House, 2nd Floor Oxford Street, Kitwe, Ph: +260-212-222231 Mobile: +260-95-501590, Mobile: 0955849020; Email: mesdamessubatafeni@gmail.com. In practice for over 34 years.

Speaks: French and Lozi

Partners: Clement F. Tafeni, Mambwe Lungu, Willie Banda and Alex Muyebe

LIVINGSTONE

Suba Tafeni and Associates

Specializes in all disciplines of Law

Inutu Etambuyu Suba: 1st Floor Sackville house, Akapelwa Street PO Box 61078 Livingstone, Ph: 03 323924, Lusaka; Mobile: +260-95-501590, Mobile: 0955849020;

Email: mesdamessubatafeni@gmail.com. In practice for over 34 years.

Speaks: French and Lozi

Partners: Clement F. Tafeni, Mambwe Lungu, Willie Banda and Alex Muyebe.

LUSAKA

AB & David

The firm specializes in commercial /business law, foreign investments, intellectual property law, taxes, Government Relations, Labor Relations, Immigration law, adoptions, insurance, banking and financial, marketing agreements, collections, commercial law, contracts, foreign claims and estates.

Dumisani James Tembo: AB & David, ground floor Mamco Hse, Madison office complex, plot 316B Independence Ave Lusaka, Zambia. Ph: +260-211-258403; Mobile: +260-97-7-754565; Fax: +260-211-258404; Email: dumisani.tembo@abdavid.com

Speaks: Nyanja, Bemba and Zulu

Brenda Mutale Chanda: AB & David, ground floor Mamco Hse, Madison office complex, plot 316B Independence Ave Lusaka, Zambia. Ph:+260-211-258403; Mobile: +260-97-2-565540; Fax: +260-211-258404; Email: brenda.chanda@abdavid.com

Speaks: Bemba

Isaac and Partners

The firm specializes in family law, marriage/ divorce, insurance, banking/financial, commercial/business law, foreign investments, marketing agreements, intellectual property law, civil law, collections, commercial law, contracts, corporations, foreign claims, estates, labor relations, immigrations and auto/accidents.

Mwenya Andrew Mukupa: Isaac and partners, Lusaka-Plot 3792 Kwacha Rd, Olympia Ext , Tel:021-1-259015; Mobile +260- 97-7-774747, Email: mam@isaacandpartners.com. In Practice for 14 years.

Speaks: Bemba and French.

Partner: Natalie Mwenya Mulenga

Lusitu Chambers

The firm specializes in family law, adoption, child protection, marriage/divorce, commercial/business law, foreign investments, marketing agreements, intellectual property law, civil law, contracts, estates, labor relations and immigration law.

Peter Matimba: Lusitu Chamber. Plot 33, House No1 corner of Joseph mwila and Great East Road, Phodes park, P/bag 91 woodlands Post Office, Lusaka. Email: matimba_1@yahoo.co.uk.

Mobile: 097-7-254972. In practice for over 2years.

In addition the law firm administers the project agreed outputs of the USAID Anti -Gender Based Violence project under Women and Law in Southern Africa.

Speaks: Bemba, Nyanja, Tonga and Portuguese

Partner: Maimbo Ziela

Nchito and Nchito Advocates

The firm specializes in family law, adoptions, insurance, banking/financial, commercial /business law, foreign investments, marketing agreement, patents/trademarks/copyright, contracts, civil law, damages, collections, commercial Law, contracts, corporations, foreign claims, estates, taxes, labor relations, immigration and Auto/ Accidents.

Nchima Nchito (State Counsel): Nchima Nchito 5th Floor Godfrey House Longolongo Rd, Lusaka, Zambia. Ph:+260-211-226920/1, Mobile:+260-979-789789, Mobile:+260-966-861295, Fax +260-211-236134, Email: info@nchito.co.zm or nhima@nchito.co.zm.

In practice for over 30 years and he is the managing partner, his primary focus is corporate and commercial law. In addition he served as Legal Counsel for Zambia Consolidated Copper Mines which was Zambia's State owned mining Conglomerate and worked on assignments with what is now the Zambia Development Agency and the World Bank.

Speaks: Bemba and Nyanja.

Mutembo Nchito (State Counsel): Nchito and Nchito Advocates 5th Floor Godfrey House Longolongo Rd, Lusaka, Zambia. Ph:+260-211-226920/1, Mobile:+260-979-789789, Mobile:+260-966-861295, , Fax +260-211-236134, Email: info@nchito.co.zm or Mutembo@nchito.co.zm.

Educated in Zambia and the United Kingdom, has been in practice for over 24 years, his primary focus is on private and public banking law, corporate insolvency, securities regulations and international commercial arbitration. In addition he received international recognition for his work as the lead prosecutor of the special task force on corruption for over 8 years. He was appointed Director pf Public prosecutions and then returned to private practice. Mr. Nchito is involved in peer review for the World Bank and is a serving member of the Executive Committee of The Hague based International Association of Prosecutors.

Speaks: Bemba and Nyanja.

P.W. Mwikisa & Co

Specializes in family law, adoptions, child custody, parental child abductions, child protection, marriage/divorce, insurance, banking/financial, commercial/business law, foreign investments, marketing agreement, civil, criminal law, damages, collections, commercial law, contracts, transportation law, corporations, foreign claims, estates, government relations, labor relations, immigration and auto/accidents.

Paul W. Mwikisa: P.W Mwikisa and Company, 3rd Floor Tazara Hse, cnr of Independence and Dedan Kimathi Rds, Lusaka, Zambia; PH: + 260-211-222790; Mobile; +260-96-1-877117; FAX: 260-211-222790; Email: plmwikisa@gmail.com or plmwikisa1@yahoo.com. In practice for over 30 years. He has vast experience and worked for a major bank in Zambia. His focus is banking and finance, civil litigation and conveyancing.

Speaks: English, French and Major Local Languages in Zambia

Partners: Mulenga Kapambwe, Catherine Banda and Bernadette Gibbons

Sharpe & Howard Legal Practitioners

Specializes in family law, child custody, marriage/ divorce, insurance, banking/financial, commercial/business law, foreign investments, marketing agreements, intellectual property law, labor relations, commercial law, contracts and estates

Tiziana Marietta: Sharpe & Howard Legal Practitioners, Stand 8235 Nangwenya Road, P/Bag RW175X Lusaka. Ph:+260-211-256426/30, Mobile: +260-97-7-597512, Fax:+260-211-256431, Email: enquiries@sharpehoward.com. In practice for 12 years,

Speaks: Italian

Partner: Andrew Howard

Suba Tafeni and Associates

Specializes in all disciplines of Law

Inutu Etambuyu Suba: Plot 2837 Los Angeles Boulevard Longraces, Mobile: +260-95-501590, Mobile: 0955849020; Email: mesdamessubatafeni@gmail.com. In practice for over 34 years.

Speaks: French and Lozi

Partners: Clement F. Tafeni, Mambwe Lungu, Willie Banda and Alex Muyebe

TCJ Legal Practitioners

Specializes in insurance, Banking/Financial, commercial/business law, foreign investments, civils law, damages, collections, commercial law, contracts, corporates, foreign claims, estates, labor relations, auto/ accidents.

Judith Tembo: TCJ Legal Practitioners; 1st floor Zimbabwe House, Haile Selaise Ave Lusaka, Zambia. PH: +260-211-258181; Mobile: +260-97-2-047677, Email: tcj@zamnet.zm. In practice for over 29 years. Trained in Both Zambia and the United Kingdom.

Speaks: French, Bemba and Nyanja

Ventus Legal Practitioners

Specializes in family law, adoptions, marriage/divorce, insurance, banking/financial, commercial/business law, foreign investments, marketing agreements, intellectual property law, civil law, collections, commercial law, contracts, corporates, aeronautical/maritime, estates, government relations, labor relations, auto/accidents

Victor Musabula: Ventus Legal Practitioners, Plot 5 Bwinjimfumu Rd, Rhodes Park Osidian Hse, Post Net Box 8, P/Bag E891 Manda Hill Lusaka PH: +260-211-258692, Mobile:+260-961907907,

Email: ventus@ventus.co.zm or victor.musabula@ventus.co.cm. In practice for over 11years.

Speaks: Nyanja

Partner: Kaungo Musonda

NDOLA

Kafunda and Company

Specializes in family law, adoptions, child custody, marriage/divorce, banking/financial, commercial/business law, Intellectual property law, civil law, criminal law, damages, collections, commercial law, contracts, labor relations, auto/accidents

Malaro Nyirenda: Kafunda and Company; Salem House, Buteko Ave Ndola, Zambia.PH:+260-212-620986, Mobile: +260-97-7-787117, FAX. +260-212-620986, Email: kafundalaw@zamtel.zm. In practice for over 22 years

ABHA Patel & Associates

The firm Specializes in family law, marriage/divorce, commercial / business law, criminal law, damages, commercial law, contracts, corporations, estates, labor relations and immigration. The firm has been in existence for over 21years

Daniel S. Libati: ABHA Patel and Associates, 35 Kabinga Ave, Northrise Ndola, Zambia, PH: +260-212-621976, Mobile: 260-95-5-566509, Email: abha@abhapatel.co.zm .

Partner: Mrs. Abha N. Patel (State Counsel)

J.M. Kapasa & Company

The firm specializes in family law, adoptions, child custody, marriage/divorce, insurance, banking /financial, commercial/business law, foreign investments, marketing agreements, civil law, criminal law, damages, narcotics, commercial law, contracts, corporations, foreign claims, estates, labor relations, immigration and auto/accidents

John M Kapasa: J.M. Kapasa &Co, 1 st floor Canada Hse, president Ave Ndola, Zambia, PH: + 260-212-620961, Mobile: 260-96-6-627414; Emails: jmkapasa@gmail.com or jmkap@zamtel.zm. In Practice for over 37 years.

Speaks: French and Local languages

Vincent K Mwewa & Company

The firm specializes in family law, marriage/divorce, commercial/business law, civil law, criminal law, damages, narcotics, commercial law, contracts, corporations, estates, labor relations

Vincent Kaunda Mwewa: Trinity Hse, 1st floor Buteko Ave, Ndola; PH: +260-212-621208, Mobile: 260-96-8-444498; Fax: 260-212-621208, Email: vkmwewa@gmail.com. In Practice for over 31 years.

Speaks: Bemba and Nyanja

GOVERNMENT OFFICES

MINISTRY	TELEPHONE
Agriculture, Food and Fisheries	Tel: 251537
Auditor General	Tel: 25241
Commerce, Trade and Industry	Tel: 228301
Communications and Transport	Tel: 251444
Community Development and Social Services	Tel:227840
Defence	Tel: 251211
Education	Tel: 227636
Energy and Water Development	Tel: 263870
Environment and Natural Resources	Tel: 229410/229419
Finance	Tel: 250544
Foreign Affairs	Tel: 252666
Health	Tel: 253040/45
Home Affairs	Tel: 254261
Information and Broadcasting	Tel: 227840
Labour and Social Security	Tel: 227840
Lands	Tel: 252288
Legal Affairs	Tel: 251588

Local Government and Housing	Tel: 253077
Mines and Minerals development	Tel: 252990
Office of the President	Tel: 260312
Science, Technology and Vocational Training	Tel: 229673
Sports, Youth and child Development	Tel: 227158
Tourism	Tel: 227645
Works and Supply	Tel: 353244

US AND COUNTRY CONTACTS

U.S. Embassy Lusaka

Ambassador David B. Dunn
Deputy Chief of Mission Robert Whitehead
Economic/Commercial Chief Troy Fitrell
Commercial Officer Daniel Ebert
Commercial Specialist Vedruna Santana

U.S. mailing address: 2310 Lusaka Pl., Washington DC 20521-2310.

International mailing address: United States Embassy, PO Box 31617, Lusaka, Zambia.

Street address: Corner of United Nations and Independence Avenues, Lusaka, Zambia.

Telephone: 260 1 250-955
Fax: 260 1 252-225

ZAMBIAN GOVERNMENT AND INDUSTRY

Ministry of Commerce, Trade and Industry, Permanent Secretary Dr. Moses Banda, PO Box 31968, Lusaka, Zambia. Tel: 260 1 223-617.

Ministry of Finance, Permanent Secretaries Mrs. Stella M Chibanda and Mr. BoniFace Nonde, PO Box RW 50062, Lusaka, Zambia. Tel: 260 1 250-657 and 260 1 251-843.

Zambia Privatization Agency (ZPA), Chief Executive Stuart Cruickshank, PO Box 30819, Lusaka, Zambia. Tel: 260 1 223-859.

Zambia Investment Center (ZIC), Director Dr. Mbikusita Lewanika, PO Box 34580, Lusaka, Zambia. Tel: 260 1 255-240.

Zambia Association of Chambers of Commerce and Industry (ZACCI), Chairman George Chabwera, PO Box 30844, Lusaka, Zambia.

Tel: 260 1 252-369

COUNTRY MARKET RESEARCH

Price Waterhouse, Senior Partner Jack Ward, PO Box 30942, Lusaka, Zambia. Tel: 260 1 228-809

COMMERCIAL BANKS

1. S. Sridhar
Managing Director
Citibank Zambia Limited
Citibank House, Chachacha Road
P.O. Box 30037
Tel: 260-1-229025
Fax: 260-1-226258

2. Margaret Mwanakatwe
Managing Director
Barclays Bank of Zambia Limited
Kafue House, Cairo Road
P.O. Box 31936
Lusaka, Zambia
Tel: 260-1-228858-66
Fax: 260-1-222519
Telex: ZA 41570

3. John Janes
Managing Director
Standard Chartered Bank Limited
Cairo Road
P.O. Box 32238
Lusaka, Zambia
Tel: 260-1-229242
Fax: 260-1-222092
Telex: 260-41660 or 45420

4. Archibald Macleod
Managing Director
Stanbic Bank Zambia Limited
Corporate House, Cairo Road
P.O. Box 32111
Lusaka, Zambia
Tel: 260-1-282441
Fax: 260-1-221152

5. Jia Zaisen
Managing Director
Bank of China (Zambia) Limited

Amandra House, Ben Bella Road
P.O. Box 34550
Lusaka, Zambia
Tel: 260-1-238711
Fax: 260-1-235350

6. Keith Stewart
Managing Director
Cavmont Mercahnt Bank Limited
Mukuba Pension House, Dedan Kimathi Road
P.O. Box 32222
Lusaka, Zambia
Tel: 260-1-224280
Fax: 260-1-224304

7. M. Wadood
Managing Director
Finance Bank Zambia Limited
Chanik House, Cairo Road
P.O. Box 36762
Lusaka, Zambia
Tel: 260-1-223587
Fax: 260-1-227290
Telex; ZA 40338

8. S. Gupta
Managing Director
First Alliance Bank Limited
Chachacah Road
P.O. Box 36326
Lusaka, Zambia
Tel: 260-1-229303
Fax: 260-1-228441
Telex: ZA 40794

9. A.K. Misra
Managing Director
Indo-Zambia Bank Limited
Cairo Road,
P.O. Box 35411,
Lusaka, Zambia
Tel: 260-1-224653
Fax: 260-1-225090
Telex: ZA 40631

10. Friday C. Ndhlovu
Managing Director
Investrust Merchant Bank Limited
AFE House, Freedom Way

P.O. Box 32344,
Lusaka, Zambia
Tel: 260-1-238733
Fax: 260-1-237060

11. Godfrey Msiska,
General Manager
New Capital Bank Limited
Anchor House, Cairo Road
P.O. Box 36452
Lusaka, Zambia
Tel: 260-1-229508
Fax: 260-1-224055
Telex: ZA 43830

12.. Samuel B. Musonda
Managing Director
Zambia National Commercial Bank
Plot 33454, Cairo Road
P.O. Box 33611
Lusaka, Zambia
Tel: 260-1-228979
Fax: 260-1-223106
Telex: ZA 42360

WASHINGTON-BASED U.S. GOVERNMENT CONTACTS

Karl Albrecht, Zambia Desk Officer (AF/S), Department of State, Washington DC, 20520. Tel: 202 647-9858.

Office of the Coordinator for Business Affairs, Department of State, tel.: 202 746-1625.

Deborah Henke Rogers, Zambia Desk Officer (ANESA/OA), Department of Commerce, Washington DC, 20230. Tel: 202 482-4227.

TPCC Trade Information Center Number: 1 800 USA-TRADE.

Trade Assistance and Promotion Office, Foreign Agricultural Service, Department of Agriculture, tel.: 202 720-7420.

FOREIGN DIPLOMATIC MISSIONS

IN LUSAKA - DIALING CODE 260+1+ NUMBER

COUNTRY	ADDRESS	POST	TELEPHONE	FAX	TLX/EMAIL
ANGOLA	Plot No. 6660	Box:	Tel: 291142	292595	ZA 41940

	Mumana Rd. Olympia Park Ext	31595	290346		
BOTSWANA	Diplomatic Triangle	Box: 31910	Tel: 250555 / 250019 /	Fax: 253895	ZA 41710
CANADA	5119 United Nations Ave	Box: 31313	Tel: 250833	Fax: 254176	ZA 42480 isaka@paris03.x400.gc.ca
CHINA.	7430 Haile Selassie Ave	Box 31975.	Tel: 252410/253770	Fax: 251157	Tlx:41360
CUBA.	5574 Magoye Road.Kalundu	Box 33132	Tel:291308	91586	Tlx:40349 ssikulem@zamnet.zm
DENMARK	Dunduza Chisidza Crescent	Box 50299	Tel:254182 / 253750	Fax: 254618	ZA 43580
EGYPT	5206 United Nations Avenue	Box: 32428	Tel: 254149	Fax: 252213	Tlx: 40021
EUROPEAN UNION	Plot 4899 Los Angeles Boulevard, Lusaka		250711, 251140, 255586,255585	250906, 252336	info@zam.eudel.com
FINLAND.	74 Independence Avenue,	Box 50819	Tel: 251988 /252026	Fax: 254981	Tlx:43460 finemb@zamnet.zm
FRANCE	74 Independence Avenue	Box 30062	Tel:251332/251340	Fax: 254475	Tlx:41430 frcooparobase@zamnet.zm
GERMANY.	5209 United Nations Avenue,	Box 50120	Tel: 250644/251259 251262	Fax: 254014	Tlx.41410
GREECE	54 Joseph Mwila Rd, Rhodes Park	Box: 31587	Tel: 231020/231064	Fax: 231061	.
INDIA,	Pandit Nehru Rd	Box: 32111	Tel:253006/253158 /9/60	Fax: 254118	Tlx:41420
IRELAND.	6663 Katima Mulilo road, Olympia Park	Box 34923	Tel:290482/291124 292288	Fax: 290482	Tlx:43110

	Extension,				
ITALY	Diplomatic Triangle, Independence Ave	Box 31046	Tel 250775/250783 250781	Fax: 254929	Tlx 43380 italyzam@zamnet.zm
JAPAN.	3218 Haile Selassie Avenue.	Box 34190	Tel: 251555/252036 252039	Fax: 253488	Tlx:41470 jez@zamnet.zm
KENYA	United Nations Ave.	Box: 50298	Tel: 250772/250742	Fax: 253829	ZA 40270 kenhigh@zamnet.zm
KOREA	92 Mutandwa Rd, Roma	Box 30584	Tel:292380	Fax: 225368	.
MALAWI HIGH COMMISSION	Bishops Rd, Kabulonga	Box 50425	Tel: 265764/9	Fax: 265765	ZA 41840
MOZAMBIQUE	Plot 9592 Kacha Rd, Northmead	Box 34877	Tel: 220333/239135	Fax: 220345	Tlx:45900
NAMIBIA	6968 Kabanga Rd, Rhodes Park	Box: 30577	Tel: 252250/250968	Fax: 252497	.
NETHERLANDS	5208 United Nations Ave	Box 31905	Tel:253819/253590 253994	Fax: 253733 250200	Tlx:40211 nlgovlus@zamnet.zm
NIGERIA	5203 United Nations Ave	Box: 32598	Tel: 253177 / 253268/253265	Fax: 253560	ZA 41280
NORWAY.	Plot No.245/65 Birdcage Walk, Haile Selassie Avenue,	Box 34570	Tel:252188/252625.	Fax: 253915	ZA 40100
PORTUGAL	23 Yotem Muleya Rd Woodlands	Box 33871	Tel: 253720/260296	Fax: 253896	Tlx:40010.
ROMANIA	2 Leopards Hill Road, Kabulonga,	Box 31944	Tel:262182/262239	.	ZA 40668

RUSSIA	Plot No. 6407, Diplomatic Triangle,	Box 32355	Tel:252183/252128 /252120	Fax: 253582	Tlx:40341
SAUDI ARABIA	4896 Los Angeles Blvd	Box: 34411	Tel: 253266 /253325	Fax: 253449	Tlx:45550.
SOMALI	Plot No.G3/377A Kabulonga	Box 34051	Tel:262119/263944.	Fax: 253582	Tlx:40270
SOUTH AFRICA	D26 Cheetah Rd, Kabulonga	Private Bag W369	Tel: 260999	Fax: 263001	sahc@zamnet.zm
SWEDEN.	Alick Nkatha Ave, Longacares	Box 30788	Tel: 251711	Fax: 254049	ZA 41820 swedem@zamnet.zm
TANZANIA	Ujaama House, United Nations Ave,	Box: 31219	Tel: 253320/253222 253323/4	Fax: 254861	ZA 40118 tzrplsk@zamnet.zm
UNITED KINGDOM	Independence Ave,	Box: 50050	Tel: 251133	Fax: 253798	ZA 41150 brtn@zamnet.zm
UNITED STATES	United Nations Ave,	Box: 31617	Tel: 250955	Fax: 252225	ZA 41970 usembass@zamnet.zm
ZAIRE	1124 Parirenytwa Rd Rd. Box 71234,	Box: 31287	Tel; 213343 / 229044 /5	.	.
ZIMBABWE	Haille Selassie Rd	Box: 33491	Tel: 254006/12/18	Fax: 253582	Tlx:45800

ZAMBIAN MISSIONS ABROAD

COUNTRY	**ADDRESS**	**PHONE**	**FAX**	**TELEX/EMAIL**
ANGOLA	106/108, Run Rei Katyavala Maculusso PO Box 1496 Luanda	Tel: 244-2-331145/ 331241	Fax: 244-2-331241	Telex:998-3439
BELGIUM	1060 Brussels	Tel: 32-2-343-	Fax: 32-	Telex: 846-63102

	469 Avenue Moliere	5649	2-347-4333	ZAMNREP B
BOTSWANA	P.O. Box 362 1118 Queen's Road, Zambia House, The Mall, Gaberone	Tel: 267-351-951 267-351-952	Fax: 267-353-952	Telex: 991-2416
CHINA	Beijing (Peking) 5 Dongsijie San-Li-Tun	Tel: 8610-5321778 /5321554 8610-8610-5321891	Fax: 8610-532-1891	Telex: 085 -22388 zamem@public.bta.net.cn
DEMOCRATIC REPUBLIC OF CONGO	54-58, Avenue de L'Ecole, Gombe. B.P. 1144, Kinshasa	Cell: 48456	Fax: 2431-2123151	
	Corner Rues/Lufira, Zone Lubumbashi. B.P.596, Lubumbashi	Tel: 222309		
EGYPT	25 Abdel Monein Riad Sreet, Mohandesein. POBox 253 Dokki. Cairo 12311	TEL: 202-3610281/2/3	Fax: 20-2-361-0833	Telex: 927-2262
ETHIOPIA	Addis Ababa, Old Airport Area Higher 23 Kebele 12, Addis Ababa. P.O. Box 1909	Tel: 251-1-711-302	FAX: 2511-711566	Telex: 976-21065 zam.emb@telecom.net.et
GERMANY	5300 Bonn 2, Bad Godesberg, Mittelstrasse 39	Tel: 49-228-376-811/2/3 49-228-376-813	Fax: 49-228-379-536	Telex: 841-88551 Bosa d zambianbonn@t-online.de
INDIA	New Delhi 110057 F-8/22 Vasant Vihar	Tel: 91~1l~6847681/ 6846848/ 6845862	Fax: 91-11-6147928	zambiand@nde.vsnl.net.in
JAPAN	10-2, Ebarn 1-Chome, Shinagwa-Ku Tokyo 142,	Tel: 813-34910121	Fax: 813-34910123	zamet@crisscross.com

KENYA	Nyerere Road City Hall Annex, Box 48741, Nairobi	Tel: 254-2-724-850 254-2-724-796 254-2-724-799	Fax: 254-2-718-494	zambiacom@swiftkenya.com
MALAWI	Box 30138, Plot 40/2 Capital Hill, Lilongwe 3	Tel: 265-731-911	Fax: 784349	Telex: 988-4181
MOZAMBIQUE	Avenida Kenneth Kaunda, 1286 PO BOX 4655, Maputo.	Tel: 258-1-492-452 491307	Fax: 2581-491893	Telex: 946-6415
NAMIBIA	22 Sam Nujoma Drive CnrMandume Nddemufayo Road. POBox 22882, Windhoek	Tel: 264 61-237610/1 264-61-237611	Fax: 264-61-228-162	Telex: 964-0485
NIGERIA	18 Festival Road, Victoria Island. POBox 6119, Lagos	Tel: 2341-2690426/7	Fax: 2341-2690426	
RUSSIA	Prospect Mira 52 Moscow	Tel: 7-095-288-5001 2885092	Fax: 7-095-975-2056	zambia@online.ru
SOUTH AFRICA	P.O. Box 12234, Pretoria, 1159 Ziervogel St. Arcadia. Off Hamilton St.P.O.BOX 12234 Hartifield 0028	Tel: 27-12-3262223	Fax: 27-012-3262140	
SWEDEN	Stockholm, Engelbrektsgatan 7 Box 26013	Tel: 468-799040	Fax: 468-796850	zamembas@algonet.se
SWITZERLAND	The United Nations Office -Geneva 17-19 Chcmin Du Champ-D'anier, Geneva, 1209 Le Petit Saconnex	Tel: 41-22-788-5330 41-22-788-5331 41-22-788-5330/1	Fax: 41-022-788-5340	Telex: 415200
TANZANIA	5 & 8 Ohio/Sokoine Drive	Tel:255-27-2621	Fax: 255-112977	zhcd@rah.com

	P.O. Box 2525 Dar-es-Salaam			
UNITED KINGDOM	2 Palace Gate, Kensington, London W8 5NG	Tel: 44-171-589-6655	Fax: 44-171-581-1353	Telex: 851-263544
UNITED NATIONS	9th Floor, 800 Second Avenue. New York, NY 10017. USA	Tel: 1-212-7581110	Fax: 1-212-7581319	zmbun@undp.org
USA	Washington, D.C. 20008 2419 Massachusetts Avenue N.W.	Tel: 202-265-9717 202-265-9718 202-265-9719	Fax: 202-332-0826	zambia@purple.tmn.com
ZIMBABWE	Box 4698, Zambia House, 48 Union rd, Harare.	Tel: 263 4-773782	Fax: 263 4-776782	Telex: 987-24698

ADVETISING COMPANIES

ADVENTURE	**COMPANY**	**BASE**	**TEL**	**FAX**	**EMAIL**
ABSEILING	Abseil Zambia	Livingstone	Tel: 3-323454	3-324440	theswing@zamnet.zm
BUNJI JUMPING	African Extreme	Livingstone	Tel: 03 324156	Fax: 03 324157	extreme@zamnet.zm
FISHING	Barotseland Fishing Tours	Lusaka	Telefax: 01 222571	Fax: 01 225491	.
	Mutemwa Camp	Lusaka	Tel: 03 3213220	Fax: 03 321320	remote.africa@satmail.bt.com
	Maziba Bay River Safaris.	Sioma, Zambezi River	Mobile: +27 82-3380896 / +27 (0)82-6809876	Tel/Fax: +27(0)15-7810205	zambezia@mweb.co.za
	Maziba Bay River Safaris.	Sioma	00 264 61225762	00 264 61225762	kessler@iafrica.com.na

	Sakazima Island	W. Province	Tel: 2711 4651534	.	.
	Ndole Bay	Lake Tanganyika	Tel: + 27 (0)12 347 2499	Fax: + 27 (0)12 347 4628	sundown@iafrica.com
	Nkamba Bay	Lusaka	Tel: 01 287291	Fax: 01 287677	nkamba@zamnet.zm
MICROLIGHTING HELICOPTERS FIXED WING	Batoka Sky	Livingstone	Tel: 03 320058 cell: +263 11 407573	Fax: 03 323095	reservations @batokasky.co.zm
	Remote Africa Safaris	South Luangwa	Tel: 01 252163	Fax:062 45059	remote.africa @satmail.bt.com
	Maziba Bay River Safaris.	Sioma, Zambezi River	Mobile: +27 82-3380896 / +27 (0)82-6809876	Tel/Fax: +27(0)15-7810205	zambezia@mweb.co.za
HORSE TRAILS	Chundukwa Adventure Trails	Livingstone	Tel: 03 324006	Fax: 03 324452	chunduka@zamnet.zm
	Chaminuka Private Game Reserve	45 mins north of Lusaka	Tel: +260 1 222694 / 225432	Fax: +260 1 222815	chaminuk@aol.com
	Lilayi Game Ranch	Tel: 01 228682	Fax: 01 222906	lilayi@zamsaf.co.zm	
LAKE CAMPING	Cipembere	Siavonga	Tel: 511358	Fax: 511249	.
HOUSEBOATING	Gwembe Safaris	Lake Kariba	Tel: 032 20021	Fax: 032 20054	gwemsaf@zamnet.zm
	Hooligan	Siavonga	Lusaka,262281 /260989	250342 / 44 code 007	.
	Matusadona	Siavonga	Tel: 01 252518 Tel: 01 511358	Fax: 01 252859 Fax: 01 511249	.

CANOEING	African Experience	Lunga River, Kafue NP	Tel: 27 11 888 8015	Fax: 27 11 888 5435	safariafrica@experience.co.za lafex@icon.co.za
	Bundu Adventures	Livingstone, Zambezi	Tel:03 324407	Fax: 03 324406	zambezi@zamnet.zm
	Changa Changa Adventures	Luangwa River	Tel: 290146 Cell: 751302	Fax:295546	rshenton@zamnet.zm
	Chundukwa Adventure Trails:	Livingstone, Zambezi R	Tel: 03 23235	Fax: 03 323224/324006	chunduka@zamnet.zm
	Karibu Safaris	Lower Zambezi River	Tel: +2711 -31-839774	Fax +2711 -31-831957	karibusa@iafrica.com
	Makora Quest	Livingstone, Zambezi	Tel: 03 321679	Fax: 03 320732	quest@zamnet.zm
	Safari Par Excellence	Livingstone, Zambezi	Tel: 03 321320	Fax: 03 321320	zambezi@africaonline.co.zw
	Sobek Canoe Adventures	Zambezi Gorge and Lower Zambezi	Tel: 01 511168	Fax: 01 511168	eagles@zamnet.zm
	Tongabezi	Livingstone, Lower Zambezi	Tel: 03 323235	Fax: 03 323234	tonga@zamnet.zm
	Tafika	Luangwa River	Tel: 03 321320	Fax: 062 45059	remote.africa@satmail.bt.com
RAFTING	Bundu Adventures	Livingstone	Tel:03 324407	Fax:03 324406	zambezi@zamnet.za
	Maziba Bay River Safaris.	Sioma, Zambezi River	Mobile: +27 82-3380896 / +27 (0)82-6809876	Tel/Fax: +27(0)15-7810205	zambezia@mweb.co.za
	Raft Extreme	Livingstone	Tel: 03 322370	.	.

	Safari Par Excellence	Livingstone	Tel: 01 2236741	Fax:01 224915	atd@zamnet.zm
WALKING SAFARIS	Remote Africa Safaris	Mfuwe	Tel/Fax: 260-62-45059	.	remote.africa@satmail.bt.com
	Shiwa Safaris	Lusaka	Tel: 01 228682	Fax 222906	safcom@zamnet.zm
	Chunduk wa Adventure Trails:	Livingstone	Tel: 323235	Fax: 323224/324006	chunduka@zamnet.zm
	Robin Pope Safaris	South Luangwa	Tel: 062 45090	Fax: 062 45051	rps@super-hub.com
	Star of Africa	South Luangwa	Tel: (263-9) 41715, 41837	Fax: (263-9) 229909	star_of_africa@telconet.co.zw
SCUBA DIVING	Tanganyika Lodge	Lake Tanganyika	Tel: 224616	Fax:224915	atd@zamnet.zm
	Kalambo Lodge	Lake Tanganyika	Tel:224616	Fax: 224915	atd@zamnet.zm
RIVER BOARDING	Serious Fun	Livingstone	Tel: 260 3 323912	Fax: 321850	.
ZAMBEZI BOAT CRUISES	Bwaato Adventures	Livingstone	Tel: 03 324106	324227	.
	Victoria Falls River Safaris	Livingstone	Tel: +260 3 324115 Cell: +263 11 230655	Fax: +260 3 322083	riversafaris@zamnet.zm
HIKING TRAILS	Changa Changa	Luangwa RIver	Tel:03 324407	Fax: 03 324406	zambezi@zamnet.zm
	Taita Falcon Lodge	Batoka Gorge Victoria Falls	Tel / Fax: 260 3 321850 (office)	Cell: 263 11 208387 (lodge)	taita.falcon@outpost.co.zm
SAFARI EXPEDITIONS	African Horizons	Zambia/Botswana	Tel: 260 3 323432		ahorizon@zamnet.zm

	Africa Original Expeditions	Lusaka	Tel (2601) 265362	Fax: (2601) 261472	anzac@zamnet.zm
	Royal Barotse Safaris	Western Zambia	Tel: +264 (0)61-225949 Cell: +264 81-1241162	Fax: +264 61-225949	barotse@iafrica.com.na
	Zambia Outdoors	All Zambia	Telefax: (0)1179 606494		info@zambiaoutdoors.co.uk

HOTELS

LUSAKA AND SURROUNDS

LUSAKA	ADDRESS	TEL / FAX	E- MAIL
CHAINAMA HOTEL	Great East Rd	Tel: 292451/6 Fax: 290809	.
CHAMINUKA	45mins north of Lusaka	Tel: 01 233303/4 Fax: 01 233305	chaminuk@aol.com
PROTEA SAFARI LODGE	Chisamba	Tel: 226589 Fax: 221175	chisamba@zamnet.zm
FRINGILLA GUESTHOUSE	50kms north Lusaka	Tel: 611199	fringill@zamnet.zm
FAIRVIEW HOTEL	Church Rd	Tel: 212954	fairview@zamnet.zm
GARDEN HOUSE HOTEL	Mongu Rd	Tel: 233004/3 Fax: 251734	.
CHRISMAR HOTEL	Los Angeles Boulevard	Tel: 253036 Fax: 253036	chrismar@zamnet.zm.
HILLVIEW HOTEL	Kafue Rd Lusaka	Tel:233250 Fax: 252779	.
HOLIDAY INN	Church Rd	Tel: 251666 Fax: 253529	holinn@zamnet.zm
INTER-CONTINENTAL HOTEL	Haille Selassie Ave.	Tel: 250000/250600 Fax:251880	lusaka@interconti.com
KAFUE ROAD GARDEN HOTEL	.	Tel: 274646 Fax:252779	

LECHWE LODGE	Box 31522	Tel: 222083/84/73, Fax: 222684	kflechwe@zamnet.zm
LILAYI LODGE	Box 30093	Tel: 228682/3, Fax: 222906	lilayi@zamnet.zm
LUSAKA HOTEL	Cairo Rd	Tel: 229049, Fax: 225726	
MUMANA PLEASURE RESORT	10446 Great East Road Box 35530	Tel: 260 1 291860/3 Fax: 260 1 291863	mumana@zamnet.zm
NDEKE HOTEL	Off Los Angeles Blvd. Box 30815.	Tel:251734 Fax: 252779	
NEW LONDE HOTEL		Tel:212061/227966 Fax: 254005.	
PAMODZI HOTEL	Church RdBox 35450	Tel: 254455 Fax: 250995	pamodzi@zamnet.zm
VILLA LODGE GARDENS	Ibex Hill	Tel:260870 Fax: 260870	villa@coppernet.zm
CHISAMBA	ADDRESS	TEL / FAX	E- MAIL/website
IBIS GARDENS		Tel: 01-233766, 05 - 221950, Tel/Fax 01 - 233764.	Ibis@zamnet.zm
PLOUGHMANS ARMS HOTEL	Main Rd.	Tel 10430	
KABWE	ADDRESS	TEL / FAX	E- MAIL
TUSKERS HOTEL		Tel: 222077 222498 Fax: 222076	tuskers@zamnet.zm
Western Zambia			
SOLWEZI	ADDRESS	TEL / FAX	E- MAIL
SAKATANGO HOTEL	Box 110071, Solwezi	Tel: 821224	
MONGU	ADDRESS	TEL / FAX	E- MAIL
LYAMBAYI HOTEL	Box 910193, Mongu	Tel: 221138 Fax: 221138	
NGULU HOTEL	Box: 910308.	Tel: 221028/221258 Fax: 221286	

SIR MWANAWINA MOTEL	Box 53, Mongu	Tel: 22148 Fax: 221856	

NORTHERN ZAMBIA

KASAMA	ADDRESS	TEL / FAX	E- MAIL
KASAMA HOTEL	Main Rd	Tel: 221188	
KWACHA RELAX HOTEL	Box : 410053, Kasama	Tel:221124	
MBALA	ADDRESS	TEL / FAX	E- MAIL
ARMS HOTEL	Box 420161, Mbala	Tel: 450585	
NEW GRASSHOPPER INN	Box 420093, Mbala	Tel: 450589	
MKUSHI	ADDRESS	TEL / FAX	E- MAIL
FOREST INN	Box 810064, Mkushi	Tel/Fax: 362188	r.shenton@zamnet.zm
MPIKA	ADDRESS	TEL / FAX	E- MAIL
CRESTED CRANE HOTEL	Box 450125, Mpika	Tel: 370694	
MPULUNGU	ADDRESS	TEL / FAX	E- MAIL
KALAMBO LODGE	Box 34065 Lusaka	Tel: 235382 Lusaka, Fax: 235381	atd@zamnet.zm
NKUPI LODGE	PB 8, Port Mpulungu	Tel: 455166	
TANGANYIKA LODGE	PB 59 Mpulungu	Tel: 224248, Fax: 224265	atd@zamnet.zm
MISHEMBE	Lake Tanganyika	Tel: 04 221615.	
SHIWA NGANDU	ADDRESS	TEL / FAX	E- MAIL
KAPISHYA HOT SPRINGS SHIWA NG'ANDU	Shiwa Ng'andu Estate	Tel: 01 228682 Fax: 222906	safcom@zamnet.zm
CHIRUNDU	ADDRESS	TEL / FAX	E- MAIL
NAMBADWE MOTEL			

GWABI LODGE	Box 30813	Tel: 250772	gwabi@zamnet.zm
KANYEMBA LODGE	Box 30815, Lusaka	Tel: 252779	

SOUTHERN ZAMBIA

CHOMA	ADDRESS	TEL / FAX	E- MAIL
CHOMA HOTEL	Box 630805, Choma	Tel: 20189	
MAMBUSHI CHALETS	Gwembe Safaris Box 630162, Choma	Tel:20021 Fax: 20054	gwemsaf@zamnet.zm
KALOMO	ADDRESS	TEL / FAX	E- MAIL
KALOMO HOTEL	Box 620110	Tel: 65188	
MAZABUKA	ADDRESS	TEL / FAX	E- MAIL
MAZABUKA GARDEN HOTEL	Box 30815	Tel: 251734	
LIVINGSTONEand VICTORIA FALLS	ADDRESS	TEL / FAX	E- MAIL
KUBU CABINS	PO Box 60748, Livingstone	Tel: 324093, Fax: 324091	
LIVINGSTONE ISLAND TENTED CAMP	PB 286x, Ridgeway, Lusaka	Tel: 2601 265814 Fax: 2601 262291	tim@chilongozi.com
MUKOLO ISLAND TENTED CAMP	PB 286x, Ridgeway, Lusaka	Tel: 2601 265814 Fax: 2601 262291	tim@chilongozi.com
NGOLIDE LODGE	P.O. Box 60186 Livingstone	Tel: 3 321091/2 Fax: 3 321113 Cell: 00 263 11 406712	ngolide@zamnet.zm
MAWALA LODGE	P.O.Box 60273, Lvingstone	Fax: 260-3-324455, Tel: 260-3-321935 Cell 263-11-213720 / 263-11-724711	mawala@zamnet.zm
TAITA FALCON LODGE	Livingstone	Tel:03321850	taita-falcon@zamnet.zm

THE ROYAL LIVINGSTONE	Sun International S.A.	Tel: 2711 780-7878 Fax: 2711 780-7061	fitres@sunint.co.za
TONGABEZI LODGE	P Bag 31Livingstone	Tel: 323235, Fax: 3232242	tonga@zamnet.zm
WASAWANGE LODGE	Box 60278 Livingstone	Tel: 260-332-4066, Fax: 260-332-4067	lisbwa@zamnet.zm
ZAMBEZI RIVER TREE LODGE	Chundukwa Adventure Trails	Tel: 324452 Fax: 324006	chunduka@zamnet.zm
ZAMBEZI ROYAL CHUNDU LODGE	Box: 60889	Tel: 321772 Johannesburg: (2711)Tel: 9533224	chundu@icon.co.za
ZAMBEZI SUN	Sun International S.A.	Tel: 2711 780-7878 Fax: 2711 780-7061	fitres@sunint.co.za
MUTEMWA CAMP Upper Zambezi	50 km from the border at Katima Mulilo	Tel: +27 (0)11 888 2431 Fax: +27 (0)11 888 5798	mutemwa.lodge@mweb.co.za
MONZE	ADDRESS	TEL / FAX	E- MAIL
MONZE HOTEL	Box 660267, Monze	Tel: 50089	
SIAVONGA	ADDRESS	TEL / FAX	E- MAIL
EAGLES REST CHALETS	Box 1, Siavonga	Tel/fax: 01 511168	eagles@zamnet.zm
LAKE KARIBA INN	Box 117, Siavonga Box 33565 Lusaka	Tel: 511269/249 Fax: 511188	Tel: 01 253768 Fax: 01 252518
LEISURE BAY LODGE	Box 68 Siavonga	Tel: 01 511135/6 or Lusaka: 01 252779	
MANCHINCHI BAY LODGE	Box 115, Siavonga	Tel: 511299/399	
LAKE SAFARI LODGE	Box 30, Siavonga	Tel: 511148 / 511200 Fax: 511103	
LAKE KARIBA			
CHETE ISLAND LODGE	UTC:	Tel: 260-32-	westisl@id.co.zw

		321122,321210	
CHIKANKA ISLAND CAMPS	Gwembe Safaris Box 630162, Choma	Tel:20021 Fax: 20054	gwemsaf@zamnet.zm

BASIC TITLES ON ZAMBIA

IMPORTANT!

All publications are updated annually!

Please contact IBP, Inc. at ibpusa3@gmail.com for the latest ISBNs and additional information

TITLE
Zambia A "Spy" Guide - Strategic Informtion and Developments
Zambia A Spy" Guide"
Zambia Banking & Financial Market Handbook
Zambia Banking & Financial Market Handbook
Zambia Business and Investment Opportunities Yearbook
Zambia Business and Investment Opportunities Yearbook
Zambia Business and Investment Opportunities Yearbook Volume 1 Strategic Information and Opportunities
Zambia Business Intelligence Report - Practical Information, Opportunities, Contacts
Zambia Business Intelligence Report - Practical Information, Opportunities, Contacts
Zambia Business Law Handbook - Strategic Informtion and Basic Laws
Zambia Business Law Handbook - Strategic Informtion and Basic Laws
Zambia Business Law Handbook - Strategic Informtion and Basic Laws
Zambia Business Law Handbook - Strategic Informtion and Basic Laws
Zambia Business Law Handbook Volume 1 Srategic Information and Basic Laws
Zambia Business Success Guide - Basic Practical Information and Contacts
Zambia Clothing & Textile Industry Handbook
Zambia Company Laws and Regulations Handbook - Strategic Information and Basic Laws
Zambia Constitution and Citizenship Laws Handbook - Strategic Information and Basic Laws
Zambia Country Study Guide - Strategic Informtion and Developments
Zambia Country Study Guide - Strategic Informtion and Developments
Zambia Country Study Guide - Strategic Informtion and Developments Volume 1 Strategic Information and Developments
Zambia Criminal Laws, Regulations and Procedures Handbook - Strategic Information, Regulations, Procedures
Zambia Customs, Export-Import Regulations, Incentives and Procedures Handbook - Strategic, Practical Information, Regulations
Zambia Diplomatic Handbook - Strategic Information and Developments
Zambia Diplomatic Handbook - Strategic Information and Developments
Zambia Ecology & Nature Protection Handbook
Zambia Ecology & Nature Protection Handbook
Zambia Ecology & Nature Protection Laws and Regulation Handbook
Zambia Economic & Development Strategy Handbook
Zambia Economic & Development Strategy Handbook
Zambia Electoral, Political Parties Laws and Regulations Handbook - Strategic Information, Regulations, Procedures
Zambia Energy Policy, Laws and Regulation Handbook
Zambia Export-Import and Business Directory

TITLE
Zambia Export-Import and Business Directory
Zambia Fishing and Aquaculture Industry Handbook - Strategic Information, Regulations, Opportunities
Zambia Foreign Policy and Government Guide
Zambia Foreign Policy and Government Guide
Zambia Immigration Laws and Regulations Handbook - Strategic Information and Basic Laws
Zambia Industrial and Business Directory
Zambia Industrial and Business Directory
Zambia Insolvency (Bankruptcy) Laws and Regulations Handbook - Strategic Information and Basic Laws
Zambia Investment and Business Guide - Strategic and Practical Information
Zambia Investment and Business Guide - Strategic and Practical Information
Zambia Investment and Business Guide - Strategic and Practical Information
Zambia Investment and Business Guide - Strategic and Practical Information
Zambia Investment and Business Guide Volume 2 Business, Investment Opportunities and Incentives
Zambia Investment and Business Profile - Basic Information and Contacts for Succesful investment and Business Activity
Zambia Investment, Trade Strategy and Agreements Handbook - Strategic Information and Basic Agreements
Zambia Labor Laws and Regulations Handbook - Strategic Information and Basic Laws
Zambia Land Ownership and Agriculture Laws Handbook
Zambia Mineral & Mining Sector Investment and Business Guide - Strategic and Practical Information
Zambia Mineral & Mining Sector Investment and Business Guide - Strategic and Practical Information
Zambia Mineral, Mining Sector Investment and Business Guide - Strategic Information and Regulations
Zambia Mining Laws and Regulations Handbook
Zambia Privatization Programs and Regulations Handbook
Zambia Privatization Programs and Regulations Handbook
Zambia Recent Economic and Political Developments Yearbook
Zambia Recent Economic and Political Developments Yearbook
Zambia Recent Economic and Political Developments Yearbook
Zambia Tax Guide Volume 1 Strategic Information and Basic Regulations
Zambia Taxation Laws and Regulations Handbook
Zambia: Doing Business and Investing in ... Guide Volume 1 Strategic, Practical Information, Regulations, Contacts
Zambia: How to Invest, Start and Run Profitable Business in Zambia Guide - Practical Information, Opportunities, Contacts

BASIC LAWS AND REGULATIONS AFFECTING BUSINESS[3]

COUTRY	LAW TITLE
Zambia	Accountants Act
Zambia	Act to amend the Environment Protection and Pollution Control Act
Zambia	Action for Smoke Damage (Prohibition)(Repeal) Act
Zambia	Acts of parliament Act
Zambia	Administration of Estates (Trust Corporations) Act
Zambia	Administrator-General Act
Zambia	Adoption Act
Zambia	Affiliation and Maintenance of Children Act
Zambia	African Education Act
Zambia	African War Memorial Fund Act
Zambia	Agricultural Credits Act
Zambia	Agricultural Lands Act
Zambia	Agricultural Products Levy Act
Zambia	Agricultural Statistics Act
Zambia	Agriculture (Fertilizers and Feed) Act
Zambia	Air Passenger Service Charge Act
Zambia	Air Services Act
Zambia	Anti Money Laundering Directives 2004
Zambia	Anti-Corruption Commission Act
Zambia	Anti-Human Trafficking Act 2008
Zambia	Apprenticeship Act
Zambia	Appropriation Act No 17 of 2006
Zambia	Arbitration Act, No.19 of 2000
Zambia	Authentication of Documents Act
Zambia	Aviation Act
Zambia	Bank of Zambia Act
Zambia	Banking and Financial Services (Bureau de Change) Regulations 2003
Zambia	Banking and Financial Services (Restriction on Kwacha Lending to Non-residents) Regulations, 2009
Zambia	Banking and Financial Services Act
Zambia	Bankruptcy Act
Zambia	Benefits of Former Presidents Act
Zambia	Betting Control Act
Zambia	Bills of Sale (Registration) Act
Zambia	Bio Safety Act No 10 of 2007
Zambia	Births and Deaths Registration Act
Zambia	Boy Scouts and Girl Guides Associations Act
Zambia	Brands Act
Zambia	Bretton Woods Agreements Act
Zambia	British Acts Extension Act
Zambia	Building Societies Act
Zambia	Calculation of Taxes (Consequential Provisions) Act

[3] For ordering tests of specific laws in English or French, Please contact Global Investment Center USA at ibpusa3@gmail.com

Zambia	Carriage by Air Act
Zambia	Casino Act
Zambia	Cattle Cleansing Act
Zambia	Cattle Slaughter (Control) Act
Zambia	Census and Statistics Act
Zambia	Central African Civil Air Transport
Zambia	Central African Power Corporation (Financial Provisions) Act
Zambia	Cheques Act
Zambia	Chiefs Act
Zambia	Citizenship of Zambia Act
Zambia	Civil Courts (Attachment of Debts) Act
Zambia	Clubs' Registration Act
Zambia	Coffee Act
Zambia	Combined Cadet Force Act
Zambia	Commercial Travellers (Special Provisions) Act
Zambia	Commission for Investigations Act
Zambia	Commissioners for Oaths Act
Zambia	Common Leasehold Schemes Act
Zambia	Companies Act
Zambia	Competition and Fair Trading Act
Zambia	Competition Rules in Zambia
Zambia	Constitution of Zambia
Zambia	Constitutional Offices (Emoluments) Act
Zambia	Consular Conventions Act
Zambia	Contempt of Court (Miscellaneous Provisions) Act
Zambia	Control of Dogs Act
Zambia	Control of Dogs Act
Zambia	Control of Goods Act
Zambia	Co-operative Societies Act
Zambia	Copyright and Performance Rights
Zambia	Cotton Act
Zambia	Council of Law Reporting Act
Zambia	Criminal Procedure Code Act
Zambia	Customs and Excise Act 2006
Zambia	Dairies and Dairy Produce Act
Zambia	Dairy Produce Board Establishment Act
Zambia	Dairy Produce Marketing and Levy Act
Zambia	Dangerous Drugs Act
Zambia	Day Nurseries Act
Zambia	Debtors Act
Zambia	Deceased Brother's Widow's Marriage Act
Zambia	Decimal Currency System (Arrangements) Act
Zambia	Deeds of Arrangement Act
Zambia	Defamation Act
Zambia	Defense Act
Zambia	Development (United Kingdom Government) Loan Act
Zambia	Development Bank of Zambia Act
Zambia	Development Bond Act
Zambia	Diplomatic Immunities and privileges Act

Zambia	Disposal of Uncollected Goods Act
Zambia	District Messengers Act
Zambia	Education Act
Zambia	Electoral (Code of Conduct) Regulations, 2006.
Zambia	Electoral Act
Zambia	Electoral Commissions Act 1996
Zambia	Electricity Act
Zambia	Electronic Communications and Transaction Act 2009
Zambia	Emergency Powers Act
Zambia	Employment Act
Zambia	Employment of Young Persons and Children Act
Zambia	Energy Regulation Act
Zambia	Engineering Institution of Zambia
Zambia	English Law (Extent of Application) Act
Zambia	Entertainment Tax (Repeal) Act
Zambia	Environmental Protection and Pollution Control Act of 1990, Cap 204
Zambia	Equity Levy Act
Zambia	Estate Duty (Repeal) Act
Zambia	European Officers' Pensions Act
Zambia	Evidence (Bankers' Books) Act
Zambia	Evidence Act
Zambia	Examinations Council of Zambia Act
Zambia	Export Development Act
Zambia	Export of Pigs Act
Zambia	Extermination of Mosquitoes Act
Zambia	Extradition Act
Zambia	Factories Act
Zambia	Factories Act
Zambia	Fees and Fines Act
Zambia	Fencing Act
Zambia	Finance (Control and Management) Act
Zambia	Financial Institutions (Validation of Acts) Act
Zambia	Firearms Act
Zambia	Fisheries Act
Zambia	Flying Doctor Service Act
Zambia	Food and Drugs Act
Zambia	Food Reserve Act
Zambia	Foreign Judgments (Reciprocal enforcement) Act
Zambia	Forests Act
Zambia	Gaming Machines (Prohibition) Act
Zambia	General Cadaster Regulations 2008
Zambia	General Loan and Stock Act
Zambia	Gold Trade Act
Zambia	Government Securities Act
Zambia	Gwembe District Special (Dissolution) Act
Zambia	Health Professions Act 2009
Zambia	High Court Act
Zambia	Higher Authority for Power (Special Provisions) Act
Zambia	Hire-Purchase Act

Zambia	Home Guard Act
Zambia	Honours and Decorations (Prevention of abuse) Act
Zambia	Hotels Act
Zambia	Housing (Statutory and Improvement Areas) Act
Zambia	Human Rights Commission Act
Zambia	Human Tissue Act
Zambia	Immigration and Deportation Act
Zambia	Income Tax Act
Zambia	Independent Broadcasting Act 2002
Zambia	Industrial and Labor Relations Act 2008
Zambia	Information and Communication Technology Act 2009
Zambia	Inland Waters Shipping Act
Zambia	Inquests Act
Zambia	Insurance Act 1997
Zambia	Insurance Levy Act
Zambia	Insurance Regulations
Zambia	International Bank Loan Act
Zambia	International Development Association Act
Zambia	International Finance Corporation Act
Zambia	Interpretation and General
Zambia	Intestate Succession Act
Zambia	Investment Act
Zambia	Investment Disputes Convention Act
Zambia	Ionizing Radiation Act
Zambia	Judges (Conditions of Service) Act
Zambia	Judgments Act
Zambia	Judicature Administration Act
Zambia	Judicial Code of Conduct 2006
Zambia	Jugdes (conditions of service) (Amendment) Act No. 15 of 2006
Zambia	Juveniles Act
Zambia	Landlord and Tenant (Business Premises) Act
Zambia	Lands Act
Zambia	Lands and Deeds Registry Act
Zambia	Law Association of Zambia Act
Zambia	Legal Aid Act
Zambia	Legal Practitioners Act
Zambia	Legitimacy Act
Zambia	Limitation of Liability (Passengers in Government Aircraft) Act
Zambia	Liquor Licensing Act
Zambia	Loan Act
Zambia	Local Authorities Superannuation Fund Act
Zambia	Local Courts Act
Zambia	Local Government Act
Zambia	Local Government Elections Act
Zambia	Local Loans (Registered Stock and Securities) Act
Zambia	Lotteries Act
Zambia	Maintenance Orders Act
Zambia	Management Services Board Act
Zambia	Markets Act

Zambia	Marriage Act
Zambia	Mashona Railway Company Limited Act
Zambia	Medical Aid Societies and Nursing Homes (Dissolution and Prohibition) Act
Zambia	Medical and Allied Professions Act
Zambia	Medical Examination of Young Persons (Underground Work) Act
Zambia	Mental Disorders Act
Zambia	Merchandise Marks Act
Zambia	Merchant Shipping (Temporary Provisions) aact
Zambia	Mineral Royalty Tax (Repeal) Act
Zambia	Mines Acquisition (Special Provisions) Act
Zambia	Mines and Minerals Act 2003
Zambia	Mines and Minerals Act Environmental Regulations
Zambia	Mines and Minerals Development Act No 7 of 2008
Zambia	Minimum Wages and Conditions of Employment Act
Zambia	Minister of Finance (Incorporation) Act
Zambia	Ministerial and Parliamentary Offices (Emoluments) Act
Zambia	Misrepresentation Act
Zambia	Money-lenders Act
Zambia	Mufulira-Mokambo Railway Act
Zambia	Mutual Legal Assistance In Criminal Matters Act, 1993
Zambia	Narcotic Drugs And Psychotropic Substances Act, 1993
Zambia	National Achieves Act
Zambia	National Anthem Act
Zambia	National Arts Council of Zambia Act
Zambia	National Assembly (Powers and Priviliges) Act
Zambia	National Assembly Staff Act
Zambia	National College for Management and development studies Act
Zambia	National Council for Scientific Research Act
Zambia	National Flag and Armorial Ensigns Act
Zambia	National Food and Nutrition Commission Act
Zambia	National Health Services Act
Zambia	National Heritage Conservation Act
Zambia	National Housing Authority Act
Zambia	National Museums Act
Zambia	National Pension Scheme Act
Zambia	National Registration Act
Zambia	National Road Fund Act 2006
Zambia	National Road Safety Council Act
Zambia	National Savings and Credit Bank of Zambia (Dissolution)
Zambia	National Youth Development Council Act
Zambia	Nkana-Nchanga Branch Railway Act
Zambia	Non-Designated Expatriate Officers (Retiring Benefits) Act
Zambia	Notaries Public and Notarial Functions Act
Zambia	Noxious Weeds Act
Zambia	Nurses and Midwives Act
Zambia	Occupiers' Liability Act
Zambia	Official Oaths Act
Zambia	Organizations (Control of Assistance) Act
Zambia	Ozone Depleting Substances Regulations, 2000

Zambia	Parliamentary and Ministerial Code conduct Act
Zambia	Patents Act
Zambia	Penal Code Act
Zambia	Pension Scheme Regulation
Zambia	Pensions (Increase) Act
Zambia	Personal Levy Act
Zambia	Persons with Disabilities Act
Zambia	Petroleum Act
Zambia	Pharmacy and Poisons Act
Zambia	Pig Industry Act
Zambia	Plant Pests and Diseases Act
Zambia	Plant Variety and Seeds Act
Zambia	Plant Variety and Seeds Regulations (1997)
Zambia	Pneumoconiosis Act
Zambia	Pools Act
Zambia	Postal Services Act 2009
Zambia	Preferential Claims in Bankruptcy Act
Zambia	Preservation of Public Security Act
Zambia	Presidential Emoluments Act
Zambia	Prevention of Cruelty to Animals Act
Zambia	Printed Publications Act
Zambia	Prisons Act
Zambia	Privatisation Act
Zambia	Probates (Resealing) Act
Zambia	Probation of Offenders Act
Zambia	Professional Boxing and Wrestling Control Act
Zambia	Prohibition and Prevention of Money Laundering Act 2001
Zambia	Property Transfer Tax Act
Zambia	Protected Places and Areas Act
Zambia	Protection of Names, Uniforms and Badges Act
Zambia	Provincial and District Boundaries Act
Zambia	Public Audit Act
Zambia	Public Health Act
Zambia	Public Holidays Act
Zambia	Public Officers (Change of Titles) Act
Zambia	Public Officers' Pensions (Zambia) Agreement (Implementation) Act
Zambia	Public Order Act
Zambia	Public Pounds and Trespass Act
Zambia	Public Private Partnership Act 2009
Zambia	Public Procurement Act 2008
Zambia	Public Seal Act
Zambia	Public Service Pensions
Zambia	Quantity Surveyors Act
Zambia	Radio communications Act
Zambia	Railways (Deviations) Act
Zambia	Railways Act
Zambia	Railways Transfer of Statutory Powers Act
Zambia	Rating Act
Zambia	Referendum Act

Zambia	Refugees (Control) Act
Zambia	Registered Designs Act
Zambia	Registration and Development of Villages Act
Zambia	Registration of Business Names Act
Zambia	Rent Act
Zambia	Rhodesia Railways Act, 1949
Zambia	Rhodesia Railways Loans Guarantee Act
Zambia	Roads and Road Traffic Act
Zambia	Roan Antelope Branch Railway Act
Zambia	Rural Councils (Beer Surtax) Fund Act
Zambia	Safety of Civil Aviation Act
Zambia	Savings Certificates Act
Zambia	Science & Technology Act
Zambia	Scrap Metal Dealers Act
Zambia	Securities Act 1993
Zambia	Securities and Exchange Commission Anti-Money Laundering Directives, 2009
Zambia	Self-Management Enterprises Act
Zambia	Service Commissions Act
Zambia	Service of Process and Execution of Judgments Act
Zambia	Sheriffs Act
Zambia	Small Claims Courts Act
Zambia	Small Claims Courts Amendment Act 2008
Zambia	Small Enterprises Development Act
Zambia	Societies Act
Zambia	Specific Loan (Rhodesia Railways) Act
Zambia	Sports Council of Zambia Act
Zambia	Standardization of Soap Act
Zambia	Standards Act
Zambia	State Lotteries Act
Zambia	State Proceedings Act
Zambia	State Security Act
Zambia	Statutory Functions Act
Zambia	Stock Diseases Act
Zambia	Subordinate Courts Act
Zambia	Suicide Act
Zambia	Supreme Court and High Court (number of judges) Act (Vol 3 ch 26)
Zambia	Supreme Court of Zambia Act
Zambia	Tanganyika Victoria Memorial Institute Act
Zambia	Tanzania-Zambia Railway Act
Zambia	Tax Reserve Certificates Act
Zambia	Taxation (Provisional Charging) Act
Zambia	Technical Education and Vocational Training Act
Zambia	Technical Education, Vocational and Entrepreneurship Training Act No 13 of 1998
Zambia	Telecommunications Act
Zambia	Termination of Pregnancy Act
Zambia	The Air Pollution Control (Licencing and Emissions Standards) Regulations, 1996.
Zambia	The Anti-corruption Commission Act
Zambia	The Banking and Financial Services Act
Zambia	The Competition And Fair Trading Act

Zambia	The Dangerous Drugs Act 1967
Zambia	The Electoral Act 2006
Zambia	The Environmental Protection and Pollution Control (Environmental Impact Assessment) Regulations, 1997
Zambia	The Hazardous Waste Management Regulations 2001
Zambia	The Law Association Act 2006
Zambia	The Minimum Wages And Conditions Of Employment Act
Zambia	The National Hiv/Aids/Sti/Tb Council Act 2002
Zambia	The National Institute Of Public Administration Act
Zambia	The Pesticides And Toxic substances Regulations, 1994.
Zambia	The Public Finance Act 2004
Zambia	The Water Pollution Control (Effluent and Waste Water) Regulations 1993
Zambia	The Water Supply And Sanitation Act, 1997
Zambia	The Zambia Development Agency Act 2006
Zambia	The Zambia Wildlife Act, No.12 Of 1998
Zambia	Theatres and Cinematograph Exhibition Act
Zambia	Therapeutic Substances Act
Zambia	Tobacco Act
Zambia	Tobacco Levy Act
Zambia	Tokyo Convention Act
Zambia	Tolls Act
Zambia	Tourism Act
Zambia	Tourism and Hospitality Act No 23 of 2007
Zambia	Town and Country Planning Act
Zambia	Trade Marks Act
Zambia	Trades Charges Act
Zambia	Trades Licensing Act
Zambia	Trading with the Enemy Act
Zambia	Traditional Beer (Levy) Act
Zambia	Traditional Beer Act
Zambia	Transferred Federal Officers (Dependants) Pensions Act
Zambia	Treasury Bills Act
Zambia	Tropical Diseases Research Centre Act
Zambia	Trusts Restriction Act
Zambia	Tsetse Control Act
Zambia	University Act
Zambia	Uranium & Radioactive Mineral Ores Regulations
Zambia	Valuation Surveyors Act
Zambia	Value Added Tax Act
Zambia	Veterinary Surgeons Act
Zambia	Victoria Memorial Institute (repeal) Act
Zambia	War Graves and Memorials Act
Zambia	Water Act
Zambia	Weights and Measures Act
Zambia	Widows and Orphans Pension Act
Zambia	Wills and Administration of Testate Estates Act
Zambia	Witchcraft Act
Zambia	Workers' Compensation Act No 10 of 1999
Zambia	Zambezi River Authority Act
Zambia	Zambia Centre for Accountancy Studies Act

Zambia	Zambia Constitution
Zambia	Zambia Development Agency Act No 11 of 2006
Zambia	Zambia Educational Publishing House Act
Zambia	Zambia Institute of Advanced Legal Education Act
Zambia	Zambia Institute of Architects Act
Zambia	Zambia Institute of Diplomacy and International studies Act
Zambia	Zambia Institute of Human Resources Management Act
Zambia	Zambia Institute of Mass Communications (Repeal) Act
Zambia	Zambia Law Development Commission Act
Zambia	Zambia National Broadcasting Corporation Act
Zambia	Zambia National Commission for UNESCO Act
Zambia	Zambia National Provident Fund
Zambia	Zambia National Service Act
Zambia	Zambia National Tender Board Act
Zambia	Zambia Police Act
Zambia	Zambia Police Reserve Act
Zambia	Zambia Red Cross Society Act
Zambia	Zambia Security Intelligence Service Act
Zambia	Zambia Tanzania Pipeline Act
Zambia	Zambia Youth Service Act
Zambia	Zambian Mines Local Pension Fund (Dissolution) Act

WORLD COUNTRY STUDY GUIDES LIBRARY

Strategic political, geographic, economic, business information, contacts and important developments

Price: $99.95 each

1.	Abkhazia (Republic of Abkhazia) Volume 1 Strategic Information and Developments
2.	Afghanistan Country Study Guide Volume 1 Strategic Information and Developments
3.	Aland Country Study Guide Volume 1 Strategic Information and Developments
4.	Albania Country Study Guide Volume 1 Strategic Information and Developments
5.	Algeria Country Study Guide Volume 1 Strategic Information and Developments
6.	Andorra Country Study Guide Volume 1 Strategic Information and Developments
7.	Angola Country Study Guide Volume 1 Strategic Information and Developments
8.	Anguilla Country Study Guide Volume 1 Strategic Information and Developments
9.	Antigua and Barbuda Country Study Guide Volume 1 Strategic Information and Developments
10.	Antilles (Netherlands) Country Study Guide Volume 1 Strategic Information and Developments
11.	Argentina Country Study Guide Volume 1 Strategic Information and Developments
12.	Armenia Country Study Guide Volume 1 Strategic Information and Developments
13.	Aruba Country Study Guide Volume 1 Strategic Information and Developments
14.	Australia Country Study Guide Volume 1 Strategic Information and Developments
15.	Austria Country Study Guide Volume 1 Strategic Information and Developments
16.	Azerbaijan Country Study Guide Volume 1 Strategic Information and Developments
17.	Bahamas Country Study Guide Volume 1 Strategic Information and Developments
18.	Bahrain Country Study Guide Volume 1 Strategic Information and Developments
19.	Bangladesh Country Study Guide Volume 1 Strategic Information and Developments
20.	Barbados Country Study Guide Volume 1 Strategic Information and Developments
21.	Belarus Country Study Guide Volume 1 Strategic Information and Developments
22.	Belgium Country Study Guide Volume 1 Strategic Information and Developments
23.	Belize Country Study Guide Volume 1 Strategic Information and Developments
24.	Benin Country Study Guide Volume 1 Strategic Information and Developments
25.	Bermuda Country Study Guide Volume 1 Strategic Information and Developments
26.	Bhutan Country Study Guide Volume 1 Strategic Information and Developments
27.	Bolivia Country Study Guide Volume 1 Strategic Information and Developments
28.	Bosnia and Herzegovina Country Study Guide Volume 1 Strategic Information and Developments
29.	Botswana Country Study Guide Volume 1 Strategic Information and Developments
30.	Brazil Country Study Guide Volume 1 Strategic Information and Developments
31.	Brunei Country Study Guide Volume 1 Strategic Information and Developments
32.	Bulgaria Country Study Guide Volume 1 Strategic Information and Developments
33.	Burkina Faso Country Study Guide Volume 1 Strategic Information and Developments
34.	Burundi Country Study Guide Volume 1 Strategic Information and Developments
35.	Cambodia Country Study Guide Volume 1 Strategic Information and Developments
36.	Cameroon Country Study Guide Volume 1 Strategic Information and Developments
37.	Canada Country Study Guide Volume 1 Strategic Information and Developments

38.	Cape Verde Country Study Guide Volume 1 Strategic Information and Developments
39.	Cayman Islands Country Study Guide Volume 1 Strategic Information and Developments
40.	Central African Republic Country Study Guide Volume 1 Strategic Information and Developments
41.	Chad Country Study Guide Volume 1 Strategic Information and Developments
42.	Chile Country Study Guide Volume 1 Strategic Information and Developments
43.	China Country Study Guide Volume 1 Strategic Information and Developments
44.	Colombia Country Study Guide Volume 1 Strategic Information and Developments
45.	Comoros Country Study Guide Volume 1 Strategic Information and Developments
46.	Congo Country Study Guide Volume 1 Strategic Information and Developments
47.	Congo, Democratic Republic Country Study Guide Volume 1 Strategic Information and Developments
48.	Cook Islands Country Study Guide Volume 1 Strategic Information and Developments
49.	Costa Rica Country Study Guide Volume 1 Strategic Information and Developments
50.	Cote d'Ivoire Country Study Guide Volume 1 Strategic Information and Developments
51.	Croatia Country Study Guide Volume 1 Strategic Information and Developments
52.	Cuba Country Study Guide Volume 1 Strategic Information and Developments
53.	Cyprus Country Study Guide Volume 1 Strategic Information and Developments
54.	Czech Republic Country Study Guide Volume 1 Strategic Information and Developments
55.	Denmark Country Study Guide Volume 1 Strategic Information and Developments
56.	Djibouti Country Study Guide Volume 1 Strategic Information and Developments
57.	Dominica Country Study Guide Volume 1 Strategic Information and Developments
58.	Dominican Republic Country Study Guide Volume 1 Strategic Information and Developments
59.	Ecuador Country Study Guide Volume 1 Strategic Information and Developments
60.	Egypt Country Study Guide Volume 1 Strategic Information and Developments
61.	El Salvador Country Study Guide Volume 1 Strategic Information and Developments
62.	Equatorial Guinea Country Study Guide Volume 1 Strategic Information and Developments
63.	Eritrea Country Study Guide Volume 1 Strategic Information and Developments
64.	Estonia Country Study Guide Volume 1 Strategic Information and Developments
65.	Ethiopia Country Study Guide Volume 1 Strategic Information and Developments
66.	Falkland Islands Country Study Guide Volume 1 Strategic Information and Developments
67.	Faroes Islands Country Study Guide Volume 1 Strategic Information and Developments
68.	Fiji Country Study Guide Volume 1 Strategic Information and Developments
69.	Finland Country Study Guide Volume 1 Strategic Information and Developments
70.	France Country Study Guide Volume 1 Strategic Information and Developments
71.	Gabon Country Study Guide Volume 1 Strategic Information and Developments
72.	Gambia Country Study Guide Volume 1 Strategic Information and Developments
73.	Georgia Country Study Guide Volume 1 Strategic Information and Developments
74.	Germany Country Study Guide Volume 1 Strategic Information and Developments
75.	Ghana Country Study Guide Volume 1 Strategic Information and Developments
76.	Gibraltar Country Study Guide Volume 1 Strategic Information and Developments
77.	Greece Country Study Guide Volume 1 Strategic Information and Developments
78.	Greenland Country Study Guide Volume 1 Strategic Information and Developments
79.	Grenada Country Study Guide Volume 1 Strategic Information and Developments
80.	Guam Country Study Guide Volume 1 Strategic Information and Developments
81.	Guatemala Country Study Guide Volume 1 Strategic Information and Developments
82.	Guernsey Country Study Guide Volume 1 Strategic Information and Developments
83.	Guinea Country Study Guide Volume 1 Strategic Information and Developments
84.	Guinea-Bissau Country Study Guide Volume 1 Strategic Information and Developments
85.	Guyana Country Study Guide Volume 1 Strategic Information and Developments
86.	Haiti Country Study Guide Volume 1 Strategic Information and Developments
87.	Honduras Country Study Guide Volume 1 Strategic Information and Developments
88.	Hungary Country Study Guide Volume 1 Strategic Information and Developments
89.	Iceland Country Study Guide Volume 1 Strategic Information and Developments
90.	India Country Study Guide Volume 1 Strategic Information and Developments

91. Indonesia Country Study Guide Volume 1 Strategic Information and Developments
92. Iran Country Study Guide Volume 1 Strategic Information and Developments
93. Iraq Country Study Guide Volume 1 Strategic Information and Developments
94. Ireland Country Study Guide Volume 1 Strategic Information and Developments
95. Israel Country Study Guide Volume 1 Strategic Information and Developments
96. Italy Country Study Guide Volume 1 Strategic Information and Developments
97. Jamaica Country Study Guide Volume 1 Strategic Information and Developments
98. Japan Country Study Guide Volume 1 Strategic Information and Developments
99. Jersey Country Study Guide Volume 1 Strategic Information and Developments
100. Jordan Country Study Guide Volume 1 Strategic Information and Developments
101. Kazakhstan Country Study Guide Volume 1 Strategic Information and Developments
102. Kenya Country Study Guide Volume 1 Strategic Information and Developments
103. Kiribati Country Study Guide Volume 1 Strategic Information and Developments
104. Korea, North Country Study Guide Volume 1 Strategic Information and Developments
105. Korea, South Country Study Guide Volume 1 Strategic Information and Developments
106. Kosovo Country Study Guide Volume 1 Strategic Information and Developments
107. Kurdistan Country Study Guide Volume 1 Strategic Information and Developments
108. Kuwait Country Study Guide Volume 1 Strategic Information and Developments
109. Kyrgyzstan Country Study Guide Volume 1 Strategic Information and Developments
110. Laos Country Study Guide Volume 1 Strategic Information and Developments
111. Latvia Country Study Guide Volume 1 Strategic Information and Developments
112. Lebanon Country Study Guide Volume 1 Strategic Information and Developments
113. Lesotho Country Study Guide Volume 1 Strategic Information and Developments
114. Liberia Country Study Guide Volume 1 Strategic Information and Developments
115. Libya Country Study Guide Volume 1 Strategic Information and Developments
116. Liechtenstein Country Study Guide Volume 1 Strategic Information and Developments
117. Lithuania Country Study Guide Volume 1 Strategic Information and Developments
118. Luxembourg Country Study Guide Volume 1 Strategic Information and Developments
119. Macao Country Study Guide Volume 1 Strategic Information and Developments
120. Macedonia,Country Study Guide Volume 1 Strategic Information and Developments
121. Madagascar Country Study Guide Volume 1 Strategic Information and Developments
122. MadeiraCountry Study Guide Volume 1 Strategic Information and Developments
123. Malawi Country Study Guide Volume 1 Strategic Information and Developments
124. Malaysia Country Study Guide Volume 1 Strategic Information and Developments
125. Maldives Country Study Guide Volume 1 Strategic Information and Developments
126. Mali Country Study Guide Volume 1 Strategic Information and Developments
127. Malta Country Study Guide Volume 1 Strategic Information and Developments
128. Man Country Study Guide Volume 1 Strategic Information and Developments
129. Marshall Islands Country Study Guide Volume 1 Strategic Information and Developments
130. Mauritania Country Study Guide Volume 1 Strategic Information and Developments
131. Mauritius Country Study Guide Volume 1 Strategic Information and Developments
132. Mayotte Country Study Guide Volume 1 Strategic Information and Developments
133. Mexico Country Study Guide Volume 1 Strategic Information and Developments
134. Micronesia Country Study Guide Volume 1 Strategic Information and Developments
135. Moldova Country Study Guide Volume 1 Strategic Information and Developments
136. Monaco Country Study Guide Volume 1 Strategic Information and Developments
137. Mongolia Country Study Guide Volume 1 Strategic Information and Developments
138. Monserrat Country Study Guide Volume 1 Strategic Information and Developments
139. Montenegro Country Study Guide Volume 1 Strategic Information and Developments
140. Morocco Country Study Guide Volume 1 Strategic Information and Developments
141. Mozambique Country Study Guide Volume 1 Strategic Information and Developments
142. Myanmar Country Study Guide Volume 1 Strategic Information and Developments
143. Nagorno-Karabakh Republic Country Study Guide Volume 1 Strategic Information and Developments

144. Namibia Country Study Guide Volume 1 Strategic Information and Developments
145. Nauru Country Study Guide Volume 1 Strategic Information and Developments
146. Nepal Country Study Guide Volume 1 Strategic Information and Developments
147. Netherlands Country Study Guide Volume 1 Strategic Information and Developments
148. New Caledonia Country Study Guide Volume 1 Strategic Information and Developments
149. New Zealand Country Study Guide Volume 1 Strategic Information and Developments
150. Nicaragua Country Study Guide Volume 1 Strategic Information and Developments
151. Niger Country Study Guide Volume 1 Strategic Information and Developments
152. Nigeria Country Study Guide Volume 1 Strategic Information and Developments
153. Niue Country Study Guide Volume 1 Strategic Information and Developments
154. Northern Cyprus (Turkish Republic of Northern Cyprus)
155. Northern Mariana Islands Country Study Guide Volume 1 Strategic Information and Developments
156. Norway Country Study Guide Volume 1 Strategic Information and Developments
157. Oman Country Study Guide Volume 1 Strategic Information and Developments
158. Pakistan Country Study Guide Volume 1 Strategic Information and Developments
159. Palau Country Study Guide Volume 1 Strategic Information and Developments
160. Palestine (West Bank & Gaza) Country Study Guide Volume 1 Strategic Information and Developments
161. Panama Country Study Guide Volume 1 Strategic Information and Developments
162. Papua New Guinea Country Study Guide Volume 1 Strategic Information and Developments
163. Paraguay Country Study Guide Volume 1 Strategic Information and Developments
164. Peru Country Study Guide Volume 1 Strategic Information and Developments
165. Philippines Country Study Guide Volume 1 Strategic Information and Developments
166. Pitcairn Islands Country Study Guide Volume 1 Strategic Information and Developments
167. Poland Country Study Guide Volume 1 Strategic Information and Developments
168. Polynesia French Country Study Guide Volume 1 Strategic Information and Developments
169. Portugal Country Study Guide Volume 1 Strategic Information and Developments
170. Qatar Country Study Guide Volume 1 Strategic Information and Developments
171. Romania Country Study Guide Volume 1 Strategic Information and Developments
172. Russia Country Study Guide Volume 1 Strategic Information and Developments
173. Rwanda Country Study Guide Volume 1 Strategic Information and Developments
174. Sahrawi Arab Democratic Republic Volume 1 Strategic Information and Developments
175. Saint Kitts and Nevis Country Study Guide Volume 1 Strategic Information and Developments
176. Saint Lucia Country Study Guide Volume 1 Strategic Information and Developments
177. Saint Vincent and The Grenadines Country Study Guide Volume 1 Strategic Information and Developments
178. Samoa (American) A Country Study Guide Volume 1 Strategic Information and Developments
179. Samoa (Western) Country Study Guide Volume 1 Strategic Information and Developments
180. San Marino Country Study Guide Volume 1 Strategic Information and Developments
181. Sao Tome and Principe Country Study Guide Volume 1 Strategic Information and Developments
182. Saudi Arabia Country Study Guide Volume 1 Strategic Information and Developments
183. Scotland Country Study Guide Volume 1 Strategic Information and Developments
184. Senegal Country Study Guide Volume 1 Strategic Information and Developments
185. Serbia Country Study Guide Volume 1 Strategic Information and Developments
186. Seychelles Country Study Guide Volume 1 Strategic Information and Developments
187. Sierra Leone Country Study Guide Volume 1 Strategic Information and Developments
188. Singapore Country Study Guide Volume 1 Strategic Information and Developments
189. Slovakia Country Study Guide Volume 1 Strategic Information and Developments
190. Slovenia Country Study Guide Volume 1 Strategic Information and Developments
191. Solomon Islands Country Study Guide Volume 1 Strategic Information and Developments
192. Somalia Country Study Guide Volume 1 Strategic Information and Developments
193. South Africa Country Study Guide Volume 1 Strategic Information and Developments
194. Spain Country Study Guide Volume 1 Strategic Information and Developments
195. Sri Lanka Country Study Guide Volume 1 Strategic Information and Developments

196. St. Helena Country Study Guide Volume 1 Strategic Information and Developments
197. St. Pierre & Miquelon Country Study Guide Volume 1 Strategic Information and Developments
198. Sudan (Republic of the Sudan) Country Study Guide Volume 1 Strategic Information and Developments
199. Sudan South Country Study Guide Volume 1 Strategic Information and Developments
200. Suriname Country Study Guide Volume 1 Strategic Information and Developments
201. Swaziland Country Study Guide Volume 1 Strategic Information and Developments
202. Sweden Country Study Guide Volume 1 Strategic Information and Developments
203. Switzerland Country Study Guide Volume 1 Strategic Information and Developments
204. Syria Country Study Guide Volume 1 Strategic Information and Developments
205. Taiwan Country Study Guide Volume 1 Strategic Information and Developments
206. Tajikistan Country Study Guide Volume 1 Strategic Information and Developments
207. Tanzania Country Study Guide Volume 1 Strategic Information and Developments
208. Thailand Country Study Guide Volume 1 Strategic Information and Developments
209. Timor Leste (Democratic Republic of Timor-Leste) Country Study Guide Volume 1 Strategic Information and Developments
210. Togo Country Study Guide Volume 1 Strategic Information and Developments
211. Tonga Country Study Guide Volume 1 Strategic Information and Developments
212. Trinidad and Tobago Country Study Guide Volume 1 Strategic Information and Developments
213. Tunisia Country Study Guide Volume 1 Strategic Information and Developments
214. Turkey Country Study Guide Volume 1 Strategic Information and Developments
215. Turkmenistan Country Study Guide Volume 1 Strategic Information and Developments
216. Turks & Caicos Country Study Guide Volume 1 Strategic Information and Developments
217. Tuvalu Country Study Guide Volume 1 Strategic Information and Developments
218. Uganda Country Study Guide Volume 1 Strategic Information and Developments
219. Ukraine Country Study Guide Volume 1 Strategic Information and Developments
220. United Arab Emirates Country Study Guide Volume 1 Strategic Information and Developments
221. United Kingdom Country Study Guide Volume 1 Strategic Information and Developments
222. United States Country Study Guide Volume 1 Strategic Information and Developments
223. Uruguay Country Study Guide Volume 1 Strategic Information and Developments
224. Uzbekistan Country Study Guide Volume 1 Strategic Information and Developments
225. Vanuatu Country Study Guide Volume 1 Strategic Information and Developments
226. Vatican City (Holy See) Country Study Guide Volume 1 Strategic Information and Developments
227. Venezuela Country Study Guide Volume 1 Strategic Information and Developments
228. Vietnam Country Study Guide Volume 1 Strategic Information and Developments
229. Virgin Islands, British Country Study Guide Volume 1 Strategic Information and Developments
230. Wake Atoll Country Study Guide Volume 1 Strategic Information and Developments
231. Wallis & Futuna Country Study Guide Volume 1 Strategic Information and Developments
232. Western Sahara Country Study Guide Volume 1 Strategic Information and Developments
233. Yemen Country Study Guide Volume 1 Strategic Information and Developments
234. Zambia Country Study Guide Volume 1 Strategic Information and Developments
235. Zimbabwe Country Study Guide Volume 1 Strategic Information and Developments

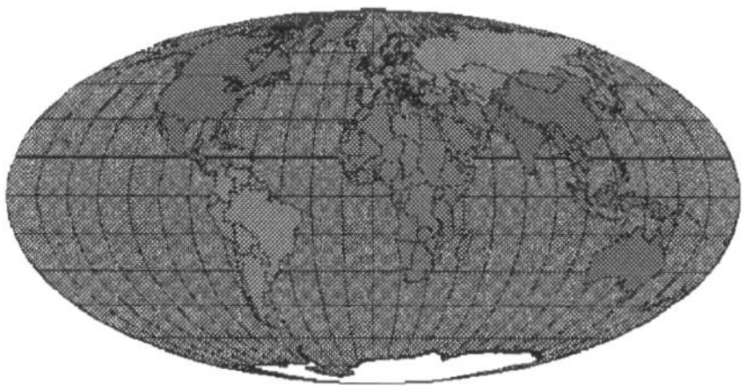

WORLD CRIMINAL LAWS, REGULATIONS AND PROCEDURES HANDBOOKS LIBRARY

Price: $99.95 Each

World Business Information Catalog: http://www.ibpus.com

TITLE
Afghanistan Criminal Laws, Regulations and Procedures Handbook - Strategic Information, Regulations, Procedures
Albania Criminal Laws, Regulations and Procedures Handbook - Strategic Information, Regulations, Procedures
Algeria Criminal Laws, Regulations and Procedures Handbook - Strategic Information, Regulations, Procedures
Angola Criminal Laws, Regulations and Procedures Handbook - Strategic Information, Regulations, Procedures
Argentina Criminal Laws, Regulations and Procedures Handbook - Strategic Information, Regulations, Procedures
Armenia Criminal Laws, Regulations and Procedures Handbook - Strategic Information, Regulations, Procedures
Aruba Criminal Laws, Regulations and Procedures Handbook - Strategic Information, Regulations, Procedures
Australia Criminal Laws, Regulations and Procedures Handbook - Strategic Information, Regulations, Procedures
Austria Criminal Laws, Regulations and Procedures Handbook - Strategic Information, Regulations, Procedures
Azerbaijan Criminal Laws, Regulations and Procedures Handbook - Strategic Information, Regulations, Procedures
Bahamas Criminal Laws, Regulations and Procedures Handbook - Strategic Information, Regulations, Procedures
Bahrain Criminal Laws, Regulations and Procedures Handbook - Strategic Information, Regulations, Procedures
Bangladesh Criminal Laws, Regulations and Procedures Handbook - Strategic Information, Regulations, Procedures
Barbados Criminal Laws, Regulations and Procedures Handbook - Strategic Information, Regulations, Procedures
Belarus Criminal Laws, Regulations and Procedures Handbook - Strategic Information, Regulations, Procedures
Belgium Criminal Laws, Regulations and Procedures Handbook - Strategic Information, Regulations, Procedures
Belize Criminal Laws, Regulations and Procedures Handbook - Strategic Information, Regulations, Procedures
Benin Criminal Laws, Regulations and Procedures Handbook - Strategic Information, Regulations, Procedures
Bermuda Criminal Laws, Regulations and Procedures Handbook - Strategic Information, Regulations, Procedures
Bhutan Criminal Laws, Regulations and Procedures Handbook - Strategic Information, Regulations, Procedures
Bolivia Criminal Laws, Regulations and Procedures Handbook - Strategic Information, Regulations, Procedures
Bosnia and Herzegovina Criminal Laws, Regulations and Procedures Handbook - Strategic Information, Regulations, Procedures
Botswana Criminal Laws, Regulations and Procedures Handbook - Strategic Information, Regulations, Procedures
Brazil Criminal Laws, Regulations and Procedures Handbook - Strategic Information, Regulations, Procedures
Brunei Criminal Laws, Regulations and Procedures Handbook - Strategic Information, Regulations, Procedures
Bulgaria Criminal Laws, Regulations and Procedures Handbook - Strategic Information, Regulations, Procedures
Burkina Faso Criminal Laws, Regulations and Procedures Handbook - Strategic Information, Regulations, Procedures
Burundi Criminal Laws, Regulations and Procedures Handbook - Strategic Information, Regulations, Procedures
Cambodia Criminal Laws, Regulations and Procedures Handbook - Strategic Information, Regulations, Procedures
Cameroon Criminal Laws, Regulations and Procedures Handbook - Strategic Information, Regulations, Procedures
Canada Criminal Laws, Regulations and Procedures Handbook - Strategic Information, Regulations, Procedures
Cape Verde Criminal Laws, Regulations and Procedures Handbook - Strategic Information, Regulations, Procedures
Caribbean Countries Crime Prevention and Security Strategy Handbook - Strategic Information, Programs and Regulations
Cayman Islands Criminal Laws, Regulations and Procedures Handbook - Strategic Information, Regulations, Procedures
Central African Republic Criminal Laws, Regulations and Procedures Handbook - Strategic Information, Regulations, Procedures
Chad Criminal Laws, Regulations and Procedures Handbook - Strategic Information, Regulations, Procedures
Chile Criminal Laws, Regulations and Procedures Handbook - Strategic Information, Regulations, Procedures

**For additional analytical, business and investment opportunities information,
Please contact Global Investment & Business Center, USA
at (202) 546-2103. Fax: (202) 546-3275. E-mail: rusric@erols.com**

China Criminal Laws, Regulations and Procedures Handbook - Strategic Information, Regulations, Procedures
Colombia Criminal Laws, Regulations and Procedures Handbook - Strategic Information, Regulations, Procedures
Comoros Criminal Laws, Regulations and Procedures Handbook - Strategic Information, Regulations, Procedures
Congo Criminal Laws, Regulations and Procedures Handbook - Strategic Information, Regulations, Procedures
Congo, Democratic Republic Criminal Laws, Regulations and Procedures Handbook - Strategic Information, Regulations, Procedures
Cook Islands Criminal Laws, Regulations and Procedures Handbook - Strategic Information, Regulations, Procedures
Costa Rica Criminal Laws, Regulations and Procedures Handbook - Strategic Information, Regulations, Procedures
Cote d'Ivoire Criminal Laws, Regulations and Procedures Handbook - Strategic Information, Regulations, Procedures
Croatia Criminal Laws, Regulations and Procedures Handbook - Strategic Information, Regulations, Procedures
Cuba Criminal Laws, Regulations and Procedures Handbook - Strategic Information, Regulations, Procedures
Cyprus Criminal Laws, Regulations and Procedures Handbook - Strategic Information, Regulations, Procedures
Czech Republic Criminal Laws, Regulations and Procedures Handbook - Strategic Information, Regulations, Procedures
Denmark Criminal Laws, Regulations and Procedures Handbook - Strategic Information, Regulations, Procedures
Djibouti Criminal Laws, Regulations and Procedures Handbook - Strategic Information, Regulations, Procedures
Dominica Criminal Laws, Regulations and Procedures Handbook - Strategic Information, Regulations, Procedures
Dominican Republic Criminal Laws, Regulations and Procedures Handbook - Strategic Information, Regulations, Procedures
Ecuador Criminal Laws, Regulations and Procedures Handbook - Strategic Information, Regulations, Procedures
Egypt Criminal Laws, Regulations and Procedures Handbook - Strategic Information, Regulations, Procedures
El Salvador Criminal Laws, Regulations and Procedures Handbook - Strategic Information, Regulations, Procedures
Equatorial Guinea Criminal Laws, Regulations and Procedures Handbook - Strategic Information, Regulations, Procedures
Eritrea Criminal Laws, Regulations and Procedures Handbook - Strategic Information, Regulations, Procedures
Estonia Criminal Laws, Regulations and Procedures Handbook - Strategic Information, Regulations, Procedures
Ethiopia Criminal Laws, Regulations and Procedures Handbook - Strategic Information, Regulations, Procedures
Fiji Criminal Laws, Regulations and Procedures Handbook - Strategic Information, Regulations, Procedures
Finland Criminal Laws, Regulations and Procedures Handbook - Strategic Information, Regulations, Procedures
France Criminal Laws, Regulations and Procedures Handbook - Strategic Information, Regulations, Procedures
Gabon Criminal Laws, Regulations and Procedures Handbook - Strategic Information, Regulations, Procedures
Gambia Criminal Laws, Regulations and Procedures Handbook - Strategic Information, Regulations, Procedures
Georgia Criminal Laws, Regulations and Procedures Handbook - Strategic Information, Regulations, Procedures
Germany Criminal Laws, Regulations and Procedures Handbook - Strategic Information, Regulations, Procedures
Ghana Criminal Laws, Regulations and Procedures Handbook - Strategic Information, Regulations, Procedures
Greece Criminal Laws, Regulations and Procedures Handbook - Strategic Information, Regulations, Procedures
Guatemala Criminal Laws, Regulations and Procedures Handbook - Strategic Information, Regulations, Procedures
Guinea Criminal Laws, Regulations and Procedures Handbook - Strategic Information, Regulations, Procedures
Guinea-Bissau Criminal Laws, Regulations and Procedures Handbook - Strategic Information, Regulations, Procedures
Guyana Criminal Laws, Regulations and Procedures Handbook - Strategic Information, Regulations, Procedures
Haiti Criminal Laws, Regulations and Procedures Handbook - Strategic Information, Regulations, Procedures
Honduras Criminal Laws, Regulations and Procedures Handbook - Strategic Information, Regulations, Procedures
Hungary Criminal Laws, Regulations and Procedures Handbook - Strategic Information, Regulations, Procedures
Iceland Criminal Laws, Regulations and Procedures Handbook - Strategic Information, Regulations, Procedures
India Criminal Laws, Regulations and Procedures Handbook - Strategic Information, Regulations, Procedures
Indonesia Criminal Laws, Regulations and Procedures Handbook - Strategic Information, Regulations, Procedures
Iran Criminal Laws, Regulations and Procedures Handbook - Strategic Information, Regulations, Procedures
Iraq Criminal Laws, Regulations and Procedures Handbook - Strategic Information, Regulations, Procedures
Ireland Criminal Laws, Regulations and Procedures Handbook - Strategic Information, Regulations, Procedures
Israel Criminal Laws, Regulations and Procedures Handbook - Strategic Information, Regulations, Procedures
Italy Criminal Laws, Regulations and Procedures Handbook - Strategic Information, Regulations, Procedures
Jamaica Criminal Laws, Regulations and Procedures Handbook - Strategic Information, Regulations, Procedures
Japan Criminal Laws, Regulations and Procedures Handbook - Strategic Information, Regulations, Procedures
Jordan Criminal Laws, Regulations and Procedures Handbook - Strategic Information, Regulations, Procedures
Kazakhstan Criminal Laws, Regulations and Procedures Handbook - Strategic Information, Regulations, Procedures
Kenya Criminal Laws, Regulations and Procedures Handbook - Strategic Information, Regulations, Procedures
Korea, North Criminal Laws, Regulations and Procedures Handbook - Strategic Information, Regulations, Procedures

Korea, South Criminal Laws, Regulations and Procedures Handbook - Strategic Information, Regulations, Procedures
Kosovo Criminal Laws, Regulations and Procedures Handbook - Strategic Information, Regulations, Procedures
Kurdistan Criminal Laws, Regulations and Procedures Handbook - Strategic Information, Regulations, Procedures
Kuwait Criminal Laws, Regulations and Procedures Handbook - Strategic Information, Regulations, Procedures
Kyrgyzstan Criminal Laws, Regulations and Procedures Handbook - Strategic Information, Regulations, Procedures
Laos Criminal Laws, Regulations and Procedures Handbook - Strategic Information, Regulations, Procedures
Latvia Criminal Laws, Regulations and Procedures Handbook - Strategic Information, Regulations, Procedures
Lebanon Criminal Laws, Regulations and Procedures Handbook - Strategic Information, Regulations, Procedures
Lesotho Criminal Laws, Regulations and Procedures Handbook - Strategic Information, Regulations, Procedures
Liberia Criminal Laws, Regulations and Procedures Handbook - Strategic Information, Regulations, Procedures
Libya Criminal Laws, Regulations and Procedures Handbook - Strategic Information, Regulations, Procedures
Liechtenstein Criminal Laws, Regulations and Procedures Handbook - Strategic Information, Regulations, Procedures
Lithuania Criminal Laws, Regulations and Procedures Handbook - Strategic Information, Regulations, Procedures
Luxembourg Criminal Laws, Regulations and Procedures Handbook - Strategic Information, Regulations, Procedures
Macao Criminal Laws, Regulations and Procedures Handbook - Strategic Information, Regulations, Procedures
Macedonia, Criminal Laws, Regulations and Procedures Handbook - Strategic Information, Regulations, Procedures
Madagascar Criminal Laws, Regulations and Procedures Handbook - Strategic Information, Regulations, Procedures
Madeira Criminal Laws, Regulations and Procedures Handbook - Strategic Information, Regulations, Procedures
Malawi Criminal Laws, Regulations and Procedures Handbook - Strategic Information, Regulations, Procedures
Malaysia Criminal Laws, Regulations and Procedures Handbook - Strategic Information, Regulations, Procedures
Maldives Criminal Laws, Regulations and Procedures Handbook - Strategic Information, Regulations, Procedures
Mali Criminal Laws, Regulations and Procedures Handbook - Strategic Information, Regulations, Procedures
Malta Criminal Laws, Regulations and Procedures Handbook - Strategic Information, Regulations, Procedures
Marshall Islands Criminal Laws, Regulations and Procedures Handbook - Strategic Information, Regulations, Procedures
Mauritania Criminal Laws, Regulations and Procedures Handbook - Strategic Information, Regulations, Procedures
Mauritius Criminal Laws, Regulations and Procedures Handbook - Strategic Information, Regulations, Procedures
Mexico Criminal Laws, Regulations and Procedures Handbook - Strategic Information, Regulations, Procedures
Micronesia Criminal Laws, Regulations and Procedures Handbook - Strategic Information, Regulations, Procedures
Moldova Criminal Laws, Regulations and Procedures Handbook - Strategic Information, Regulations, Procedures
Monaco Criminal Laws, Regulations and Procedures Handbook - Strategic Information, Regulations, Procedures
Mongolia Criminal Laws, Regulations and Procedures Handbook - Strategic Information, Regulations, Procedures
Morocco Criminal Laws, Regulations and Procedures Handbook - Strategic Information, Regulations, Procedures
Mozambique Criminal Laws, Regulations and Procedures Handbook - Strategic Information, Regulations, Procedures
Myanmar Criminal Laws, Regulations and Procedures Handbook - Strategic Information, Regulations, Procedures
Namibia Criminal Laws, Regulations and Procedures Handbook - Strategic Information, Regulations, Procedures
Nauru Criminal Laws, Regulations and Procedures Handbook - Strategic Information, Regulations, Procedures
Nepal Criminal Laws, Regulations and Procedures Handbook - Strategic Information, Regulations, Procedures
Netherlands Criminal Laws, Regulations and Procedures Handbook - Strategic Information, Regulations, Procedures
New Zealand Criminal Laws, Regulations and Procedures Handbook - Strategic Information, Regulations, Procedures
Nicaragua Criminal Laws, Regulations and Procedures Handbook - Strategic Information, Regulations, Procedures
Niger Criminal Laws, Regulations and Procedures Handbook - Strategic Information, Regulations, Procedures
Nigeria Criminal Laws, Regulations and Procedures Handbook - Strategic Information, Regulations, Procedures
Northern Mariana Islands Criminal Laws, Regulations and Procedures Handbook - Strategic Information, Regulations, Procedures
Norway Criminal Laws, Regulations and Procedures Handbook - Strategic Information, Regulations, Procedures
Oman Criminal Laws, Regulations and Procedures Handbook - Strategic Information, Regulations, Procedures
Pakistan Criminal Laws, Regulations and Procedures Handbook - Strategic Information, Regulations, Procedures
Palestine (West Bank & Gaza) Criminal Laws, Regulations and Procedures Handbook - Strategic Information, Regulations, Procedures
Panama Criminal Laws, Regulations and Procedures Handbook - Strategic Information, Regulations, Procedures
Papua New Guinea Criminal Laws, Regulations and Procedures Handbook - Strategic Information, Regulations, Procedures
Paraguay Criminal Laws, Regulations and Procedures Handbook - Strategic Information, Regulations, Procedures
Peru Criminal Laws, Regulations and Procedures Handbook - Strategic Information, Regulations, Procedures
Philippines Criminal Laws, Regulations and Procedures Handbook - Strategic Information, Regulations, Procedures
Pitcairn Islands Criminal Laws, Regulations and Procedures Handbook - Strategic Information, Regulations, Procedures

Poland Criminal Laws, Regulations and Procedures Handbook - Strategic Information, Regulations, Procedures
Portugal Criminal Laws, Regulations and Procedures Handbook - Strategic Information, Regulations, Procedures
Qatar Criminal Laws, Regulations and Procedures Handbook - Strategic Information, Regulations, Procedures
Romania Criminal Laws, Regulations and Procedures Handbook - Strategic Information, Regulations, Procedures
Russia Criminal Laws, Regulations and Procedures Handbook - Strategic Information, Regulations, Procedures
Rwanda Criminal Laws, Regulations and Procedures Handbook - Strategic Information, Regulations, Procedures
Samoa (Western) Criminal Laws, Regulations and Procedures Handbook - Strategic Information, Regulations, Procedures
Sao Tome and Principe Criminal Laws, Regulations and Procedures Handbook - Strategic Information, Regulations, Procedures
Saudi Arabia Criminal Laws, Regulations and Procedures Handbook - Strategic Information, Regulations, Procedures
Senegal Criminal Laws, Regulations and Procedures Handbook - Strategic Information, Regulations, Procedures
Serbia Criminal Laws, Regulations and Procedures Handbook - Strategic Information, Regulations, Procedures
Seychelles Criminal Laws, Regulations and Procedures Handbook - Strategic Information, Regulations, Procedures
Sierra Leone Criminal Laws, Regulations and Procedures Handbook - Strategic Information, Regulations, Procedures
Singapore Criminal Laws, Regulations and Procedures Handbook - Strategic Information, Regulations, Procedures
Slovakia Criminal Laws, Regulations and Procedures Handbook - Strategic Information, Regulations, Procedures
Slovenia Criminal Laws, Regulations and Procedures Handbook - Strategic Information, Regulations, Procedures
Solomon Islands Criminal Laws, Regulations and Procedures Handbook - Strategic Information, Regulations, Procedures
Somalia Criminal Laws, Regulations and Procedures Handbook - Strategic Information, Regulations, Procedures
South Africa Criminal Laws, Regulations and Procedures Handbook - Strategic Information, Regulations, Procedures
Spain Criminal Laws, Regulations and Procedures Handbook - Strategic Information, Regulations, Procedures
Sri Lanka Criminal Laws, Regulations and Procedures Handbook - Strategic Information, Regulations, Procedures
Sudan Criminal Laws, Regulations and Procedures Handbook - Strategic Information, Regulations, Procedures
Suriname Criminal Laws, Regulations and Procedures Handbook - Strategic Information, Regulations, Procedures
Swaziland Criminal Laws, Regulations and Procedures Handbook - Strategic Information, Regulations, Procedures
Sweden Criminal Laws, Regulations and Procedures Handbook - Strategic Information, Regulations, Procedures
Switzerland Criminal Laws, Regulations and Procedures Handbook - Strategic Information, Regulations, Procedures
Syria Criminal Laws, Regulations and Procedures Handbook - Strategic Information, Regulations, Procedures
Taiwan Criminal Laws, Regulations and Procedures Handbook - Strategic Information, Regulations, Procedures
Tajikistan Criminal Laws, Regulations and Procedures Handbook - Strategic Information, Regulations, Procedures
Tanzania Criminal Laws, Regulations and Procedures Handbook - Strategic Information, Regulations, Procedures
Thailand Criminal Laws, Regulations and Procedures Handbook - Strategic Information, Regulations, Procedures
Togo Criminal Laws, Regulations and Procedures Handbook - Strategic Information, Regulations, Procedures
Trinidad and Tobago Criminal Laws, Regulations and Procedures Handbook - Strategic Information, Regulations, Procedures
Tunisia Criminal Laws, Regulations and Procedures Handbook - Strategic Information, Regulations, Procedures
Turkey Criminal Laws, Regulations and Procedures Handbook - Strategic Information, Regulations, Procedures
Turkmenistan Criminal Laws, Regulations and Procedures Handbook - Strategic Information, Regulations, Procedures
Uganda Criminal Laws, Regulations and Procedures Handbook - Strategic Information, Regulations, Procedures
Ukraine Criminal Laws, Regulations and Procedures Handbook - Strategic Information, Regulations, Procedures
United Arab Emirates Criminal Laws, Regulations and Procedures Handbook - Strategic Information, Regulations, Procedures
United Kingdom Criminal Laws, Regulations and Procedures Handbook - Strategic Information, Regulations, Procedures
United States Criminal Laws, Regulations and Procedures Handbook - Strategic Information, Regulations, Procedures
Uruguay Criminal Laws, Regulations and Procedures Handbook - Strategic Information, Regulations, Procedures
Uzbekistan Criminal Laws, Regulations and Procedures Handbook - Strategic Information, Regulations, Procedures
Venezuela Criminal Laws, Regulations and Procedures Handbook - Strategic Information, Regulations, Procedures
Vietnam Criminal Laws, Regulations and Procedures Handbook - Strategic Information, Regulations, Procedures
Yemen Criminal Laws, Regulations and Procedures Handbook - Strategic Information, Regulations, Procedures
Zambia Criminal Laws, Regulations and Procedures Handbook - Strategic Information, Regulations, Procedures
Zimbabwe Criminal Laws, Regulations and Procedures Handbook - Strategic Information, Regulations, Procedures

Made in United States
Orlando, FL
04 November 2026

90207779R00153